THE STREAKS OF THE TULIP

Also by William Jay Smith

POETRY

Poems • Celebration at Dark • Poems 1947–1957
The Tin Can and Other Poems • New & Selected Poems
(FOR CHILDREN) Laughing Time • Boy Blue's
Book of Beasts • Puptents and Pebbles • Typewriter
Town • What Did I See? • Big and Little: *Little
Dimity, Big Gumbo, Big and Little* • Ho for a
Hat! • If I Had a Boat • Mr. Smith and Other Nonsense

TRANSLATIONS

Poems of a Multimillionaire, by Valery Larbaud
Selected Writings of Jules Laforgue
(FOR CHILDREN) The Children of the Forest, by
Elsa Beskow • The Pirate Book, by Lennart Hellsing

CRITICISM

The Spectra Hoax • Herrick, *Selected
with an Introduction and Notes*

ANTHOLOGIES

(with Louise Bogan) The Golden Journey: *Poems
for Young People* • Poems from France • Poems from
Italy • Two Plays by Charles Bertin: *Christopher
Columbus* and *Don Juan*

WILLIAM
JAY SMITH

THE
STREAKS
OF THE
TULIP

SELECTED CRITICISM

DELACORTE PRESS / SEYMOUR LAWRENCE

Certain of these essays, articles, and reviews have
appeared in the following newspapers and magazines;
grateful acknowledgment is made to the editors:
*Accent, Américas, The Bennington Banner, The Berkshire
Eagle, Book Week, Harper's, The Hollins Alumnae Quarterly,
The Hollins Critic, Horizon, The Horn Book, The Nation,
The New Republic, The New York Times Book Review, Poetry,
The Prairie Schooner, The Red Balloon (Williams College),
Saturday Review, The Sewanee Review, What's New (Abbott
Laboratories), Woman's Day, The Yale Literary Magazine.*

Certain essays appeared, in whole or in part,
in the following books:
Herrick, edited with an introduction and notes by William
Jay Smith; (Laurel Poetry Series Dell Books), *Poets on
Poetry,* edited by Howard Nemerov (Basic Books, Inc.),
The Spectra Hoax by William Jay Smith (Wesleyan University
Press). Copyright © 1961 by William Jay Smith. Reprinted by permission.
"The Skies of Venice" was first published by André
Emmerich Gallery.

Library of Congress Catalog Card Number: 77–37661
Manufactured in the United States of America
First printing

Library of Congress Cataloging in Publication Data

Smith, William Jay, 1918–
    The streaks of the tulip.

    I. Title.
PS3537.M8693S8   809   77–37661

Acknowledgments

Excerpts from *The Anathemata* by David Jones: Reprinted by permission of Chilmark Press and Faber & Faber, Ltd.

Excerpts from *Questions of Travel* by Elizabeth Bishop and from *The Blue Estuaries* by Louise Bogan: Reprinted by permission of Farrar, Straus & Giroux, Inc.

Excerpts from *Spectra* poems: Reprinted by permission of Mrs. Gladys Ficke.

Excerpt from "The Waste Land" by T. S. Eliot: Reprinted by permission of Harcourt Brace Jovanovich, Inc. and Faber & Faber, Ltd.

Excerpt from Poem #621 from *The Poems of Emily Dickinson,* edited by Thomas H. Johnson. Copyright © 1951, 1955 by The President and Fellows of Harvard College. Reprinted by permission of The Belknap Press of Harvard University Press and the Trustees of Amherst College.

Excerpts from *The Poetry of Robert Frost,* edited by Edward Connery Lathem. Copyright © 1958, 1962 by Robert Frost, copyright © 1969 by Holt, Rinehart and Winston, Inc. Reprinted by permission of Holt, Rinehart and Winston, Inc.

Excerpts from *The Complete Poetical Works of Amy Lowell* and from *All My Pretty Ones* by Anne Sexton: Reprinted by permission of Houghton Mifflin Company.

Excerpt from *The Lost World* by Randall Jarrell. Copyright © 1965 by Randall Jarrell. Reprinted by permission of The Macmillan Company.

Excerpt from *Collected Poems* by James Stephens. Copyright 1938, 1954 by The Macmillan Company. Reprinted by permission of The Macmillan Company, Mrs. Iris Wise, Macmillan & Co. Ltd., London, and Basingstoke, and The Macmillan Company of Canada, Ltd.

Excerpts from *Collected Poems* by Marianne Moore. Copyright 1935 by Marianne

ACKNOWLEDGMENTS

Moore, renewed 1963 by Marianne Moore and T. S. Eliot. Reprinted by permission of The Macmillan Company.

"The Rainy Summer" by Alice Meynell: Reprinted by permission of Mrs. Sylvia Mulvey.

Excerpts from "Journey Around My Room" by Louise Bogan, from *The New Yorker*, January 14, 1933. Reprinted by permission of The New Yorker Magazine, Inc.

Excerpts from *The Burning Perch* by Louis MacNeice: Reprinted by permission of Oxford University Press and Faber & Faber, Ltd.

Excerpt from *Nights and Hours* by Reginald Pole: Reprinted by permission of Rupert Pole.

Excerpts from *Oh, Millersville!* by Fern Gravel. Copyright 1940 by The Prairie Press. Reprinted by permission of The Prairie Press.

Excerpt from *Eloges and Other Poems* by St.-John Perse, translated by Louise Varese, Bollingen Series LV. Copyright © 1956 by The Bollingen Foundation. Reprinted by permission of Princeton University Press.

Excerpt from *George Seferis: Collected Poems 1924-1955*, translated, edited and introduced by Edmund Kelley and Philip Sherrard. Copyright © 1967 by Princeton University Press. Supplemented Edition 1969. Reprinted by permission of Princeton University Press and Jonathan Cape, Ltd.

Excerpts from *The Beginning and the End and Other Poems* by Robinson Jeffers, and from *About the House* and *Homage to Clio* by W. H. Auden: Reprinted by permission of Random House, Inc.

Excerpts from the works of Walter de la Mare: Reprinted by permission of The Society of Authors as the representative of The Literary Trustees of Walter de la Mare.

Excerpts from *Under the Tree* by Elizabeth Madox Roberts. Copyright 1922 by B. W. Huebsch, renewed 1950 by Ivor S. Roberts; from *New Poems 1965-1969* by A. D. Hope. Copyright © 1968, 1969 by A. D. Hope, All Rights Reserved; and from *Collected Poems 1930-1965* by A. D. Hope. Copyright 1963, 1966 in all countries of the International Copyright Union by A. D. Hope. All reprinted by permission of The Viking Press.

Excerpts from "I've Been Thinking": Copyright © 1963 by Marianne Moore; from "Leonardo da Vinci's": Copyright © 1959 by Marianne Moore. "I've Been Thinking" originally appeared in *The New York Review of Books*, "Leonardo da Vinci's" in *The New Yorker;* both are from *Complete Poems* by Marianne Moore. Reprinted by permission of The Viking Press.

Excerpts from *At the End of the Open Road* by Louis Simpson: Reprinted by permission of Wesleyan University Press.

Excerpt from *Spring, Summer and Autumn* by Hans Zinsser: Reprinted by permission of Ruby Handforth Zinsser.

"The business of the poet," said Imlac, "is to examine, not the individual, but the species; to remark general properties and large appearances; he does not number the streaks of the tulip, or describe the different shades in the verdure of the forest."

SAMUEL JOHNSON, *Rasselas*

Dr. Johnson has said that the poet is not concerned with the minute particulars, with "the streaks of the tulip." This, I thought, was just where he was wrong. . . .

LOUIS MACNEICE, *The Strings are False*

To
Allen Tate
and
Malcolm Cowley
masters and friends

CONTENTS

I. A PLACE FOR THE GENUINE

II. A POETRY CHRONICLE: 1963–1966

X. EPITAPHS

XI. A FRAME FOR POETRY

I

A PLACE
FOR THE
GENUINE

THE BLACK CLOCK:
THE POETIC ACHIEVEMENT
OF LOUIS MACNEICE

LOUIS MACNEICE's last volume of poems, *The Burning Perch*, went to press in January 1963; he died suddenly in September of the same year at the age of fifty-six. Critics since have generally acknowledged that he was a poet of genius, and that much of his finest work was produced in the three years immediately preceding his death. While granting him his place in the front rank among the poets who came to prominence in the thirties—W. H. Auden, Stephen Spender, Cecil Day Lewis—they have had considerable difficulty in assessing the nature of his achievement. On his death, T. S. Eliot commented that he "had the Irishman's unfailing ear for the music of verse." During his lifetime, however, many readers felt that his ear did indeed fail him, that his rhythms were frequently too easy, and his parodies and imitations of jazz lyrics too flat and mechanical in nature to hold one's interest for long. While he had much in common with his contemporaries, he was, in many ways, totally unlike them. His poems are easy to understand on the surface (seemingly far less complicated than those of W. H. Auden or Dylan Thomas), but they present deeper, less obvious, difficulties. They appear to be the open, easy expression of an engaging and intelligent personality, but basically that personality, and the poems through which it manifests itself, is not easy to grasp.

Stephen Spender, who knew MacNeice at Oxford, has spoken of him, as have many of his contemporaries, as one who was brilliant but aloof. "He had a way," Mr. Spender writes, "of leaning back and gazing at one through half-closed eyes which scarcely covered a mocking glance. Secrets he surmised about oneself he did not intend to share, the glance said . . . That this detachment of MacNeice's was noticeable enough is notorious. A famous occasion at which I happened to be present was when, late in the war, Archibald Clerk-Kerr (later Lord Inverchapel), the British ambassador at Moscow, returning to London for a visit attended a party given by John Lehmann for the young English poets of the thirties and forties. Throughout the party MacNeice, holding a glass in his hand, leaned against a piece of furniture, and gazed around him disdainfully without addressing a word to anyone. Finally Clerk-Kerr went up to him and told him there was a matter about which he would like to be informed. Did MacNeice come from the northern coast of Ireland? MacNeice acknowledged that he did. 'Ah,' said Clerk-Kerr, 'well that corroborates a legend I heard in my youth that a school of seals had landed on that part of the coast, cohabited with the natives, and produced a special race, half-seal, half-human.' MacNeice did look a bit taken aback, as Clerk-Kerr left the room." (*The New Republic*, 28 January 1967)

MacNeice's friend John Hilton, in an appendix to *The Strings are False*, an unfinished autobiography now published, speaks of him in similar, if more sympathetic, terms: "On the whole at that time he preferred to study mankind indirectly. He liked—or perhaps this came on a bit later—to read the 'small ads' in the papers. Meeting people face to face he was apt to make too clear that he was treating them—head thrown slightly back, eyes quizzically narrowed—as specimens, bearers of the potentialities of the race, concrete universals perhaps. A remark ventured by the specimen would be visibly rolled around his mental palate and mental ear; and the response if any would be less than whole-hearted. He practiced in this way a certain spiritual economy that I take to have been necessary to the protection of his inner world. He was afraid—as in the *Prayer before Birth* —of being spilled. He did not mind at times appearing sly; and he did not always choose to recognize people he had met before (though his increasing shortsightedness was probably responsible for many imagined offenses of the kind) ." I felt when I met MacNeice myself several times in London in the spring of 1948 that he was treating me, through his narrowed eyes, as a specimen of the sort of poet America produced, for whom he appeared to feel only disdain. I discovered from his friends Reggie Smith and Ernest Stahl, whom I saw often, that this was not true. I did not meet him again until a year or so before his death: he came in out of the rain in Greenwich Village to a party at Howard Moss's apartment looking literally like the half-seal that Clerk-Kerr had encountered in London. Soon dry and warmed by liquor, he appeared far more human than I had remembered him, the brilliant and engaging person one expected from his poems.

There is in everything that Louis MacNeice wrote a surface brilliance, an extraordinary verbal dexterity, a poise that shows itself in a command of complicated verse forms. There is a distance maintained, even when he is being most personal, that gives his poetry, at its best, a cold classical power, and, at its worst, the casualness of an uncommitted poetic journalist. MacNeice during his career engaged in many literary pursuits that took him away from the writing of poetry. But he was never deceived, no matter how well he succeeded in journalism, criticism, translation, or radio work, that these were anything but diversions from his main course. Of the prose books for which he accepted commissions from publishers during the late thirties he writes: "It flattered me that publishers should ask me to do something unsuitable. The more unsuitable, the more it was a sign of power. Many of us were still reacting overmuch against Art for Art's Sake, against the concept of the solitary pure-minded genius saving his soul in a tower without doors. Our reaction drove us to compete with the Next Man. But once you come up against the Next Man you begin to lose sight of the sky. The Next Man swells to a giant, you find your face buried in his paunch and on his paunch is a watch ticking louder and louder, urging you to hurry, get on with the job—when the job is finished there will always be another. In commercial writing, in 'bookmaking', one comes to think of carelessness and speed as virtues." His extensive work for the BBC served to accentuate his desire for the use of direct and colloquial speech, but for the trained classicist that he was, the virtues of harmony and measure were ingrained.

It was important for MacNeice to look at the world from a certain distance in order to view it, and himself as part of it, with honesty and without self-pity. MacNeice was interested in the concrete, as true lyric poets always are; he wanted to get things straight. (He believed that a critic should not speak of poetry in the abstract, but should point out specific qualities, merits in individual poems.) Dr. Johnson was wrong, he remarks at one point, when he said that the poet is not concerned with minute particulars, with "the streaks of the tulip." MacNeice was passionate about particulars; in "Autumn Sequel" he writes:

> Everydayness is good; particular-dayness
> Is better, a holiday thrives on single days.
> Thus Wales with her moodiness, madness, shrewdness,
>   lewdness, feyness,
>
> Daily demands a different color of praise;

Absorbed in the dailiness of life, he could not tolerate lofty rhetoric, the grand gesture: he was not to be taken in. His last

6

poems in *The Burning Perch* showed that he could "let common-place be novelty," and that he had the power, with the lightness of his touch and the bite of his wit, to create a lasting resonance.

John Hilton describes a speech that MacNeice made at the Marlborough School in November 1925: "It really was simply astounding; an amazing and magnificent conglomeration of dreams, fables, parables, allegories, theories, quotations from Edward Lear and Edith Sitwell, the sort of thing that you want to howl with laughter at, but are afraid to for fear of missing a word. He spoke in a loud, clear, fast, matter-of-fact voice going straight on without a pause from a long story about two ants who fell into a river and went floating down in company with two old sticks and a dead dog, until they met a fish to whom they said 'stuff and nonsense; it's contrary to common sense to swim upstream; we won't believe it' and went on and were drowned in a whirlpool, while the fish swam on upstream until he met St. Francis of Assisi preaching to the fishes and gained eternal happiness." Mr. Hilton concludes, in a letter, that Mac-Neice was undoubtedly "a great genius," even though he "stands for nonsense."

MacNeice's gift for nonsense was given full play at Oxford. He describes his verbal collaboration at Oxford with his friend Graham Shepard, "not that we had ever heard of Joyce or sur-realism or automatic writing; we just liked to play about with words." Their experiments took such forms as this: "Mr. Little Short of Extraordinary was little short of extraordinary. He went to bed with his wife and dislocated his jaw. And that was the Night the Isms came to Auntie. General Useless MacNess was always in a mess. The Boy stood in the Burning Bush. 'What are ye doin' the day?' Quoth the cat. I'm minding my pees and peeing my queues. Oh the Harp that Once and never got over it!" He was especially fond, he said, of parodying hymns: "every little blasphemy a blow for the better Life." He could look at the grotesques who typified Oxford with the eye of a Lewis Carroll: "When I think of Oxford dons I see a

Walspurgisnacht, a zoo—scraggy-necked baldheads in gown and hood looking like marabou storks, giant turtles reaching for a glass of port with infinitely weary flippers, sad chimpanzees, codfish, washing blown out on a line. Timid with pipes or boisterous with triple chins. Their wit and themselves had been kept too long, the squibs were damp, the cigars were dust, the champagne was flat." The verbal play was a means of keeping his distance.

MacNeice made technical use of nonsense right up to the end. In *The Burning Perch*, the poem "Children's Games," written in 1962, is a playful handling of children's nonsense phrases, but even the simplest one, such as "Keep your fingers crossed when Tom Tiddler's ground is over you," takes on a deeper significance. In "Sports Page," he observes his Doppelgänger as a participant in games:

> Nostalgia, incantation, escape,
> Courts and fields of the Ever Young:
> On your Marks! En garde! Scrum Down! Over!
> On the ropes, on the ice, breasting the tape,
> Our Doppelgänger is bounced and flung
> While the ball squats in the air like a spider
> Threading the horizon round the goalposts
> And we, though never there, give tongue.
> Yet our Doppelgänger rides once more
> Over the five-barred gates and flames
> In metaphors filched from magic and music
> With a new witch broom and a rattling score
> And the names we read seem more than names,
> Potions or amulets, till we remember
> The lines of print are always sidelines
> And all our games funeral games.

The "metaphors filched from magic and music" in *The Burning Perch* build up a nightmare world from which there is no

8

escape; and distance—the objectivity of the artist—is of no help. The iceberg is a favorite figure in MacNeice's poetry (he always remembered seeing the *Titanic* as a child in Belfast on her maiden voyage) but in these later poems he explores the iceberg's underside. The nonsense world of childhood has become the real world, the grotesque figures that could once be laughed at are now omnipresent in a packaged and plastic, dehumanized scene:

> On the podium in lieu of a man
> With fallible hands is ensconced
> A metal lobster with built-in tempi;
> The deep-sea fishermen in lieu of
> Battling with tunny and cod
> Are signing their contracts for processing plankton.
>
> On roof after roof the prongs
> Are baited with faces, in saltpan and brainpan
> The savour is lost, in deep
> Freeze after freeze in lieu of a joint
> Are piled the shrunken heads of the past
> And the offals of unborn children.
>
> In lieu therefore of choice
> Thy Will be undone just as flowers
> Fugues, vows and hopes are undone
> While the weather is packaged and the spacemen
> In endless orbit and in lieu of a flag
> The orator hangs himself from the flagpost.

The poems depict a world in which "Greyness is all":

> But, as it is, we needs must wait
> Not for some demon but some fate
> Contrived by men and never known
> Until the final switch is thrown
> To black out all the worlds of men

And demons too but even then
Whether that black will not prove grey
No one may wait around to say.

"Budgie" presents a final grotesque vision of existence:

The budgerigar is baby blue,
Its mirror is rimmed with baby pink,
Its cage is a stage, its perks are props,
Its eyes black pins in a cushionette,
Its tail a needle on a missing disc,
Its voice a small I Am. Beyond
These wires there might be something different—
Galaxy on galaxy, star on star,
Planet on planet, asteroid on asteroid,
Or even those four far walls of the sitting room—
But for all this small blue bundle could bother
Its beak, there is only itself and the universe,
The small blue universe, so *Let me attitudinize*,
Let me attitudinize, let me attitudinize,
For all the world is a stage is a cage
A hermitage a fashion show a crèche an auditorium
Or possibly a space ship. *Earth, can you hear me?*
Blue for Budgie calling Me for Mirror:
Budgie, can you hear me? The long tail oscillates,
The mirror jerks in the weightless cage:
Budgie, can you see me? The radio telescope
Picks up a quite different signal, the human
Race recedes and dwindles, the giant
Reptiles cackle in their graves, the mountain
Gorillas exchange their final messages,
But the budgerigar was not born for nothing,
He stands at his post on the burning perch—
I twitter Am—and peeps like a television
Actor admiring himself in the monitor.

10

In *The Strings are False* MacNeice writes about the
break-up of his first marriage: "Sometimes in the nights I woke
and wondered where we were going, but most of the time I was
doped and happy, most of the time except when I thought about
time that most of the time is waste but whose is not? When I
started again to write poems they were all about time. We had
an old record of 'The Blue Room', one of the most out-and-out
jazz sentimentalizations of domestic felicity—far away upstairs
but the blue began to suffocate. I wrote a novel which was basically dishonest and ended in a blue room as if that solved everything." After his wife had left him, he writes of not being able
to sleep. In a large room with a ten-foot skylight he "felt the
skylight encroaching, tried to dodge it; sometimes it was a falling tent and sometimes it was the gap that cannot be closed." In
this room he had "two precise visions, both by electric light,
both solidly planted in the air about five feet up from the floor.
The first was a human eye a yard or so long; the rest of the face
was invisible but on both the upper and the under eyelid there
were worms instead of eyelashes, transparent worms curling and
wriggling. The second vision was of a sky-blue little beast like
a jackal but with horns; he sat there pat on the air, his front feet
firmly together."

In "Budgie" he confronts the same "sky-blue little beast,"
the same "small blue bundle," the same suffocating blue of "The
Blue Room," but now in broad daylight, close-up and with an
honesty that is terrifying. Life, reflecting upon itself, is reduced
to a blue and pink babylike vision, utterly nonsensical; but its
nonsense parroting of its own parroting echoes through an expanding universe. "Budgie," in its mad vision and its alliterative
and obsessive *b*'s, reminds one of "The Hunting of the Snark"
by Lewis Carroll: Budgie is a space-age Boojum, and its twitter-
ing "I Am" comes from every TV screen.

The image of the bird on the burning perch calls to mind
also an earlier poem by MacNeice, one of the finest of his war

11

poems, "The Springboard," in which the poet contemplates
man, called upon to sacrifice himself:

> He never made the dive—not while I watched.
> High above London, naked in the night
> Perched on a board. I peered up through the bars
> Made by his fear and mine but it was more than fright
> That kept him crucified among the budding stars.

and concludes:

> And yet we know he knows what he must do.
> There above London where the gargoyles grin
> He will dive like a bomber past the broken steeple,
> One man wiping out his own original sin
> And, like ten million others, dying for the people.

In "Budgie" the poet again looks through the bars, but sees not
a human perched on a board ready to spring, but the "sky-blue
beast" on its burning perch, sailing totally without meaning
through a meaningless universe while the gargoyles—now real
beasts—cackle and grin, and the human race "recedes and
dwindles."

MacNeice speaks at one point of the importance that his
generation attached to personal relationships. "It is better," he
says, agreeing with his friend E. R. Dodds, the editor of both his
poems and his unfinished autobiography, "to be like Rilke and
capitalize your own loneliness and neuroses, regard Death as the
mainspring. Or it is better—if you can do it—to become the
servant of an idea. But if you take either of these courses, you
have got to commit yourself utterly; if you give yourself to
Loneliness or Otherness it must not be a negative thing—a mere
avoiding of other troubles, mere sublimation—but it must be
positive, an End. Thus people have become monks sometimes in
order to avoid the trouble of sex, sometimes out of perverse sexu-
ality, but that is not how people become saints. Not real saints.
In spite of analytical researches into the pathology of sainthood,

the saint, like the mathematician, has got hold of something positive. And so have the real hero and the real artist."

Beneath the bright and lively surface of his poems, death seems to have haunted MacNeice throughout his work. He tells of dreaming of a house that was a skeleton, the walls and floors of which were gone. (He speaks elsewhere of having enjoyed climbing over ruined houses, of fearing blindness, long corridors, and light glancing off a mirror.) The dream ends with a vision of Dr. Mabuse, from the film that he had just seen, with a "great bush of orange red hair," cackling and leering at him. The war poems of the forties present a panoramic vision of death and destruction, as in the masterful "Brother Fire":

> O delicate walker, babbler, dialectician Fire,
> O enemy and image of ourselves,
> Did we not on those mornings after the All Clear,
> When you were looting shops in elemental joy
> And singing as you swarmed up city block and spire,
> Echo your thought in ours? "Destroy! Destroy!"

At the same time he wrote a far more personal poem, "Prayer in Mid-passage," which addresses death, in its "fierce impersonality" ("O Thou my monster, Thou my guide"), as the mainspring of his work:

> Take therefore, though Thou disregard,
> This prayer, this hymn, this feckless word,
> O Thou my silence, Thou my song,
> To whom all focal doubts belong
> And but for whom this breath were breath—
> Thou my meaning, Thou my death.

In a later poem "A Hand of Snapshops: The Left-Behind" the poet asks, peering into his glass of stout, a series of riddles:

> Where can you find a fire that burns and gives no warmth?
> Where is the tall ship that chose to run on a rock?

13

Where are there more fish than ever filled the ocean?
Where can you find a clock that strikes when it has stopped?

Oh, poverty is the fire that burns and gives no warmth.
My youth is the tall ship that chose to run on a rock.
Men yet unborn could more than fill the ocean,
And death is the black clock that strikes when it has stopped.

In much of his work his obsession with his past, with memories that "flitter and champ in a dark cupboard," seems to predominate. Often he tries to regain the bright particularity, the sensuous awareness, of childhood; and to do so he uses childlike playful rhythms and metrical devices. With sparkling nonsense and satiric savagery he hacks away at the deadness of language and of life; and many of his poems are verbal triumphs. But often, as he expresses it in the dedicatory poem to his first (1948) *Collected Poems*, he "is content if things would image/ Themselves in their own dazzle, if the answers came quick and smooth . . ." It is not until the poems in *The Burning Perch* that he listens with full attention to "the black clock that strikes when it has stopped," and confronts his Loneliness and Otherness head-on. The poems in *The Burning Perch* are more direct and terrifying than any he had written. He goes over the same ground, treating the same subjects and frequently in the same manner, but with greater honesty and intensity. He uses the "same tunes that hang on pegs in the cloakrooms of the mind," but "off the peg seems made to measure now." And in the direct confrontation of loneliness and death, he became, with greater dimension than one would have thought possible, not only a real, but also a great, artist:

THE INTRODUCTION

They were introduced in a grave glade
And she frightened him because she was young

And thus too late. Crawly crawly
Went the twigs above their heads and beneath
The grass beneath their feet the larvae
Split themselves laughing. Crawly crawly
Went the cloud above the treetops reaching
For a sun that lacked the nerve to set
And he frightened her because he was old
And thus too early. Crawly crawly
Went the string quartet that was tuning up
In the back of the mind. You two should have met
Long since, he said, or else not now.
The string quartet in the back of the mind
Was all tuned up with nowhere to go.
They were introduced in a green grave.

[1967]

A PLACE
FOR THE GENUINE
(Marianne Moore)

THERE IS a Chinese saying that translation is the reverse side of the brocade, and all Marianne Moore's poetry is in that paradoxical sense translation. It is a carefully wrought imaginative fabric of observation and experience, based on common sense, with which she tries, in Conrad's phrase, "to render the highest kind of justice to the visible world." If she seems to shun "that radiance which poets/are supposed to have," it is because, as she states in a recent poem:

> Nothing mundane is divine;
> Nothing divine is mundane.

The true, original side of the brocade is never glimpsed, only suggested, but it is always there:

> The power of the visible
> is the invisible; as even where
> no tree of freedom grows,
> so-called brute courage knows.

Her protector is Saint Jerome, the patron saint of translators:

> Pacific yet passionate—
> for if not both, how
> could he be great?
> Jerome—reduced by what he'd been through—
> with tapering waist no matter what he ate,
> left us the Vulgate. . .

The present volume,[1] containing in addition to previously collected poems, four hitherto uncollected ones along with nine translations from *The Fables of La Fontaine,* is prefaced by Miss Moore's admonition to her reader: "Omissions are not accidents." What then has been left out? Several poems like "Half Deity," "See in the Midst of Fair Leaves," "Walking-Sticks and Paper-Weights and Water Marks," and earlier ones like "Roses Only," all omitted from *Collected Poems,* are again omitted here. Another much discussed poem that appeared in *Selected Poems* as "Black Earth" and again in *Collected Poems* as "Melancton" is dropped, I suppose because Miss Moore now finds its stanzas contrived and facile. There are omissions of individual lines from many poems; usually ones that seem flat and prosaic and will not be missed. There are happily some additions as well as omissions. "The Student," dropped from *Collected Poems,* is back. The section cut from "The Steeple Jack" has been restored. And an early poem "To a Prize Bird" (addressed to Bernard Shaw) is happily revived.

The most serious omission, and the one that is certain to baffle many readers, is the major portion of one of her best known poems. "Poetry" now retains only its first three lines, and these are amended to read:

> I, too, dislike it.
> Reading it, however, with a perfect contempt for it,
> one discovers in

[1] *The Complete Poems of Marianne Moore* (New York: Macmillan; Viking).

it, after all, a place for the
  genuine.

In this instance, Miss Moore, perhaps anticipating the disappointment of those readers who have made so much of her "liter-
alists of the imagination" and "imaginary gardens with real
toads in them," appends the complete original version, along
with the notes to it, in a new note. The first three lines of the
poem originally read:

> I, too, dislike it: there are things
>   that are important beyond all
> this fiddle.
>   Reading it, however, with a
>   perfect contempt for it, one
>   discovers in
>   it after all, a place for the
>   genuine.

If we are to take Miss Moore seriously, and I think we must,
since, however playful, "omissions are not accidents," why has
she transformed what was essentially an essay into an epigram?
Is it that she is weary of what many pompous critics have made
of her poetic dictum? Or is it her feeling that the entire poem
merely defines the word "genuine" in a rather prosaic, tedious,
and insistent editorial manner; that it is merely illustrative of
the phrase "all this fiddle"; that, in a word, it lacks the gusto
that she feels poetry should have? I have always thought that
this poem was little more than an epigram, and I am happy to
see that Miss Moore seems to agree. It may be that she wishes
these lines to stand as a kind of coda, an ironic footnote to this
complete volume; "after all," set off as it now is by commas,
takes on a new emphasis and significance at the time of her
eightieth birthday.

18

Sentir avec ardeur—to feel with ardor—Miss Moore quotes the words (of Madame Boufflers, a contemporary of Rousseau's) in speaking of Tom Fool, the race horse, who has the quality of "submerged magnificence," magnetized by feeling. Many critics, speaking of Miss Moore's work, have done precisely what she has asked them not to do, that is, placed "too stern an intellectual emphasis upon this quality or that," and have failed to see that her best poems are all a framework of feeling. It is no accident that she admires the ballet, that art form which seems at times inhuman, lacking in feeling only because it is *all* feeling. Many years ago Miss Moore wrote of Pavlova that her "humor, esprit, a sense of style—and also a moral quality—make it impossible for her to show off, to be hard, to be dull; the same thing that in life made her self-controlled so that she was not a prison to what she prized." And more recently she addressed Arthur Mitchell, who danced the role of Puck in Balanchine's *A Midsummer Night's Dream*, as a "contagious gem of virtuosity." Mobility is for her not only necessary; it is magical.

In a lecture, referring to her poetic practice, Miss Moore has said: "When I began writing verse, I regarded flowing continuity as indispensable." Rhythm was her primary objective. "If I succeeded in embodying a rhythm that preoccupied me, I was satisfied. Uniform line length seemed to me essential as accrediting the satisfactory model stanza and I sometimes ended a line with a hyphen, expecting the reader to maintain the line unbroken (disregarding the hyphen). I have found readers misled by the hyphen, mistaking it as an arcane form of emphasis, so I seldom use it today." Miss Moore apparently now feels that uniform line length is less important than the overall rhythm; she has not hesitated, in many poems reprinted here, to break up a uniform line or stanza in order to avoid hyphenated end words. At times, she goes too far in her revision, I think, but she appears determined to show that she has not just been counting syllables all these years, as many critics have insisted. "Poetry is a magic of pauses . . ." she maintains. "I do not know what syllabic verse is. I find no appropriate application for it."

Miss Moore's poetry is indeed a translation of emotion, an attempt to objectify feeling, to see, like the hero of her poem, "the rock/crystal thing to see—the startling El Greco/brimming with inner light—that covets nothing that it has let go." It is all wonderfully precise and rewarding. It is only in her actual translation—of *The Fables of La Fontaine*—that the threads of her fabric become confused, jumbled, and frayed, and the suggestion of the luminous original disappears. "The rhythm of a translation as motion," she has written, "should suggest the rhythm of the original." Miss Moore's rhythm often does so ingeniously, but more often, I think, she forgets what Alexander Fraser Tytler pointed out in his eighteenth-century *Essay on the Principles of Translation*, namely, that an imitation of the style of the original text, while always desirable, must always be regulated by the nature or genius of the languages of the original and of the translation. The greater brevity that French admits of by its nature cannot be approximated in English by a heavily Latinate diction. The simple dramatic impact of La Fontaine is often impeded in her English versions by affectation and mannerism, which are very far from the natural conversational tone that Miss Moore advocates in her own work. It is unfortunate that among the nine examples of her translations given here she did not choose to include "The Dog Who Dropped Substance for Shadow," a real triumph.

Yet the years Miss Moore spent translating La Fontaine were certainly not lost, for they helped bring to her own poetry greater directness and vigor, as evidenced in the poems written since. We should all be grateful for the courage, independence, and moral sense that have produced *The Complete Poems*. The book is not just "the approved triumph" that may easily be honored "because something else is small"; it is great because, a result of lifelong restraint and discipline, it so clearly acknowledges "the spiritual forces which have made it."

[1968]

WHEN POETS RISE
TO THE OCCASION

THE SUBTITLE of this volume,[1] "An anthology of occasional poetry by people better known in other walks of life and designed to be enjoyed by people from any walk of life," leads one to ask what "occasional poetry" is, and how and by whom it gets written.

Yeats's poem on visiting schoolchildren is sometimes given as an example of an occasional poem. It is certainly one growing out of an occasion, and although the occasion is not of itself profound, the sentiments that it evokes are anything but shallow. But then, in this sense, Keats also wrote occasional poems—when looking into Chapman's Homer or when listening to a nightingale. Indeed, if we were to list those poems in any language beginning with "when," whether directly stated or implied, we would find that the greatest lyric poetry is by its nature occasional.

What the anthologist here means is something else, however. "The spirit of poetry lives in every human heart, as Emer-

[1] *Poetry from Hidden Springs*, selected and edited by Paul Jordan-Smith (New York: Doubleday).

22

son forcibly suggested long ago," he writes. "And almost every man at some time in the course of his life, has been lifted out of himself by some rare experience which awakens his sense of wonder, when self-consciousness falls away and, for a moment at least, he is caught up in a state of ecstasy; and while under that spell any man—lawyer, doctor, merchant, chief—may feel compelled to write a poem." As examples of those who have been lifted, caught up, and compelled, Mr. Jordan-Smith gives us the noted bacteriologist, Dr. Hans Zinsser:

> For I have widely wandered and
>   have been
> Blessed with high tasks and dear
>   companionships;
> Warm hearts and noble courage
>   have I seen
> And tender curving of beloved lips.

He offers also samples of the work of Dr. Franklin Henry Giddings, the noted sociologist, who wrote in a preface to his *Pagan Poems* (1914) : "I have made the book because it bade me make it!" Included also is a poem (not a bad one, either) by Harold S. Hartley, a Northville (Michigan) carpenter, on the occasion of hearing the Italian poet, Salvatore Quasimodo. There is also a Connecticut housewife who is frustrated at the kitchen sink while her soul "is chiming to the bay of hounds." And Ruth Guthrie Harding, also known as Guthrie Burton, an authority (unacknowledged) on metrics, who was born at Tunkhannock, Pennsylvania, and, according to the editor, "rejoices in it." There is the bridge builder, David Barnard Steinman, the industrialist, Hyman Jordan Sobiloff, the "Father of Radio," Dr. Lee De Forest. And then, also, Reginald Pole, the British composer, director of Shakespeare's plays, and friend of Rupert Brooke, who ended up not surprisingly in southern California, where on the edge of the Coachella Desert near Palm Springs, he discovered in the white sands an abandoned can of Prince Albert tobacco and, on this occasion, composed a poem that concludes:

> Who wrought this strangely way-
>   ward meeting
> Under a desert sky,
> Staring grotesquely, each at other,
>   The tailored prince and I? . . .
>
> Yet here was a man of blood and
>   passion
>   Who loved, and laughed—like
>   me;
> Once king of a far off foreign
>   country
> Called England, over the sea.

It does not matter that Prince Albert was never king of England. Clearly many have been called.

All children are geniuses, said Jean Cocteau—with the exception, he added, of the child poetess, Minou Drouet. She, he maintained, was an eighty-year-old midget. At the age of four or five, the child is not put off by placing impossibles together: he is unselfconscious, and he can often achieve in his spontaneous rhymes, as in his drawings, far more than he realizes; but as the intellect and the emotions develop, the problem begins. Child prodigies in poetry are hard to take because the reader is painfully aware of the occasion that gave rise to the poem, and of the inability of the poet's craft to cope with his subject. He is also aware of the adult presence looking over the child's shoulder, guiding, and attempting to control, the result. With the adult amateur "occasional" poet something of the same thing happens: looking over his shoulder, however, are all the poets, past and present, whom he has read. And no matter how moved he may be by some particular occasion, what he pours forth in his moment of ecstasy is apt to be a poem that had been written long ago by a poet of talent and training. Only genius can afford the risk of accident.

The beat poets have given the go-ahead signal to thousands of untrained versifiers; their arrogance knows no bounds, and their pronouncements on poetics are of unequalled pretension. Side by side with the beat self-expressionist stands the genteel traditionalist, as represented in this anthology; his arrogance is also transcendent. To him all modern poetry is a betrayal: nothing, Mr. Jordan-Smith would have us believe, has really happened in poetry since Kipling. There have been a few volumes that have "crept quietly out," to use Mr. Jordan-Smith's phrase, over the past fifty years; but apparently it takes more than these few undetected swallows to make a summer. The beat poet and the genteel traditionalist share the same pompous concern for poetics, for in reality they have almost nothing to say. Each feels that he alone, in the one case by throwing out all tradition and in the other by preserving what he mistakenly believes to be tradition, can bring poetry back to life.

Occasional verse—*vers d'occasion*—verse written for occasions manages to get written all the time. The occasion may be slight or it may be solemn: the best recent example is the poem composed by Robert Frost for President Kennedy's inauguration. (The fact that he could not see to read it only served to heighten the occasion.) Mr. Frost's new volume contains many such remarkable occasional brevities. In more formal societies than ours the occasion always called for poetry. It still often does, and there are those who can rise to it. Not all of them are poets and not all of them pretend to be, but the level of their verse is high— higher, I think, than is evidenced by some of the examples in this anthology. Whether or not what they produce is poetry of lasting merit is another matter.

[1962]

TOUGH-MINDED
AND HUMBLE
(A. D. Hope)

A MERICAN READERS who came to know the work of
Australia's leading poet, A. D. Hope, after he visited here in 1967 for the Lincoln Center Festival
and again in 1969 at the invitation of the Library of Congress,
will welcome the publication of his new book of poems.[1] Some
may be disappointed that this volume contains less savage satire
than they had encountered in his *Collected Poems*. There is only
one real satiric piece, "The Great Baboons," and although it is
beautifully executed, as one would expect from Mr. Hope, it is
less impressive than many of the other poems. The satiric bite
and the savage wit are still present, but they are tempered in this
collection by a great and moving tenderness.

Irony, of course, is not absent from these pages. Mr. Hope,
in a series of delightful "Sonnets to Baudelaire," pays tribute to
the poet who, more than any other, he says, drank "deepest of
that pure sardonic draught," and knew best what laws forge
"Irony to Beauty":

[1] A. D. Hope, *New Poems: 1965-1969* (New York: Viking).

26

> You, naked, the first gardener under God,
> Who tilled our rotting paradise, from its
>   sod
> Raised monstrous blooms and taught my
>   tongue the craft.

Mr. Hope likewise forges irony to beauty here at every turn, especially in the "Six Songs for Chloë," a marvelous sequence exploring every aspect of love, where wit informs from every angle a compelling exploration of *"luxe, calme, et volupté."* There is greater attention, however, to music; Mr. Hope has never written more musical verse. Music itself is the subject of two of the finest poems, "Vivaldi, Bird and Angel or Il Cardellino" and "Moschus Moschiferus, A Song for St. Cecilia's Day." Both poems are triumphs of the poet's exquisite inner ear, one treating the perverse and evil use of music and the other its divine and proper use. "Moschus Moschiferus" is one of his most brilliant poems and, to my mind, one of the truly great poems of the century. A close look at it shows something of the peculiar nature of A. D. Hope's craftsmanship and the special quality of his genius.

The poem describes the destruction of the Kastura, the small deer hunted for their musk pods in the jungles of Assam on the border of Tibet. The animals are lured by the playing of a flute into a jungle glade, where hunters await them hidden in the trees. The deer, enchanted by the music and "an ecstasy that conquers fear," are drawn into "a net of crystalline sound," then shot by the hidden archers who remove the musk glands and leave the carcasses to rot. The poem concludes:

> A hundred thousand or so are killed each year;
> Cause and effect are very simply linked:
> Rich scents demand the musk, and so the deer,
> Its source, must soon, they say, become extinct.

Divine Cecilia, there is no more to say!
Of all who praised the power of music, few
Knew of these things. In honor of your day
Accept this song I too have made for you.

Mr. Hope remarked on reading this poem publicly that he had taken the facts from an article in a scientific journal. But who else could have realized so magnificently the possibilities of the subject, so richly sensuous and at the same time so supremely ironic—the irony of Baudelaire forged to the greatest beauty?

A. D. Hope in *The Cave and the Spring*,[2] first published in 1965 and now made available in this country for the first time, says that he takes the Cave and the Spring to stand in his essays principally for the sensory and the verbal imagination respectively. "Wordsworth had one of the two essential gifts of the poet," he writes, "the sensory imagination. What he touched with his senses fired him and combined in forms of beauty and vision. He was often defective in the other essential gift of the poet, the verbal imagination. With Coleridge it was almost the other way about. Ideas, books, things put into words were the true source of his imagination. . . ." Coleridge stopped writing poetry, Mr. Hope contends, because of the disastrous influence of Wordsworth, who tried to make him respond to natural scenery, which was simply not his way. One feels that Mr. Hope is very much on the side of Coleridge; he is also a very bookish man, responding in full to his reading, as in the case of "Moschus Moschiferus." He has said that when not composing, or writing about, poetry, he enjoys reading books on biology and other sciences. (Somewhat like Allen Tate, who once remarked to me that at one point in his life he never traveled without several books on astronomy in his luggage.) One of the finest poems in this collection is "On an Engraving by Casserius," inspired by turning the leaves of "this majestic book." A. D. Hope's imagination is primarily ver-

2 A. D. Hope, *The Cave and the Spring: Essays on Poetry* (Chicago: University of Chicago Press).

bal, but at his best the two gifts combine, and the sensory imagination is equally strong. Certainly no one who had not carefully observed the natural scene (his childhood in Tasmania perhaps here comes into play) could communicate sensuous detail as he does in so many fine passages.

The essays in *The Cave and the Spring* represent, Mr. Hope says, "a poet's occasional reflections on different aspects of his craft and they are written much as poems are written, to show forth and to illuminate an idea rather than to argue and demonstrate a truth." He is excellent in examining the art of Coleridge, Marlowe, and Dryden, in the case of the latter praising the art of modulation, of which A. D. Hope is himself the modern master. Whenever he is discussing harmony and clarity in poetry, he is as lucid and as rewarding as in his poems. He only goes astray, it seems to me, when, as in "Free Verse: A Post-Mortem," he argues rather than illuminates. Free verse, he says, is a disease, which began with Whitman and, having gone through a period of incubation in France at the end of the nineteenth century, was transported back to England by the Americans, Eliot and Pound. And Mr. Hope has some pretty harsh words for Eliot's "prosodic nonsense." With Eliot finished off in a sentence or two, he informs us that we have nothing more to fear since free verse is now dead. Poets of the world—and doctors of literature—please note. It is only here, and later when he is discussing "creative writing" courses in universities, that he sounds shrill and a little silly. One may agree with him basically, but his tone is wrong and his point is lost. (And somebody, incidentally, at the University of Chicago Press ought to go hide his head in the polluted sand of Lake Michigan for allowing a book to appear in which there is a reference to "Marion [*sic*] Moore's journal *Poetry*, published in Chicago.")

For A. D. Hope there are three faces of love—the active, the contemplative, and the creative. It is the creative life that he admirably explores in his essays and demonstrates brilliantly in his poems. He is, as a critic as well as a poet, both tough-minded and humble, one who has written poems that we may wish to question closely because of the care and skill with which they were composed, but poems that also raise questions that may indeed be, as he says of those raised by poems in general, "more searching than our own."

[1970]

LOUISE BOGAN:
A WOMAN'S WORDS

W HEN Louise Bogan died suddenly on 4 February
1970, at the age of seventy-two, there were
many tributes to her in the press. None of these
said more about her in a direct and moving way and with an
economy that matched the economy so characteristic of Miss
Bogan's own work than that published in *The New Yorker*, the
magazine with which she had been associated for some thirty-
seven years:

The first poetry review that Louise Bogan did for *The
New Yorker* appeared in the issue of 21 March 1931, and
the last in the issue of 28 December 1968. In this magazine, between those two dates—that is to say, for thirty-
eight years—poets good, bad, and indifferent came under
a perceptive and just scrutiny. Out of what they did or
didn't do with language she often constructed a kind of
portrait of them of lasting value. Their work was also,
when this was relevant, placed in a line of descent or a

tradition. Aesthetic experiments were viewed with an open mind, inflation was punctured, and entrepreneurism was put in its place. At times, the exactness and lucidity of her criticism suggested that she was attempting to create a new kind of lyric poetry out of statements *about* poetry.

Louise Bogan was born in Livermore Falls, Maine. Both her parents were of Irish descent. Her father's father was a sea captain who sailed out of Portland. Though she returned to New England periodically, when she was tired and wanted to refresh her spirit, her home for most of her adult life was New York City. She lived quietly, almost anonymously, in Washington Heights, in an apartment full of books, with a photograph of Mozart's birthplace on one wall and, from a living-room window, a narrow view, between apartment buildings, of the Hudson River. She published six volumes of poetry and two volumes of literary criticism. A third is now in the process of being printed. She also did a number of distinguished collaborative translations, which include Goethe's "Elective Affinities" and a selection from the "Journal" of Jules Renard.

All the literary honors that *are* an honor to receive she received.[1] To say that she was one of the finest lyric poets of our time is hardly to do her justice; her best poems have an emotional depth and force and a perfection of form that owe very little to the age she lived in and are not likely to go out of style, being a matter of nobody's style but her own. She was a handsome, direct, impressive, vulnerable woman. In whatever she wrote, the line of truth was exactly superimposed on the line of feeling. One look at her work—or sometimes one look at her—made any number of disheartened artists take heart and go on being the kind

---

[1] Louise Bogan's final book of poetry, *The Blue Estuaries, Poems 1923-1968*, received neither the National Book Award nor the Pulitzer Prize; this injustice distinctly diminished the honor of both these awards in the eyes of many of her fellow poets.

of dedicated creature they were intended to be. In defense
of the true artist, she wrote:

Come, drunks and drug-takers; come perverts unnerved!
Receive the laurel, given, though late, on merit; to whom
    and wherever deserved.

Parochial punks, trimmers, nice people, joiners true-blue,
Get the hell out of the way of the laurel. It is deathless
    And it isn't for you.[2]

To certain elements of her life and work that are touched on
here—and clearly by someone who knew her well both as a
woman and an artist—I would like to return in a moment.

There were other tributes from poets old and young. One
of the most interesting was a poem by Daniel Hoffman that
presents her character in cameo; he read it at the Library of
Congress shortly after her death:

THE SONNET
(REMEMBERING LOUISE BOGAN)

The Sonnet, she told the crowd of bearded
        youths, their hands exploring
            rumpled girls
            is a sacred

vessel: it takes a civilization
        to conceive its shape or know
            its uses. The kids
            stared as though

A Sphinx now spake the riddle of
        a blasted day. And few,
            she said, who would
            be *avant-garde*

2 "Several Voices Out of a Cloud."

consider that the term is drawn
> from tactics in the Prussian
>> War, nor think
>>> when once they've breached

the fortress of a form, then send
> their shock troops yet again
>> to breach the form,
>> there's no form—

. . . they asked for her opinion of
> 'the poetry of Rock.'
>> After a drink
>> with the professors

she said, This is a bad time,
> bad, for poetry.
>> Then with maenad
>> gaze upon

the imaged ghost of a comelier day:
> I've enjoyed this visit,
>> your wife's sheets
>> are Irish linen.

Usually when a poet of Miss Bogan's distinction dies, there has already over the years grown up around his or her body of work an even greater body of fact and fiction about the poet's life. So insistent was Miss Bogan, however, on maintaining her privacy during her lifetime, so reticent about making public any of the details of her private life, that on her death there was no residue of legend for her critics to call upon in writing about her; and that is just the way she wanted it. A collection of the major part of her prose pieces was in her publisher's hands when she died and has now appeared (*A Poet's Alphabet*, New York, 1970). One of the editors of the volume, Robert Phelps, in the draft of an introduction had made a number of personal references—all very laudatory—and had included an entertaining account of a visit he and she had made to Melville's tomb in the Bronx. Louise Bogan was adamant that the entire piece be re-written and that all personal references be removed. John Hall Wheelock, one of Miss Bogan's oldest friends, spoke at the memorial service held for her at the Academy of Arts and Letters in New York on 11 March 1970.[3] Mr. Wheelock, quoting W. H. Auden's "In Memory of W. B. Yeats," said that on her death Louise Bogan, like Yeats, had become her poems. And yet another friend, Glenway Wescott, said to me later that it is time now that a legend begin to grow up around those magnificent poems, which seem assured of a long life and which no biographical bits of information are going to damage in any way. I hope that I may be forgiven, therefore, for mentioning first a few personal details about this extraordinary woman whom I knew for almost twenty-five years.

When I first met Louise Bogan in 1947, she was for me already a living legend. I had discovered her poetry in the middle thirties in college. It should be remembered, however, that the woman poet who was then most admired by undergraduates was Edna St. Vincent Millay. Tennessee Williams, then Thomas Lanier Williams and a friend of mine at Washington University, wrote at this time a sonnet that concluded somewhat like this:

> Sappho, O God, has gone her soundless way,
> But spare us a while our glorious Millay!

When I discovered the poems of Louise Bogan in Louis Untermeyer's anthology and in the pages of *The New Yorker*, I looked up every piece of her work I could locate and everything, then very little, that had been written about her. Official biographies

---

[3] At this ceremony, at which I presided, the speakers were, in addition to Mr. Wheelock, Léonie Adams, Richard Wilbur, and William Maxwell; a statement from Allen Tate, who was unable to attend, was also read. I am indebted to the participants for their permission to quote extensively from a taping of this service, which is to be deposited at the Library of Congress.

said only that she was born in Maine, attended the Girls' Latin
School in Boston, and married Curt Alexander, an army officer
with whom she lived briefly in New York and later in the Pan-
ama Canal Zone. He died shortly after the birth of their only
child, a daughter; she later married the poet Raymond Holden,
from whom she was divorced after a number of years. It was the
passionate intensity and control in her work that appealed to me.
I remember on my first trip to New York in the summer of 1938
—on my way to France for three months of study—that I wandered into Scribner's and acquired a beautiful, signed copy of
The Sleeping Fury, which had just been published. I read that
book over and over night and day and quoted from it frequently
during that summer, much to the disapproval of one or two
young writers I then met, who looked down their noses at Louise
Bogan and had good words only for W. H. Auden, Stephen
Spender, and C. Day Lewis. I gave the book later to a young lady
in St. Louis with whom I thought I was in love. She had experienced, if not a passionate interest in me, a passionate interest at
least in the poetry of Louise Bogan. She became, many years
afterwards, a well-known writer of detective stories, and I often
wonder what happened to the book. I have many signed copies
of Louise Bogan's work, but I wish I had that one back.

At the time we met in the summer of 1947, Louise Bogan
was greatly appreciated among poets but had no great reputation
with the general public. For some years her work had been
neglected or overlooked, except by a few critics such as Allen
Tate and Yvor Winters. She had just been elected to the Institute
of Arts and Letters, an honor long overdue. We met in Vermont
at the home of Barbara Howes, who was to become my wife
shortly afterwards. It was Barbara's magazine *Chimera* that had
brought us together: Louise had been a contributor to that review, and a poem of mine had just appeared there. Barbara and
I sat for hours at Louise's feet as she quoted poetry and regaled
us with stories about the literary world—she always liked to
quote Oscar Wilde's description of it as that "poisoned bowl"—

that she disliked but that she knew so well. She spoke at length of the new work by her protégé Theodore Roethke, which was sure to make an impression, she said, in spite of its dependence on James Joyce.

Barbara and I left for Europe just after our marriage, and during our three years there we kept in touch with Louise. She was a marvelous letter writer. Often hers were very short letters —"very" she abbreviated as "v."—but little cameos of perceptive comment and feeling, like her poems, like her criticism. When we returned to Vermont, Louise was one of our first visitors. She came regularly, usually once in the summer and once again in the fall, and stayed never for a period of more than four days. (She liked to quote the familiar proverb that guests are like fish; after three days they stink.) We looked forward to Louise's visits; it was always a time of wonderful talk and laughter that gave us both sustenance for months afterwards. Louise was a city person—she loved New York. But the country was important to her—the New England landscape, the sea and mountains that nurtured her poems. She loved it dearly, but she had at the same time a fear of the country, a fear of being trapped there. This feeling of delight in, and terror of, the landscape runs through all her poems. The fear of being trapped perhaps owed much to an experience years earlier when she and Raymond Holden were living in the foothills of the Berkshires. They drove back home one evening to find their country house burning to the ground and all her papers—her entire output since early school days—with it.

Louise did not like to walk, but she loved being driven, and we spent hours driving over the back country roads. We had a cottage on the place, and we tried for years to persuade her to walk up to see it. Ten years went by and she never got up there because we could not drive. What we did most during those days and nights was talk, and talk was always about poetry—hers sparkling with wit and studded with indignation. "Heavenly Dinah!" she would exclaim or, again, "Great God in the foothills!" And she was the only person I ever heard use those lovely expressions. She was a lapsed Catholic, but she did say strongly at times that she felt there must be some supreme power that had shaped all this universe. We always had the feeling that this power was one we could approach only in a civilized manner —in human terms—"Great God in the foothills!"

It was Louise Bogan who introduced Barbara and me to the lovely game of *bouts rimés*. This she had played with her friends Rolfe Humphries, Léonie Adams, Allen Tate, Ford Madox Ford, and others in the twenties. (*Bouts rimés*, of course, means rhymed ends: we would choose the end words, the rhyme scheme, and then as quickly as possible, each produce a poem. I understand that in some of the sessions in the twenties the poets played by the clock, seeing who could first whip off a sonnet. We were not quite that exacting about it but did try to be as quick as possible.) Louise was always fastidious about her writing. She used to say, looking over some of the surrealist rubbish that was then as now being poured out, that any one of us could write that kind of thing in the middle of the night with our hands tied behind our backs. It was wonderful to see what she could produce within a few minutes—often lines of great beauty and depth as well as ones of great wit. Somewhere among my papers I have kept the best of these *bouts rimés;* I wish I had been able to find a few examples to offer. I remember a sonnet she wrote once with amazing speed, using the absurdly difficult rhyme words we had forced upon her. Entitled "Henry James," it concluded with a line that went somewhat like this:

He put on and took off and put on and took off his hat.

Once when Louise was with us in Vermont, she and I went into a small country store to get some supplies. She wanted to purchase some paper on which to work. I offered her what was available—a filler of looseleaf notebook paper. She turned it down firmly and rather grandly, saying, "I could never write poems on paper that has holes in it."

38

During the period when Barbara Howes and I lived in Greenwich Village, we saw Louise more often. She would come down to dinner on the subway from Washington Heights and then in the early morning hours take a taxi back uptown. A friend of hers and mine has remarked that as an evening of conversation went on, Louise Bogan would become increasingly Irish. She did often come up with stories about her family. She told us a number of times that for years her mother had claimed there were a number of dishes that she could not prepare because she did not possess a double boiler. "Now you know that was silly," Louise said. "Never, never in your life lead a double boiler existence!" There was in Louise Bogan's conversation the same elegance that is in her poems. I have been listening during the past few days to her recordings in the Library of Congress Archive of Recorded Poetry and Literature. With her rich contralto voice, she has the most perfect enunciation that you will encounter among poets today: every consonant, every vowel, every syllable is given its proper value, and then there are the pauses around which the poems are constructed, all carefully observed. She says in her poem "St. Christopher":

The middle class is what we are.

And in her personal life she prided herself on her middle-class background. When she received some unexpected but deserved honor, she would often remark, but of course only to her closest friends, "Not bad for a little Irish girl from Boston."

Louise Bogan was a warm and generous person, and although she was not easy to know, how rewarding it was to those who knew her well. She was independent, and although she loved seeing people, she did not like to see them in a casual manner. After several enraged and threatening telephone calls from irate, untalented poets whose work she had dismissed in the pages of *The New Yorker*, she had obtained an unlisted phone number. (She disliked the telephone and used it rarely.) I remember that in the early years of our friendship I sometimes called her when I was passing through New York, and each time she would say at once, "I'd love to see you, I'd love to see you, but I've just had a tooth extracted. . . ." After hearing this a few times, I was tempted to say that she wouldn't have any teeth left if she kept having them extracted; but what I understood was that she did not at the moment feel up to seeing anyone, even someone she approved of. We often met for lunch at the Oyster Bar in Grand Central Station, a favorite spot of hers near the New York Public Library, where she enjoyed working, and not far from the trains she loved. (Her daughter persuaded her to fly for the first time a few years ago. I met her after her first flight and she exclaimed, "I have flown through the air like a bird!" as if flying were the most natural thing in the world to a lyric poet. She never really learned, however, to like being *inside* an airplane.) With the trains at hand she felt secure, able perhaps to make a quick getaway if something dreadful developed and in the meantime to relax and enjoy the conversation and the seafood.

John Hall Wheelock tells of meeting Louise Bogan in the twenties when Scribner's, for which he worked as an editor, became her publisher. Scribner's brought out three of her books, but after several years passed, Mr. Wheelock says, her innate distrust of publishers—a distrust shared with Lord Byron and many other poets—asserted itself. She summoned him one day to meet her at a Child's Restaurant near the publishing house. Then for several hours he was forced to listen to the most terrible accusations. She told him that she was going to leave Scribner's for another publisher. "I don't feel like quarreling today, Louise," Mr. Wheelock pleaded, "and if I did, I think I'd like to quarrel with William Carlos Williams, perhaps, or with Wallace Stevens or someone else, but not with you." Her sense of humor, however, had deserted her, and her decision was final. The house of Scribner lost one of its most illustrious authors, but Mr. Wheelock had not lost a friend. Yet for years afterwards, he says, she would sometimes in a mischievous mood taunt him in the pres-

ence of others with what she liked to call "our old quarrel." Even
a few weeks before her death she introduced Mr. Wheelock at a
meeting of the National Institute of Arts and Letters to an
acquaintance and described him as the man who was her publisher before their quarrel.

Allen Tate, also aware of her independent spirit, says:
"Louise Bogan ignored literary fashion, went her own way, and
as early as the mid-1920s was a lyric poet in the Elizabethan-
metaphysical mode—traditional yet wholly original. For the
originality is not in the exacerbating image, but in the subtle
and elusive vision. No influences can be discerned." It is indeed
difficult to point to any clearly defined influences, but it may be
interesting to try to pin down one or two. Louise Bogan and I
collaborated a few years ago in compiling *The Golden Journey:
Poems for Young People* (Chicago, 1965), a happy and rewarding venture for us both. Of our collaboration, in an unpublished
account, she had this to say, and I think her remarks may give
some clues to her early reading (she said many times that she
could not remember what on earth she had done before she
learned to read) :

> One evening, as I remember, quite casually and in a
> completely unplanned way, we began the game of "Do you
> remember?"—and we soon were surprising each other by
> early enthusiasms that we discovered we shared. Tenny-
> son's "Brook," for example, the first poem which had ex-
> cited me, around the age of nine or ten. Chesterton's "Song
> of Quoodle," more or less lost in one of his prose books. An
> exquisite Kipling lyric, also more or less mislaid in *Puck of
> Pook's Hill.* The wonderful children's verse of Christina
> Rossetti and Elizabeth Madox Roberts. . . . We went on and
> on and sometime after midnight decided that we should do
> the anthology together.
>
> We had other meetings—one on the outskirts of the
> MacDowell Colony, where we spent some mornings and

afternoons surrounded by piles of books which Bill had transported thither in a station wagon—separate works, for the most part, of this poet or that—for we prided ourselves in *not* anthologizing from anthologies. We laughed a great deal; we were never for one moment bored; and we kept on "remembering."

We took our title from James Elroy Flecker, a poet we both admired. What Louise did not say here—but what she did sometimes relate to friends—was that because guests were not permitted within the MacDowell Colony itself I stayed at a fine motel just below it in a room overlooking a lovely millstream. It was here that Louise joined me each day to work on our anthology. The room was equipped with two extremely large double beds which were just the right height so that we could spread out all our books and materials in front of us. And the motel was equipped with a most efficient bar from which we could order cold drinks, and so looking over the poems and out over the stream, we spent several delightful days. Louise, with her New England sense of propriety, enjoyed the rather *louche* and suggestive notion of having compiled an anthology for young people in a motel bedroom with a younger man.

For the Library of Congress Festival of Poetry held in connection with National Children's Book Week last year, Louise Bogan, on a panel with William Cole to discuss poetry for children, chose to read two poems from *The Golden Journey*. The first, "Ferry Me Across the Water" by Christina Rossetti, she said, was one that means absolutely nothing, perhaps, but one toward which she felt a shock of recognition each time she came on it anew:

> "Ferry me across the water,
>   Do, boatman, do."
> "If you've a penny in your purse
>   I'll ferry you."

42

"I have a penny in my purse,
    And my eyes are blue;
So ferry me across the water,
    Do, boatman, do!"

"Step into my ferryboat,
    Be they black or blue,
And for the penny in your purse
    I'll ferry you."

Louise pointed out that there are in this poem, simple as it is, overtones of death, the river of Lethe. These are the facts we realize as adults but which the little girl who is speaking does not, and implicit in it is a kind of magic. The other poem she chose to read was one more explicitly concerned with death, "The Midnight Skaters" by Edmund Blunden. In this poem skaters are described on a frozen winter pond while death watches them from the dark waters below. The poem ends:

Court him, elude him, reel and pass,
And let him hate you through the glass.

It is significant, surely, that Louise, who had been severely ill not long before, should choose two poems on death.

Critics usually place Louise Bogan as a metaphysical poet, stemming from the seventeenth century, but it is well to remember that as a student at the Girls' Latin School she was nurtured on the poetry of the Victorian era, and to certain Victorian poets she never lost her allegiance. In teaching, she referred students constantly to "In Memoriam," a great poem that she felt was not sufficiently appreciated today. When asked how to get young people interested in poetry, she answered without hesitation: "Read to them until they can read themselves." There were in her day teachers—"women who were wild about poetry." She had one teacher who introduced the girls to the poetry of A. E. Housman, "who was," she said, "very hot stuff in those days." There was a good deal of nudging and giggling in the classroom, but the teacher insisted that this was *serious*. Another lesser figure whom she then discovered was Arthur Symons; and it was through Arthur Symons that she, like T. S. Eliot, discovered the French poets—Mallarmé, Laforgue, and, of course, Baudelaire. Another poem in *The Golden Journey* that she especially liked was "The Rainy Summer," by Alice Meynell:

> There's much afoot in heaven and earth this year;
>   The winds hunt up the sun, hunt up the moon,
> Trouble the dubious dawn, hasten the drear
>   Height of a threatening noon.
>
> No breath of boughs, no breath of leaves, of fronds,
>   May linger or grow warm; the trees are loud;
> The forest, rooted, tosses in her bonds,
>   And strains against the cloud.
>
> No scents may pause within the garden-fold;
>   The rifled flowers are cold as ocean-shells;
> Bees, humming in the storm, carry their cold
>   Wild honey to cold cells.

If we examine it alongside a poem of Louise Bogan's middle period, "Dark Summer," I think we can recognize certain parallels:

> Under the thunder-dark, the cicadas resound.
> The storm in the sky mounts, but is not yet heard.
> The shaft and the flash wait, but are not yet found.
>
> The apples that hang and swell for the late comer,
> The simple spell, the rite not for our word,
> The kisses not for our mouths,—light the dark summer.

Léonie Adams has spoken brilliantly of some of the early influences and directions in Louise Bogan's work:

> Louise Bogan's first book, which was called *Body of This Death*, had for its underlying theme the redemption of life as in art, music, poetry, and perhaps most of all in a kind of living, of choice. It appeared in 1923, almost fifty years ago, and the obituaries have all quoted poems from it —the ones I've seen. It was not then precocious to have a collection of poems at twenty-five or twenty-six although for some it was unwise; it was precocious to have a volume in which there was almost no taint of the ungainliness of youth. . . . I met Louise Bogan at about the time of its appearance and although I was dazzled by its accomplishment, I did not then realize—and perhaps it was not until just now when I was reading over all her work and thinking of her over the years that I named to myself—what was perhaps its most extraordinary precocity, her certainty of self-discernment as poet. Perhaps she herself was not aware of it then, but had made the secret compact—as in the old legendary bonds, unbreakable though made unawares—which came to light years later in the words:
>
> Ignorant, I took up my burden in the wilderness.
> Wise with great wisdom, I shall lay it down upon flowers.[4]
>
> . . . To say that the first book is still quoted from is not to say there is any lack of growth in the work. I think that each new book or portion of a book was an advance of the peculiarly living sort which becomes "apparent by invisible stages." . . . I wrote a time ago and feel as strongly or more strongly now that hers was an art of limits, the limits of the inner occasion and of the recognized mode. These are formal limits; but with the discernment of which I have spoken I should say she accepted with some others of the

[4] "After the Persian," part IV.

45

best of her poetic generation that that generation was not to be so abundant as its predecessor, and later within her work as critic she would welcome a generation that would be more abundant again. . . . I was not then aware that *she* was so aware that she must function not only as a poet of her own time but within the limits accorded a woman poet . . . For the poet of intensity, the lyric poet, awaiting the inner occasion, it is truly rare to manage those occasions with a continuing discretion and to work toward what is to be perfectly achieved and is in the central and tragic mode . . . There was still at the time not a little of the Matchless Orinda syndrome in readers of women's poetry. It was easy for one of her probity to avoid the mistakes some others had made—those she used to call (after the late Clinch Calkins) the "O God, the pain girls." There could not be the confusion of the role of woman and the role of poet, or any exploitation of the role of woman. She knew, moreover, that she should not model herself upon the women she admired and who were closest to her in time. But she read good women writers, contemporaries such as Viola Meynell, who were not poets but writers of prose and noted in them a marvelous delicacy and restraint at employing the feminine sensibility for the scene. There was no need for a woman to justify this attachment by a philosophy of nature or a metaphysic of angels: she took it for granted. Perhaps to respond effectively to whatever is—the landscape, the room, the scene around—is to love it perceptively, as we love people. This was a part of the feminine way, and one could easily be quite lax and overdo it. In the writers just alluded to, such perceptions were subsidiary to the larger narrative structure, and in the poem she would make them subsidiary to the sequence of unstated statement. Thus she could achieve the lyric intensity without indulging, because it was natural to her, the true voice of woman's feeling.

Louise Bogan herself had much to say about the role of woman as poet. In 1947 she wrote in an essay, "The Heart and the Lyre":

> Certainly it is not a regression to romanticism to remember that women are capable of perfect and poignant song; and that when this song comes through in its high and rare form, the result has always been regarded not only with delight but with a kind of awe. It is a good thing for young women to bring to mind the fact that lost fragments of the work of certain women poets—of Emily Dickinson no less than of the Sappho quoted by Longinus as an example of "the sublime"—are searched for less with the care and eagerness of the scholar looking for bits of shattered human art, than with the hungry eyes of the treasure hunters looking for some last grain of a destroyed jewel. Though she may never compose an epic or a tragic drama in five acts, the woman poet has her singular role and precious destiny. And, at the moment, in a time lacking in truth and certainty and filled with anguish and despair, no woman should be shamefaced in attempting to give back to the world, through her work, a portion of its lost heart.

And in an unpublished essay, written in 1962, entitled "What the Women Said" (first delivered as a lecture at Bennington College), she went into greater detail on the subject of women poets:

> To tell the truth, there is very little that one can say about women poets, past, present, and (presumably) to come. One truth about them is an open secret: when they are bad they are very, very bad, and when they are good, they are magnificent. . . . The problem of the woman artist remains unchanged. Henry James, in *The Tragic Muse*, spoke of "that oddest of animals, the artist who happens to

47

be born a woman." Robert Graves has more recently said that women poets have a distinctly difficult problem, since they must be their own Muse. Farther back in time, in ancient manuscripts, in inscriptions chiseled into rock and marble, in ideograms, in hieroglyphics, and, of course, in print, the discussion has gone on: woman's nature, her place in society, her charm and her wiles, her physiological and economic dilemmas, her open and her hidden powers—attracting, from men and women alike (but chiefly from men), overweening praise as well as blame; temper, contempt; false and true witness; and spite. . . .

In this remarkable essay Louise Bogan discusses many aspects of women writers and calls attention in particular to certain prose writers such as Dorothy Richardson and Virginia Woolf. She has also certain sharp words for Simone de Beauvoir, in the pages of whose large book *The Second Sex* she was, she felt, at one point in her reading trapped:

> Mme. de Beauvoir cherishes, in the deep recesses of her existentially trained self, a dislike, even a contempt, for the enigmatic, the intuitive, the graceful, the tender, the opalescent, the mercurial side of women's nature—the side that truly complements the virtues of the male. The side that has always been involved centrally in the production of women's art, the side that contributes, as one critic has said, "to the deeply feminine appeal and enchantment of Berthe Morisot's [and Mary Cassatt's] pictures"; the side upon which the great women poets have drawn; the side which sustains the great women novelists. This feeling is reinforced as, just before we close the book, we glance at its formidable index. I recommend to you, on some afternoon of rain and incipient boredom, the perusal of this index, and the ticking off of the names of women artists listed therein. The gaps and *lacunae* are shocking.

She mentions a number of them, and among the most shocking, she says, is that of Louise Labé, one of the greatest French women poets, known in the city of Lyon as *la belle cordelière*, because she was the wife of a ropemaker. Louise Labé, whom Louise Bogan very much admired, wrote some of the finest and most passionate sonnets in any language. Louise Bogan concludes with some careful admonitions:

> In women's deportment, we can agree, the brutal, rough, swaggering, masculinized gesture never, somehow, works, the cigars of the young George Sand and the middle-aged Amy Lowell to the contrary notwithstanding. And in her writing, the gentle, tender, nurturing feminine nature certainly precludes ultimate coarseness and harshness, either in tone or in choice of material. Women have never succeeded, for example, in writing true surrealism, except, perhaps, in the case of Djuna Barnes (who is more Joycean than surrealist) —a style closely involved with the hallucinatory, the shocking, and the terrifying effect; with the calculated irrational and the direct or indirect erotic. A younger generation of women poets has allied itself with "far-out" poetic procedures; unsuccessfully. For (and I have looked into this subject with some care) these younger women writers, although published side by side, in anthologies and elsewhere, with their far-out brothers, cannot bring themselves to use Anglo-Saxon monosyllables of a sexual or scatological kind. They swear a little, instead— even Mary McCarthy, even Caitlin Thomas. (An exception to this rule has recently appeared in England. In her long and rather chaotic novel *The Golden Notebook*, Doris Lessing, born in Persia and brought up in Southern Rhodesia, permits herself every license of language. I recommend the results to your attention.)

Fortunately, this limitation in vocabulary does not mean that young women writers today are in any way limited in regard to subject matter. In fact, only recently a young woman of nineteen broke through several taboos formerly prevalent in the British theater. This was Shelagh Delaney, whose play *A Taste of Honey* after a great success, both in London and New York, has been made into a most poignant motion picture. "Down from Salford came this splendid young prophetess," Colin MacInnes, in *Encounter*, recently remarked.

Like all prophetesses Shelagh Delaney tells the truth —her own truth, both observed and suffered through. For in the case of the woman writer and particularly of the woman poet, every lie—every fib, even—shows, like a smutch on a child's (or on a woman's) cheek. We can, perhaps, at this point draw up a short list of tentative rules. First, in literature (or in any other art) women must not lie. Second, they must not whine. Third, they must not attitudinize (in the role of the *femme fatale* least of all). And they must neither theatricalize nor coarsen their truths. They must not be vain, and they must not flight or kite in any witchlike way. Nor, on the other hand, go in for little girlishness and false naiveté. Nor "stamp a tiny foot at the universe."

So far as form is concerned, they should consider themselves free to move about unhampered by strict rules, keeping in mind, however, the fact that women can be, and have been, superb technicians. Perhaps the long *souffle* —*the big machine*, as the French say—is not for them; on the other hand it may lie ahead of them, in the discernible future.

Louise Bogan adhered so rigidly and so brilliantly to her own critical principles that any poem chosen at random from her work serves as an example of her artistic probity. When she speaks of the *Don Giovanni* of Mozart as refracted "as though from a dark crystal," she might be speaking of her own poems.

All the great joy of her life—and its great sorrow (and there was terrible suffering toward the end)—"has been translated into treasure. . . ." [5]

Music—"speech proud in sound"—is central to her work. Barbara Howes has said of Louise Bogan that she was "so finely honed by her writing and sensitivity and lifetime of addiction to reading that she was almost a musical instrument." The poem "Musician," in both substance and form, speaks eloquently of what Louise Bogan calls elsewhere "the ordered strings":

> Where have these hands been,
> By what delayed,
> That so long stayed
> Apart from the thin
>
> Strings which they now grace
> With their lonely skill?
> Music and their cool will
> At last interlace.
>
> Now with great ease, and slow,
> The thumb, the finger, the strong
> Delicate hand plucks the long
> String it was born to know.
>
> And, under the palm, the string
> Sings as it wished to sing.

This poem represents one of the most extraordinary achievements of sound that I know in modern poetry. Note the vowels—the short *i* sounds throughout; and the rhythm hovering between two and three beats to the line; and then the final sense of the actual plucking of the strings. It is a poem about resonance that resounds in the mind long after it is read. And, of course, the poem is much more than just music about music; it is about the

[5] "After the Persian," part III.

artistic process itself, which Louise Bogan examines in so many of her poems, and about the artist who has waited to return to his craft.

Another poem concerned with music is "To Be Sung on the Water":

> Beautiful, my delight,
> Pass, as we pass the wave.
> Pass, as the mottled night
> Leaves what it cannot save,
> Scattering dark and bright.
>
> Beautiful, pass and be
> Less than the guiltless shade
> To which our vows were said;
> Less than the sound of the oar
> To which our vows were made—
> Less than the sound of its blade
> Dipping the stream once more.

Of this piece Richard Wilbur says: "This poem is very lilting, very lulling; it approaches pure music, yet it contains an implicit narrative and a specific mood, which if I read it rightly is a mood of consent to passion upon whatever bitter terms may be necessary." Mr. Wilbur is right in this connection, and he is right in saying, I think, that "as a poet faithful to the theme of passion Louise Bogan is more comparable to Ahkmatova than to many Americans of her time"; and here he cites "Kept":

> Time for the wood, the clay,
> The trumpery dolls, the toys
> Now to be put away:
> We are not girls and boys.
>
> What are these rags we twist
> Our hearts upon, or clutch

Hard in the sweating fist?
They are not worth so much.

But we must keep such things
Till we at length begin
To feel our nerves their strings,
Their dust, our blood within.

The dreadful painted bisque
Becomes our very cheek.
A doll's heart, faint at risk,
Within our breast grows weak.

Our hand the doll's, our tongue.

Time for the pretty clay,
Time for the straw, the wood.
The playthings of the young
Get broken in the play,
Get broken, as they should.

Louise Bogan, as I said earlier, wrote little in prose of an autobiographical nature, and the autobiographical elements in her poetry are carefully objectified. There is one notable exception—a piece called "Journey Around My Room," published in *The New Yorker*, 14 January 1933. (William Maxwell read this piece at the memorial service for Louise Bogan.) She took her title, of course, from the little classic *Voyage Autour de ma Chambre* of Xavier de Maistre, the eighteenth-century French writer. De Maistre, you remember, as an officer in the army of Savoy, was confined for several weeks to his barracks, and he wrote this brilliant book during that period. He describes the objects in his room, going from dresser to table to chair to bed, and each piece has its chapter. But, of course, what he is really doing is speaking of himself. And this Louise Bogan does as she describes her room in New York:

The most advantageous point from which to start this
journey is the bed itself, wherein, at midnight or early in
the morning, the adventurous traveler lies moored, the ter-
rain spread out before him. The most fortunate weather is
warm to cool, engendered by a westerly breeze, borne from
the open window toward the ashes in the grate. At midnight, moonlight lies upon the floor, to guide the traveler's
eye; in the early morning, the bleak opacity that serves the
traveler in this region as sun brightens the brick wall of the
house across the yard, and sheds a feeble reflected glow
upon all the objects which I shall presently name.

And she begins to name them as she goes around the room and
then tells how she happened to come here in the first place:

The steam shrieks out of the engine and smoke trails
out, into the clear morning, from the smokestack, blotting
out the willows and the mill dam. The conductor lifts me up
to the step. That is the reason for my presence here. I took
the Boston train in March 1909.

Having almost made the circle of the room, she concludes:

It is at this point, precisely when the end is in sight,
and the starting point almost gained, that the catastrophe
of the journey invariably occurs.

For it is here, as I nearly complete the circle set, that
at midnight and in the early morning I encounter the
dream. I am set upon by sleep, and hear the rush of water,
and hear the mill dam, fuming with water that weighs
itself into foam against the air, and see the rapids at its foot
that I must gauge and dare and swim. Give over, says this
treacherous element, the fear and distress in your breast;
and I pretend courage and brave it at last, among rocks
along the bank, and plunge into the wave that mounts like
glass to the level of my eye. O death, O fear! The universe

swings up against my sight, the universe fallen into and bearing with the mill stream. I must in a moment die, but for a moment I breathe, upheld, and see all weight, all force, all water, compacted into the glassy wave, veined, marbled with foam, this moment caught raining over me. And into the wave sinks the armoire, the green bureau, the lamps, the shells from the beach in Maine. All these objects, provisional at best, now equally lost, rock down to translucent depths below fear, an Atlantis in little, under the mill stream (last seen through the steam from the Boston train in March 1909).

In all Louise Bogan's poems she explores those "translucent depths below fear." This is especially evident in the final poems of *The Blue Estuaries*. (*The Blue Estuaries* is, of course, a brilliant title, and no one was more conscious of titles than Louise Bogan. When Wallace Stevens published *The Auroras of Autumn* she said to me: "Here is a word that has been lying around for years, and no one has ever thought of using it: auroras! *The Auroras of Autumn*. Marvelous, isn't it?" She herself had found a word like "estuaries" that had been lying around for years and used it most effectively.)

As an epigraph to *The Sleeping Fury* (1937), which was retained in all her subsequent books, Louise Bogan used the lines of Rilke:

> *Wie ist das klein, womit wir ringen;*
> *was mit uns ringt, wie ist das gross . . .*
> (How small is that with which we struggle;
> how great is that which struggles with us.)

To give some sense of what a great woman has said, I will end with her own words—with one of the greatest of her poems (I think all poets who know her work agree that it is one that will unquestionably endure).[6] It has in it all the elements of her

6 Both Mr. Wheelock and Mr. Tate chose it to read at her memorial service.

work; the seashell with its resonance, the earth, the sea, the movement, the music; it is a poem about poetry, about the poet who puts all of life, all her experience of the earth into poetry, and in the end becomes the earth itself:

HENCEFORTH, FROM THE MIND

Henceforth, from the mind,
For your whole joy, must spring
Such joy as you may find
In any earthly thing,
And every time and place
Will take your thought for grace.

Henceforth, from the tongue,
From shallow speech alone,
Comes joy you thought, when young,
Would wring you to the bone,
Would pierce you to the heart
And spoil its stop and start.

Henceforward, from the shell,
Wherein you heard, and wondered
At oceans like a bell
So far from ocean sundered—
A smothered sound that sleeps
Long lost within lost deeps,

Will chime you change and hours,
The shadow of increase,
Will sound you flowers
Born under troubled peace—
Henceforth, henceforth
Will echo sea and earth.

[1970]

II

A POETRY
CHRONICLE:
1963-1966

1963

THERE HAS BEEN much talk in the past few years about the lamentably poor quality of book reviewing in this country, but little in these discussions has been said about the reviewing of poetry. The general feeling appears to be that it makes no difference what sort of review a book of poems receives because the audience for poetry is so limited anyway. Furthermore, since poetry is usually reviewed by poets, it is thought, even with its limited coverage, to fare better than prose. The fact is that whether appearing in the book pages of the best newspapers and magazines or in the critical journals, poetry reviews are the worst written, sloppiest, and silliest critical pieces published anywhere today. Over a decade ago Elizabeth Bishop wrote: "The analysis of poetry is growing more and more pretentious and deadly. After a session with a few of the highbrow magazines one doesn't want to look at a poem for weeks, much less start writing one."

After a similar session recently, I noted down a few passages from some of these same highbrow pages. Here is one from a distinguished quarterly: "An utopian and oral poetry like his [Gregory Corso's] refuses to be an object and to be pointed at as I am now doing: it tries to be speech that does not know the negative, therefore adds instead of subtracts, and subsumes contraries in its affirmative sweep." And another from the lead review in our oldest magazine of verse: "Gresham's law applies to poetry at least part of the time, but in MacDiarmid the bad writing is just swamped by the good. The creative tap is left running and a kind of ardor pours out, an untrammeled spontaneity, and with it come tumbling the wonderful tadpoles and toads, all the small monsters of magic that more constricted writers have hidden away forever in the inaccessible shadows of themselves." It is clear that Gresham's law does indeed apply to the reviewing of poetry; bad writing drives out the good even more effectively than it did ten years ago.

Few of the older poets today write reviews of current work as they once did (Louise Bogan in *The New Yorker* is the exception); they do, however, release their capsule comments in blurb form on dust jackets. In the past year several manuscripts that I have had occasion to read have reached me subsequently in book form. Their new wrappings were studded with such a profusion of encomiums that I felt in some cases that I had been handed a small box of diamonds rather than a modest collection of uneven, unenduring, and generally pretentious verse. It is no wonder that newspaper editors, gathering at the time of the National Book Awards, said that they would be pleased to publish more reviews of poetry if publishers would only alert them to the books that were really important and were likely to receive attention. I certainly hold no brief for reviewers who cannot arrive independently at the proper judgment of a book, but in the case of poetry the publishers seem to want to bring the house down on their heads. If virtually everything published is great, is there anything really good? Whitman's unauthorized use of Emerson's statement on *Leaves of Grass* seems unusually modest alongside the quotes displayed on some first books today. The time has surely come to call for a more careful editing of volumes of verse, and for a moratorium on blurbs.

The air of prosperity evident in the critical appraisals on the dust jackets is followed through on the biographical notes on their back flaps. The young poet now is not just on his way; he has *arrived:* After receiving his doctorate from Iowa, he has published two and one-third volumes, has appeared widely in magazines and paperback anthologies, has received numerous awards (including undoubtedly the Janus medal and the Bronze Sunflower of the Kansas Poetry Society) ; he has spent the previous year in Peru on a pre-Columbian grant, and is now traveling in Europe on a Longfellow fellowship. In an address entitled "Poetic Gold," delivered before the Oxford University Philological Society and included in his *Oxford Addresses on Poetry*, Robert Graves comments wryly on his discovery that the "gold" medal awarded him in 1960 by the Poetry Society of America was only gold-plated. "To be paid in gold is to be paid *really*," Mr. Graves writes, "not in promissory notes or base metal." And he goes on to quote Chaucer : *"Hyt is not al gold that glareth."* In the gold-labeled poetic productions currently being published with *éclat*, the authors, for all their glistening credentials, pay off only intermittently in the real thing.

Recent books display every type of style from the oracular to the whispered confessional, from the women's club weeping wet to the academic dull dry, from the wild beat to the dead-beat. Although there are many of the standard Guggenheim and Fulbright metaphysical salutes to the European capitals—Rome, Paris, Athens, and even Amsterdam—the focus in most of the new poetry is clearly on the American suburban scene; its subject is the young married couple—their quarrels, children, divorces, and their moments of anguish, revelation, and delight over too many martinis. A new poetic mode has evolved that can only be described as split-level grotesque; it is replete with classical allusions (the poet has, after all, been to graduate school) but they all relate to a suburban setting; it contains all the neat ironies that readers of the critical journals have learned to expect, but it offers also some deadpan shock effects.

Frederick Seidel's *Final Solutions* attempts the grotesque on a grand scale (there is nothing split-level about it) and at times he succeeds; but much of his book has an air of Grand Guignol. Mr. Seidel's first collection has already caused quite a stir, largely because it was banned even before publication, a distinction that few poets achieve. It was awarded a prize last year by a jury consisting of Robert Lowell, Louise Bogan, and Stanley Kunitz. When officials of the organization offering the prize read the manuscript, they found certain of the poems not only shocking but libelous; the prize was withdrawn, and the jury resigned in protest. The manuscript was accepted by the publisher who had agreed to issue the prizewinner and subsequently rejected on the grounds of possible libel when Mr. Seidel refused to make any changes. It now appears under the imprint of a second publisher, intact except for the deletion of one poem concerning the private life of a prominent American woman.

All this sounds like something that could only have happened in the Soviet Union. But Mr. Seidel's poems, despite the implications of his title, are not at all political. They are in no way public utterances. Hitler's final solution to the Jewish problem was mass destruction; the final solutions of the characters in Mr. Seidel's poems lie in their personal confrontation of destruction in the private world of nightmare. Everything is seen in a cold, clear, terrible light, unrelieved by any hint of joy. Mr. Seidel speaks through many masks; and certainly he carries the dramatic monologue to new extremes (the speaker in "Heart Attack" is a long-dead mistress haranguing her aged Roman lover as he lies with another woman). But his poetry is nevertheless one of confession, as is shown in the opening poem, "Wanting to Live in Harlem," which is modeled on the Rimbaud of *"Les Poètes de sept Ans."* The power of Rimbaud's poetry, as Laforgue pointed out early on, rests "in the extraordinary power of confession, in the inexhaustible surprise of his perfectly adequate images." The failure of much of Frederick Seidel's book for me lies precisely in the lack of such adequate images, in a too heavy reliance on Robert Lowell's meters, and a theatricality that, although at first startling, does not ultimately ring true.

In the first complete revision in over a decade of his *Modern American Poetry and Modern British Poetry*, Louis Untermeyer includes, as the youngest poet represented, Anne Sexton, whose second volume, *All My Pretty Ones*, has now appeared. "Her subject matter—guilt, loss, mental distress," says Mr. Untermeyer, "will trouble the reader, yet, in its calm clarity, it delights even while it disturbs. This poetry is poignant and sometimes painful, the impact of a spirit so agitated that it has been pushed across the borders of sanity." Mrs. Sexton makes clear what she believes poetry should be in an epigraph from Kafka to the effect that "a book should serve as the ax for the frozen sea within us." She writes of "life with its terrible changes":

> My friend, my friend, I was born
> doing reference work in sin, and born
> confessing it. This is what poems are:
> with mercy
> for the greedy,
> and are the tongue's wrangle,
> the world's pottage, the rat's star.

Her poems, like Mr. Seidel's, are indeed confessional; their rhetoric is less dense than his, and their imagery generally more adequate to their subject matter. Her work is a feminine version of Mr. Lowell's *Life Studies*, and she treats baldly themes that most women writers would avoid. When she succeeds, she conveys a real sense of poignancy and power; when she fails, she is merely embarrassing. Poetry, since the time of Browning's *The*

Ring and the Book and Tennyson's *Maud,* has been making in-
roads on the novel, and rightly so; but certain of Mrs. Sexton's
less successful pieces, which seem only the raw materials of autobiography, make one wonder if some such material could not be
better dealt with in prose.

One of the most curious, difficult, and fascinating books to
reach us recently is *The Anathemata* by David Jones. It is not
unknown, having appeared over a decade ago in London; and it
is not likely ever to become widely read, although W. H. Auden
has called it "very probably the finest long poem written in English in this century." It has yet to receive the critical attention
of Pound's *Cantos,* which it superficially resembles; but it is epic
in scale, and there is certainly no other book like it.

When *The Anathemata* first appeared, Kathleen Raine
said of its author, "David Jones seems to be the only writer to
have adopted Joyce's allusive method from the same sense of
man's place in history as Joyce himself possessed." She was right
then in pointing out that most imitators of Joyce have imitated
"the accidents of his style without sharing his political sense."
Mr. Jones is a Londoner of Welsh extraction, a painter of distinction, and a Roman Catholic convert; and it is as one aware of
Britain and her long history that he approaches his subject. *The
Anathemata* bears the subtitle, "fragments of an attempted writing"; and what is it about? "I answer," says Mr. Jones in his
preface, "that it is about one's own 'thing,' which *res* is unavoid-
ably part and parcel of the Western Christian *res,* as inherited by
a person whose perceptions are totally conditioned and limited
by and dependent upon his being indigenous to this island."

One has the impression in reading it—an impression en-
hanced by the illustrations in the book and the inscriptions all
made by the author—of a mosaic composed of brilliant and
varied fragments of both past and present at a moment in time
which is now, but of a moment already receding in time. It is a
mosaic washed over and rubbed clear by the flux of time as by

the sea—and some of the finest passages in the poem are those concerned with the sea and ships. "I regard my book," says Mr. Jones, "more as a series of fragments, fragmented bits, chance scraps really, or records of things, vestiges of sorts and kinds of *disciplinae*, that have come my way by this channel or that influence. Pieces of stuffs that happen to mean something to me and which I see as perhaps making a kind of coat of many colors, such as belonged to 'that dreamer' in the Hebrew myth. Things to which I would give a related form, just as one does in painting a picture." To help the reader through these disjointed bits, Mr. Jones provides an elaborate supporting framework of notes and an intricately wrought introduction.

The author intends *The Anathemata*, the title meaning "Things set up, lifted up, or in whatever manner made over to the gods," to be said as well as viewed on the page. The punctuation marks, the line lengths, the groupings of words have "an aural and an oral intention." The poem has a circular pattern, the tale of a dark and stormy night told on a dark and stormy night. At the beginning, the reader finds himself in a church while mass is being said, and allows his mind to wander, along with that of the author, in "a kind of quasi-free association." He is taken on an endless voyage through time and space, in search of identity, a voyage paralleled in the mass, which "is precisely the argosy or voyage of the Redeemer, consisting of his entire sufferings and his death, his conquest of hades, his resurrection and his return in triumph to heaven":

> Extend your hands
>> all you *orantes*
>>> for the iron-dark shore
>> is to our lee
>> over the lead-dark sea
>> and schisted Ocrinum looms in fairish
>>> visibility

and white-plumed riders shoreward go
and
THE BIRDS DECLARE IT
that wing white and low
that also leeward go
go leeward to the tor-lands
where the tin-veins maculate the fire-
rocks.
The birds
have a home
in those rocks.

David Jones stresses the fact that it is incumbent upon the visual artist, all the way from Beatrix Potter to Picasso, just as it is upon those who practice any art, to "uncover a valid sign." He has attempted that in a more profound manner perhaps than any other poet writing today; and for those who care about poetry that offers both delight and dimension, *The Anathemata* will be well worth the effort it requires.

To turn from the epic view of David Jones to that of Robinson Jeffers, who died last year in California at the age of seventy-five, is at first seemingly to cross more than an ocean and a continent. Yet different as they are, a similar Celtic background informs the work of both. In the forty-eight short pieces in *The Beginning and The End and Other Poems*, collected after his death from his manuscripts by his sons and secretary, Jeffers, like Mr. Jones, stresses the fact that a poet works always *sub specie aeternitatis*. After the population explosion has pushed people into his Carmel retreat and they have eaten up his woods and thrown down his stonework, Jeffers says in one poem, only the little "four-foot-thick-walled" tower that he built with his own hands may remain:

That and some verse. It is curious that
flower-soft verse

66

Is sometimes harder than granite, tougher
than a steel cable, more alive than life.

But whereas David Jones is concerned primarily with man
in relation to history, Robinson Jeffers views the human race as
only "one of God's sense-organs/Immoderately alerted to feel
good and evil." Mr. Jones says also in his preface that when the
workman is dead all that will matter is the work "objectively
considered." But he adds:

> Moreover, the workman must be dead to himself while en-
> gaged upon the work, otherwise we have that sort of "self-
> expression" that is as undesirable in the painter or the
> writer as in the carpenter, the cantor, the halfback, or the
> cook. Although all this is fairly clear in principle, I have
> not found it easy to apply in practice.

Robinson Jeffers, who would surely have agreed with the
statement in principle, found it even less easy to apply in practice. The Titanic stance that he assumes in his poetry is often
marred by touches of shrillness and self-pity. But when he is
writing objectively, as he often does in these poems, of the natural scene—of the wildness of this country, the full moon, the
Pacific, sea gulls in a storm, the "enormous inhuman beauty of
things"—no one has equaled him. A poem like "Birds and
Fishes" is as fine as anything he ever wrote.

1964

American poetry of late seems to answer the description given of it in a brief poem by Pulitzer Prize-winning poet Louis Simpson in his volume, *At the End of the Open Road:*

> Whatever it is, it must have
> A stomach that can digest
> Rubber, coal, uranium, moons, poems.
>
> Like the shark, it contains a shoe.
> It must swim for miles through the desert
> Uttering cries that are almost human.

A strong stomach it certainly has, and one that contains a good many shoes; the cries that it utters are indeed human, and it appears to be swimming through an endless desert. The dry waste is relieved at moments by bits of color, bursts of turbulence, and whirlpools of activity. Much is going on; there are flashes of considerable talent, and some real achievements. One of

68

the latter is Mr. Simpson's own book. Born in the West Indies, schooled in the East, and now a resident of the West, he is able to look at America dispassionately; and the image he evokes of it, both urban and rural, spares us nothing of its ugliness while at the same time never diminishing its sweep and vision. His style is at times reminiscent of the early Spender, as when in "The Redwoods" the trees say in conclusion:

> O if there is a poet
>
> let him come now! We stand at the
>   Pacific
> like great unmarried girls,
>
> turning in our heads the stars and
>   clouds,
> considering whom to please.

At other moments Mr. Simpson is a gentler and less troubled Hart Crane, a romantic who attempts to define the reality of America, accepting the message of Walt Whitman (one poem, "Pacific Ideas," is a letter to him), but with reservations:

> Whitman was wrong about the People,
> But right about himself. The land is
>   within.
> At the end of the open road we come
>   to ourselves.

It is what he calls the "inner part," "the currents that moved from within," that he explores in language rich in imagery but always controlled by wit and regulated by irony. The longest poem in the book, "The Marriage of Pocahontas," based on John Smith's *Generall Historie*, is a successful attempt to give life and meaning to legend.

Over ten years ago the little magazine *Furioso*, striving to deflate the pretensions of aspiring poets, announced to its contributors in a black-bordered statement that Walt Whitman was dead. Louis Simpson's treatment of the "open road" serves to remind us that he is still very much alive. Whitman, filtered through the Beat poets, is indeed one of the most significant influences now being felt. Mr. Simpson himself is contemptuous of the Beats—he has written a brilliant parody entitled "Squeal" of Allen Ginsberg's *Howl*—but Ginsberg has become for some poets of stature more than just a figure of fun.

Karl Shapiro, winner of a wartime Pulitzer Prize for his *V-Letter and Other Poems*, has paid tribute to Ginsberg and the Beats; and there is no greater tribute than imitation. Mr. Shapiro, in *The Bourgeois Poet*, also takes to the open road, and, leaving Whitman behind, assumes his place proudly beside the bearded Ginsberg on the Ganges. The dust jacket of *The Bourgeois Poet* informs us that it is Mr. Shapiro's belief that the "two traditional attributes of poetry (rhyme and versification) are nonessential and artificial impediments to the poetic process." Mr. Shapiro thus sets out—in Frost's terms—to play tennis with the net down, but goes even further; he dispenses with the court as well. Such a game is maddening to watch, and however sympathetic one may be, impossible to criticize.

But this is just as Mr. Shapiro wants it; criticism is out— along with "the old chestnuts Pity and Terror, Form and Content, Good and Evil, Love and Hate." "Phone book of myself, I will call you up," Mr. Shapiro writes, and the reader is here treated to that call—incoherent, disordered, disturbing, infuriating, brilliant—and the phone-book self that is evoked is simply the long list of names, numbers and addresses that make up the psyche of the bourgeois poet. "Kill the poet in yourself," the poet exclaims, and "Longing for the Primitive I survive as a Modern, barely."

In the second section entitled "The Doctor Poet," Mr. Shapiro quotes Dr. Harry B. Lee:

The creativeness of the artist is a most efficient technique for liquidating guilt and reestablishing the function of pity. . . . This mental organization is a fortunate one for the artist in the man; but it is an unfortunate one for the man in the artist since it afflicts him with his emotional immaturity, exquisitely narcissistic character, maladjustment to life, and recurrent neurotic depressions.

It is thus this very mental organization, this very creativeness, that the creator here seeks to destroy, and in so destroying it, becomes the man he is:

> Across the iambic pentameter of the Atlantic
>   (the pilot dropped, the station wagon in
>   the hold) we sail to the kingdom of Small.
>   Is it cheaper there? Can I buy a slave?

> This is the camera with the built-in lie. This
>   is the lens that defies the truth. There's
>   nothing for it but to write the large bad
>   poem in middle-class magic. Poem con-
>   demned to wear black, be quoted in
>   churches, versatile as Greek. Condemned
>   to remain unsung by criminals.

This antipoem of destruction is the ultimate poem that tries to mean, not be, or rather to reveal itself in the process of meaning:

> I'm writing this poem for someone to see
>   when I'm not looking. This is an open
>   book. I want to be careful to startle you
>   gently. The poem is about your looking
>   at it, as one looks at a woman covertly. (I
>   wonder what she's doing in this town; it's
>   a long way from the look in her eyes.)

> The rings of my big notebook stand open
> like the rib cage of a barracuda. Careful
> with your fingers.

The open book reveals the man, and all the afflictions of the artist in him from which he cannot quite escape. Mr. Shapiro's method of, in his words, holding "the shaving mirror to all" is not unlike that of the Pop Art painters who ask us to look at rows of soup cans, bleeding hamburgers, and comic strips seen close-up as if through a magnifying glass. "Lower the standards," he writes, "Let's all play poetry . . . sabotage the stylistic approach. Let weeds grow in the subdivision." But for all Mr. Shapiro's direct assault and his attempt to get at the human situation, this work is oddly literary on almost every page: poet after poet is evoked and discussed. "They held a celebration for you, Charles, in Iowa. I was asked but I regretted." The Charles in this case is, of course, Charles Baudelaire. Another long paragraph is addressed to Randall Jarrell: "Randall, I like your poetry terribly, yet I'm afraid to say so." The bourgeois poet, however much he lowers his sights, does not escape the "poetry trap" or the "prison of Art." And despite Karl Shapiro's dismissal of tradition, he must be aware that these versets, without rhyme and without versification and frequently without rhythm, are very much in a tradition—that of the prose poem. Judged as such, they often convey a brilliant confessional power, but just as often they are flat, predictable, and definitely boring.

Another influence besides that of "The Song of Myself" that is making itself felt in recent books of poetry is that of Robert Lowell's *Life Studies*. Mr. Lowell remarked about his book that after he had completed it, he was not entirely sure whether it was an end or a beginning. For many of his fellow poets, it has been a beginning. John Berryman in his *77 Dream Songs* has perhaps taken his cue from it, as he did from the earlier Lowell in his much-praised *Homage to Mistress Bradstreet*. This is not to say that Mr. Berryman's work does not offer something very much his own. His *Dream Songs*, which he tells us in an introductory note, are sections constituting one version of a poem on which he has been working since 1955, are a fascinating, cryptic, and often impenetrable mosaic of confession. Beside them, Mr. Shapiro's prose poems seem simple indeed. The speaker in this case keeps shifting, and the reader soon becomes aware that Mr. Berryman has adopted a persona, or several personae, to communicate his explorations of the subconscious.

The title of the projected long poem, *The Dream Songs*, is ironic: the songs, which are composed of three loosely and crudely rhymed six-line stanzas, have little about them of the traditional song, and the dream alternates between daydream and nightmare with nightmare clearly predominating. Mr. Berryman has literally put his signature on this work; he may even have had in mind a pun—in that this is his "John Henry." There appear to be three characters in this little drama: John, Henry, and Mr. Bones. They merge one into the other, or rather are all parts or sides of the same person. It is a kind of mental minstrel show in which Mr. Bones, representing the blackface, the underside of consciousness, dramatically presents the actions and thoughts of Henry (or John Henry), "a human American man," who, in turn, becomes Huffy Henry, Henry Hankovitch, Henry Pussycat, and Henry House. Mr. Berryman makes much of the minstrel show metaphor, playing up all the ironies of the blackface poet-minstrel.

The second of the songs, here entitled "Big Buttons, Cornets: the advance," is dedicated to the memory of Daddy Rice, the actor Thomas D. Rice, who in the 1820s created and made popular the role of "Jim Crow." Rice's costume was picturesquely dilapidated, wrinkled all over, and ill-fitting with large patches on his breeches and gaping holes in his shoes. In his blackface, he "jumped" "Jim Crow" on both sides of the Atlantic. Mr. Bones-Henry here mimics his antics and his strut. Henry in one song is sitting in a plane when "his thought made pockets & the plane buckt." It is the pockets that thought makes with which Mr. Berryman is concerned, or more specifically, the operations that take place in the dark arena of the subconscious:

> I am obliged to perform in complete
> darkness
> operations of great delicacy
> on my self.
> —Mr. Bones, you terrifies me.

Henry is "pried/open for all the world to see." The scalpel cuts clear through in these operations on the self, and terror is always attendant.

John Berryman's metaphorical framework is highly original, and it allows him a wide range both public and private. One song is devoted to Eisenhower (the "lay of Ike"); others are tributes to Robert Frost, William Faulkner, and Theodore Roethke; still another concerns a convention of the Modern Language Association. More often, Henry is involved with his own private hell. The language of the songs is a curious mixture of baby talk (verbs shift inexplicably from singular to plural and back again and syllables are blurred and swallowed), beat lingo, droll Negro minstrel dialect bits, and donnish puns and inversions. The influence of Cummings and Pound is obvious. The songs, for all their shifting and overlapping montage effect, have little of the free flow of dreams; they are oddly angular and jagged. The minstrel breakdown, the psychic dance (and Mr. Berryman is aware of the pun on "breakdown") are always desperate; there is no joy. John Berryman is clearly a descendant of Poe rather than of Whitman, and his subject is the unrelieved nightmare of existence.

Although both Mr. Shapiro's and Mr. Berryman's books are often forthright in their diction and contain a few four-letter words, neither can be said to be in any way erotic. It is well to be reminded, in two recent anthologies, of the fact that modern poets, like those of the past, have not entirely neglected the role of Eros. *Erotic Poetry, The Lyrics, Ballads, Idyls and Epics of Love—Classical to Contemporary*, edited by William Cole, and *An Uninhibited Treasury of Erotic Poetry*, edited, with a running commentary, by Louis Untermeyer, bring together some of the greatest poems of past centuries as well as some of the finest of today concerned with the pleasures of love. If eroticism has not yet, as André Malraux would have it, been integrated with life and been made a value in itself, the sensual is no longer a forbidden topic. In the introduction to Mr. Cole's volume, Stephen Spender remarks that a young poet can today "write about nakedness, love-making, sex, as part of experience which is thought about and visualized, in the manner of other experiences, and not with shame, in whispers, or as though it belongs to dimensions of science, free thought, high courage or low outrageousness." Many of them in Mr. Cole's collection do just that, but, as Mr. Spender also points out, in our victory over the puritans, "censorship has been largely defeated, though self-consciousness has not been altogether avoided." The awkwardness of the modern efforts in these collections springs perhaps from the conscious attitude of defiance that engendered them. That attitude is absent in the works of A. D. Hope and Alex Comfort, in which wit is an important element.

William Cole divides his book into categories that range far and wide: the first is "Of Women," the last, "By-Paths and Oddities." He has included a number of modern poems that have never before been collected, many of them by unknown writers hitherto buried in the pages of little magazines; and one can only marvel at the magnitude of his labor and its amazing result. Louis Untermeyer arranges his collection chronologically, with running commentaries on the periods and writers; the collections complement each other nicely. Mr. Untermeyer has also unearthed many unusual items: along with a generous selection from *The Greek Anthology*, he includes an unusual piece by Francis Scott Key, "On a Young Lady's Going into a Shower

Bath," that is certainly far removed from "The Star Spangled Banner."

It is interesting that women, who are so often the subject of erotic poetry, are usually themselves so bad at writing it. When treating the joys of the flesh, they tend to start to talk about the birds and the bees in a most embarrassing fashion, as for example, in Katherine Hoskins's "The Bee and the Petunia" in Mr. Cole's anthology. Indeed, one can only think that both anthologists put in some of the feminine pieces with a view to showing the pitfalls of erotic writing, and with tongue in cheek. Only Isabella Gardner, in her "Gimboling," is really convincing.

The best poems by women appearing in either anthology are those by Emily Dickinson and Charlotte Mew. The erotic and the religious are, as Mr. Spender says, always closely connected. They come together in the carvings on Indian temples and in the drawings on Greek vases; they are inextricably intermingled in the poems of St. John of the Cross. While perhaps the truly erotic in poetry belongs to the Orient, as in "Black Marigolds" from the Sanskrit, it serves in Western civilization to underline the spiritual. Because love, in all its aspects, is everything to modern woman, she is unable to stand back and look at it. (She has been able to at times in the past; and it is unfortunate that neither Mr. Cole nor Mr. Untermeyer has included anything by either of the French women, Louise Labé or Marceline Desbordes-Valmore, who both wrote marvelous erotic poems.)

1965

WHEN the Association of Literary Magazines of America met in Washington in April at the Library of Congress, there was much talk of the literary situation. Having assembled under a grant from the Carnegie Foundation, the little-magazine editors considered at length their plight, their chance for survival, and their need to continue to publish new writing of merit. What was strange, as one followed the proceedings, was that such an organization should exist at all and that its members should assemble in the nation's capital. Culture is, of course, being organized in a big way in Washington—groups of writers invited for the Inauguration were shuttled to and from the events in buses marked "Cultural Leaders," and an all-day cultural jamboree was held in June for the first time at the White House—but it seemed incongruous that the last holdouts of littleness should apparently want to get into the big act. Allen Tate, honorary president of the organization, called attention to this incongruity when he remarked that he simply did not understand what was meant by the phrase "the literary situation." "There is never," he said, "a real literary situation—just people trying to write as best they can."

The little magazine has indeed been an important part of the literary scene; it has over the years published deserving work that would never have appeared elsewhere, and much of it has naturally been poetry. It is frequently doing the same thing today, but the observations of several young editors at the Washington conference left some doubt. They often seemed prouder of the fact that they had succeeded in getting certain four-letter words into print under the eyes of their university sponsors (they spoke of the words at times as they might of jewels being smuggled over borders) than they did in serving the "people trying to write as best they can." The truth is that today poetry of merit may just as often appear initially in the larger publications or even in book form as in little magazines. The slim volume of verse is not only not neglected but it rarely appears; even first books of poems are fatter than they were twenty years ago, and most of them are conspicuously unedited. Many university presses now feel compelled to have their own poetry series, and, as a result, publish some of the best, as well as the worst, poetry. Poets have taken to the lecture circuit in droves and are bringing poetry to the masses in a way previously unheard of. Unfortunately, many of the poems they read to their audiences are unwritten to begin with, and, in their unwritten form, find their way subsequently into books. Fortunately there are some notable exceptions to the thick, uneven, unedited volumes to appear during the year.

W. H. Auden, at the time of Marianne Moore's seventy-fifth birthday, admitted that he had stolen from her more treasure than he "could accurately assess." Something of the extent of his debt is shown in his new book *About the House*. The major sequence, "Thanksgiving for a Habitat," which takes the reader on a tour of Mr. Auden's new Austrian house, beginning with the writer's study and ending in the living room, is, in the very choice of subject and the essayistic treatment of it, reminiscent of Miss Moore. This is Mr. Auden *en pantoufles*, and only a poet of his stature would dare undertake so personal, direct, and indirect, a journey. His answer to the possible criticism of the slightness—and homeliness—of his subject is given in a brief postscript to one of the poems:

> Only tuneless birds,
> Inarticulate warriors,
> Need bright plumage.

"The Cave of Making," the first poem of the sequence, concerns his study, a room where, from the Olivetti portable, the best dictionaries money can buy, and the heaps of paper, "it is evident/what must go on." It is a place designed to "discourage daydreams," where all is subject "to a function," where silence "is turned into objects." Addressing Louis MacNeice—this poem is a moving elegy to his friend—Mr. Auden writes:

> For Grammar we both inherited
> good mongrel barbarian English
> which never completely succumbed to
> the Roman rhetoric
> or the Roman gravity, that non-
> sense
> which stood none.

In handling "good mongrel barbarian English"—and Mr. Auden here acknowledges his debt as well to J. R. R. Tolkien in "A Short Ode to a Philologist"—he has no equal.

In *The Lyric Impulse*, a compilation of the Charles Eliot Norton lectures he delivered this year at Harvard, C. Day Lewis speaks eloquently of the decline of lyric writing in the modern era and of the need to revive this important aspect of poetry:

Wherever we move, we are assailed or solicited by words spewing out at us from the presses, deafening us from radio and television. Can you wonder that in this almighty shindy the lyric utterance, which is a still, small voice, goes unheard, or that lyrical poets should be tempted into straining their voices in order to be heard . . . Poetry's language should be a heightening of the common language; but, when so much of that language is either vile or without flavor, the poet has no sound basis from which to work. He may try to shout down the general pandemonium, as Dylan Thomas did, by sheer weight and eccentricity of language. The same effort can be seen in much American verse of the last forty years. Vigorous and adventurous though it is, the reader cannot help noticing how desperately words are often strained, dislocated even, in order to get away from cliché and give an appearance of "originality." This distortion of language, whether it comes from complexity of thought or from a craving for novelty, goes counter to the lyric impulse, which is for simplicity both in words and in thought.

The love poem, the most fruitful and exacting type of lyric, tends to get "ignored or blasted by both sides" in the Apollonian-Dionysian warfare that has taken place in poetry in the past few decades. One of the very few modern poets to have written great love poems—Mr. Day Lewis calls him, along with Hardy and Yeats, one of the supreme love poets of our century—is Robert Graves. Most of these poems, and all the best of them, have been written in late middle age. Mr. Graves was seventy in July, and his latest book *Man Does, Woman Is* contains several love lyrics that can take their place beside the best.

One line from a poem by Randall Jarrell in *The Lost World* on the subject of women makes us conscious of his debt to Robert Graves:

> Men are what they do, women
> are what they are.

But Mr. Jarrell is no mere imitator; his style, in its vigor and freshness, is completely his own. His subject here, as in much of his previous work, may be summed up in the opening lines of "Well Water":

> What a girl called "the dailiness
>   of life"
> (Adding an errand to your errand.
>   Saying,
> "Since you're up . . ." Making you
>   a means to
> A means to a means to) is well water
> Pumped from an old well at the
>   bottom of the world.

It is from the depths of the psyche that Randall Jarrell views the "dailiness of life." In the long title poem, an evocation of the joys and terrors of childhood, real objects merge with mythic ones in a kind of fantastical cinematographic sequence that somehow never loses focus and is completely effective. Three of the poems in this book were actually written for children—they are from *The Bat-Poet*, a children's story published last year—and show that Mr. Jarrell can be simple without sacrificing any of the complex play between dream and reality that concerns him in the longer monologues. In its directness, its unity and power, this seems to me his best book to date.

Robert Lowell's much praised *For the Union Dead* deals also with persons and places, past and present, and with recollections of childhood. Mr. Lowell brings every scene he touches fully to life, whether it is modern Boston or Buenos Aires, New England or Italy. When he focuses his attention on a subject, it is always with terrible intensity; no detail is peripheral, every-

81

thing is rounded up, swept in—brought forcefully to bear—on its central core. "July in Washington" is a good example because it deals specifically with roundness, with circularity:

> The stiff spokes of this wheel
> touch the sore spots of the earth.

This is a simple enough beginning, embodying a gentle irony, but by the end of the poem the wheel of Washington has become the hub of a frightening world, a whirlpool drawing everything —personal and impersonal—into itself. Certain of the poems in this book are among the finest Robert Lowell has written, and it is no exaggeration to call the title poem truly magnificent.

1966

MANY RECENT BOOKS of poetry have been concerned in one way or another with travel and with the response of poets to new and foreign scenes and situations; never have poets seemed more peripatetic than today. After going through volumes of the past year that deal with summer in Provence as well as winter in Alaska, with South America, Japan, India, as well as Italy and Greece (those two old poetic favorites), the reader ends by asking inevitably what place has place itself in poetry. The answer is that it has a very important one. Certainly as the most sensitive and concentrated of recorders, the fine poet will give us a powerful sense of what it is like to be in a certain place at a certain time. New England will be forever associated with Robert Frost, but the San Francisco of his early childhood is equally vivid in his poems, and so—geographically and metaphorically (a rare thing, indeed)—he spans a continent. We cannot think of Hartford without thinking of Wallace Stevens, nor of Brooklyn without Marianne Moore, Paterson without William Carlos Williams.

Place is what a poet knows and makes known to us, his point of departure, the base of his particular angle of vision. Then why should the poet feel the need to move about? A house in Amherst was world enough for Emily Dickinson; why travel?

In the title poem of her new collection, *Questions of Travel*, Elizabeth Bishop asks the same question in these words:

> *Is it lack of imagination that*
> *   makes us come*
> *to imagined places, not just stay*
> *   at home?*
> *Or could Pascal have been not*
> *   entirely right*
> *about just sitting quietly in*
> *   one's room?*
>
> *Continent, city, country, society:*
> *the choice is never wide and never*
> *   free.*
> *And here, or there . . . No. Should*
> *   we have stayed at home,*
> *wherever that may be?"*

The question is answered by a question—one that every American poet seems to put to himself. The quest for home, for roots is unending; the metaphor of the journey provides the frame for the greatest imaginative literature. For the American poet the theme is central: alienated from a materialistic society, the views of which he cannot share, he nevertheless loves his country; he is the exile always returning. Each of his poems becomes a means of defining his true place, his real home.

For Emily Dickinson, Brazil was more than just a word; it was heaven on earth, all that she could ask for, and precisely the one commodity that God, "the Mighty Merchant," could not provide:

Brazil? He twirled a button
Without a glance my way
"But, Madam, is there nothing else
That we can show today?"

For Elizabeth Bishop, another New Englander by birth and up-
bringing, Brazil has actually for the past fifteen years been
home; and she writes of it in poems that make up almost half
her volume with all the precision, clarity, and wit that we have
come to expect of her. Her best poems have the sense of ease and
repose that great poems possess. They are composed, both in the
sense of being admirably constructed (she has a painter's eye
and knows how to put together the most disparate objects and
observations) and in the sense of being restful, controlled. She
is modern, a student of Hopkins, in that she is interested in the
mind in action. She is Romantic, also, a nature poet, Words-
worthian, but never allows herself to be carried away: her emotions are tranquilly recollected and her musings are made
memorable. There are several poems in the Brazilian section of
the book that any anthologist would want to include with Miss
Bishop's best work: "The Armadillo," "The Riverman" (based
on Brazilian folklore), and a ballad, "The Burglar of Babylon."
In the second section, entitled "Elsewhere," I would choose
"Filling Station" and "Visits to St. Elizabeths," the latter inspired by her visits to Ezra Pound in Washington.

But for all its brilliance, the book is oddly uneven and raises
questions in our minds about the direction of Miss Bishop's work
in general. The central part is given over to a short story, "In
the Village," a childhood reminiscence of a village in Nova
Scotia. The sick mother's scream hovers in the air throughout
the summer, and echoes on down the years in the mind of the
child who tells the story. But above it is another sound, that of
the blacksmith, hammering out a horseshoe: his pure sound like
the voice of the elements (the voice of the maker) "turns everything else to silence," even "those other things—clothes, crumbling postcards, broken china; things damaged and lost, sick-

ened or destroyed; even the frail almost-lost scream." The story ends with a plea to the blacksmith: "Oh, beautiful sound, strike again!" The reader is reminded that much of Elizabeth Bishop's work is about childhood and lost innocence—"things damaged and lost, sickened or destroyed." But too often, the pure, elemental, mastering sound becomes itself lost in the small things, in the detail. Miss Bishop is a miniaturist for whom "The world is uniquely/minute and vast and clear"; and in which there is "no detail too small." As an epigraph to "Brazil, January 1, 1502," she quotes a phrase of Sir Kenneth Clark's from *Landscape into Art*, "embroidered nature . . . tapestried landscape," and it might be applied not just to the Brazilian landscape of which she is speaking here but to her work in general. The trouble with embroidery is that it is too fine and finicky; what is "vast and clear" is frequently lost in the small stitching. Miss Bishop overworks the adjective "little": there is something little on almost every page—little pearls, little bottles, little people, little moons, a little filling station. The effect of all this is sometimes to put things in proper perspective, but by its very insistence it often becomes merely peculiar and tiresome. Miss Bishop stated in a recent interview that she is "not interested in big-scale work as such. Something needn't be large to be good."

That is certainly true, but neither is something necessarily good just because it is small. By straining to understate, to undercut, to minimize, to avoid the grandiose, Miss Bishop comes dangerously close at times to seeming as ridiculous as an earlier New England poet, Lydia Sigourney, the Sweet Singer of Hartford, was in trying to be grand. What we have always admired in Elizabeth Bishop is what she admires in Herbert, "the absolute naturalness of tone." When her work becomes muted and coy, quaint and quilted, that tone is lost. But she is so fine a poet, so individual an artist, that she can only momentarily disappoint us: we know that the simple, pure, "beautiful sound" is within her grasp, and that it will be heard again and again.

III

THINKING
IN IMAGES:
On Children's
Literature

CHILDREN
AND POETRY

CHILDREN and poetry—how naturally the two go together. Every child responds to rhythm and rhyme because they are as natural to him as breathing: saying over the old rhymes, he seems to answer some deep primitive urge. Paul Hazard has said that the English, with their nursery rhymes, which have a harmony all their own, "are not unconscious of the fact that by placing rhythm at the beginning of life they are conforming to the general order of the universe."

How natural and harmonious it all is at the beginning; and yet what happens along the way later to make poetry to many children the dullest and least enjoyable of literary expressions? It is usually along about the fifth grade in our schools that children decide poetry is not for them. It is then that they are exposed to—and often made to memorize—some insipid lines from which they never recover. A few years ago—in the fifth grade—my younger son, who had been brought up to love poetry and to read it constantly, came home from school with a poem he had been asked to memorize. It was eight lines long (some teachers now seem to think that eight is the magical number, not too much nor too little). The first quatrain of the poem, which I regret to say is to be found in many textbooks, describes how a dog begins to howl in the downstairs hallway in order to be let out; the second describes how he begins to howl as soon as he is out in order to get back in. The language used in this intended humorous observation is banal, imprecise, and devoid of any felicity; the rhymes are obvious and flat. Moreover, the whole thing reveals a dreadful condescension on the part of the author, for it is clear that he has concocted what he considers a coy turn that a child will find amusing.

The lines are typical of the deadening verse that fills many anthologies. I was distressed to find my son exposed to such rubbish, but, thinking it over, I remembered what I had had to memorize at his age. I dug up a notebook I had kept in the fifth grade, and there, copied out on page after page, along with such poems as "The Flag Goes By" and "Helping Hands," was one that I particularly recalled. Indeed, how could I forget it! The poem, "Somebody's Mother," begins:

> The woman was old and ragged and gray,
> And bent with the chill of a winter's day.
> The street was wet with the recent snow,
> And the woman's feet were aged and slow.
> She stood at the crossing and waited long,
> Alone, uncared for, amid the throng
> Of human beings who passed her by,
> Nor heeded the glance of her anxious eye.

It continues for another four stanzas until one of the boys emerging from school "like a flock of sheep" helps the old woman across. It concludes:

> And somebody's mother lowered her head
> In her room that night, and the prayer she said

Was, "God be kind to the noble boy,
Who is somebody's son and pride and joy."

I note, following my schoolboy hand, that there are places where
my pen seemed to falter, scratch, and blur; the banality of the
language was clearly too much for me. And yet I did memorize
it, and still today, as an example of truly bad poetry worthy of
inclusion in *The Stuffed Owl*, I can recite the entire poem. How
did I survive this? I suppose because I could see even then how
bad it was, and outside the classroom I was composing, or passing along with my classmates, parodies of poems like this one of
"The Village Blacksmith," in the same notebook, by changing
only a word here and there:

And the muscles of his brawny arms
Are as strong as *rubber* bands.

We were reacting as Lewis Carroll had done some eighty years
earlier to the deadening piety of much of the verse that was then
intended for children when he wrote, for his younger brother
and sister, his first book, *Useful and Instructive Poetry*, which
includes lines such as these:

"What meat is in that stew to go?"
"My sister'll be the contents." "Oh!"
"Will you lend the pan, cook?" "NO!"

Moral: "Never stew your sister."

When I look over the poetry the young are still being
offered in many textbooks, the same sentimental drivel but now
couched in forthright but unimaginative language and wreathed
or buried in lavish illustration, I despair that any feeling whatever for poetry can be kept alive. And the complaint seems to be
universal. Listen to what Kornei Chukovsky, the great children's
poet, says about students in the Soviet Union: "Together with
the works of classical poets, they have been taught hackneyed

91

lines, absurd rhythms, cheap rhymes. There are times when I could cry with disappointment. I am convinced that exposing children to such trash will cripple their aesthetic taste, disfigure their literary training, and condition them to a slovenly attitude to the written word, and that all this rubbish will block off the children's appreciation of genuine poetic works." In my own case I am sure that the result would have been exactly this had I not had access to the public library to discover other poets for myself, and had I not had a wise and sensitive teacher who early on put in my hands Palgrave's *Golden Treasury*, from which we read a poem each morning.

Poetry, especially children's poetry, always begins with the particular; and, like that of most poets who have written for children, my interest began with a particular child on a special day. When my son David was four years old, I was sitting in the living room of our Greenwich Village apartment. We had rented the apartment furnished (with massive, dark Spanish furniture) from a man who, in the course of his long years in Spain, had collected as many instruments of torture as possible; most of these we had stored away in closets, but the room was still rather somber (with something of a fairytale atmosphere about it) save for the light that poured in from a bay window overlooking a garden in back. I was working with a pad on my lap, when David, as four-year-olds will, came parading up and down the room reciting to the rhythm of his step:

> A Jack-in-the-Box
> Fell in the coffee
> And hurt himself.

At first I paid no attention and went on with my work, but he also went on, coming down hard on every syllable again and again. I can't remember whether or not I actually wrote the phrase down, but it certainly stayed with me. It stayed until that night when I lay awake—in a huge, dark, brocaded four-poster bed that made me feel a child again myself. I made up the poem:

A Jack-in-the-Box
On the pantry shelf
Fell in the coffee
And hurt himself.
Nobody looked
To see what had happened:
There by the steaming
Hot urn he lay;
So they picked him up
With the silverware,
And carried him off
On the breakfast tray.

The next morning I said the poem to David, and he was delighted with it—it was his. And indeed it was; all I had done was to complete what he had begun. What happens in the poem is what happens in the world of the four-year-old—for no reason and with no result—just as it happens at the circus, which is the child's dream of action realized. He asked me to repeat it to him several times, and then he turned to other things that interested him, and I went back to working on what seemed more serious poems. A night or two later, when we were entertaining friends, someone told a story and everyone burst out laughing. David, who had come out of his room, poked his head from behind one of the large armchairs and said, "It's laughing time!" and everybody naturally laughed all the harder. The next day I thought again about the jack-in-the-box and about laughing time. When one is four, there is a time for everything: a time for eating, a time for playing, a time for sleeping; why shouldn't there be a time for laughing as well? And so I began at once, in a kind of frenzy, to write the poems that have subsequently appeared in *Laughing Time*. It seemed rather as if the poems wrote themselves—they flowed out as I listened and watched. When I held David up to the mirror, I said:

> I look in the mirror and what do I see?
> A little of you and a lot of me!

And again he took these to be his lines, and they were. For the next few weeks I listened to my son and watched his every movement. I had, of course, watched and listened before, but now I was like a painter with his model: there was no line, no bone structure, no shadow that I did not wish to explore. I wanted to get inside him, to see things as he was seeing them—and as I could remember having seen them once myself; I wanted to give back to him the delight that he had given me, and in such a way that he would not even realize he was being given anything. And so I worked on as if all my life and training as a writer had been meant only for this moment.

When I completed my manuscript a short time later, I read it aloud to one of my closest friends, an art critic, who had first heard many of my poems. In this case he listened and gazed at me as if I had gone stark, raving mad. The leaps and connections that seemed perfectly natural to a four-year-old were ones that he had forgotten ever having made; the relationships and situations that struck the four-year-old as funny he found either embarrassing or strange, to say the least. A silence fell when I had finished, and I began to wonder whether or not I had been misguided in thinking that I had understood and captured a four-year-old's view of the world. I am happy to say that I do not think I had been, for David's poems have now been read by thousands of children, many of whom have written me to say that the book made them "laugh out loud"; and what better response could anyone wish?

I like to think that what I discovered instinctively in the course of composition was what Chukovsky in *From Two to Five* has so brilliantly described as the requirements for poetry for small children. Their poems, he says, must be graphic, for children think in images, and there must be a rapid shift of imagery. The verbal painting must be lyrical, with a lilt, heightened music, and frequent and lively rhymes. The poems must be carried forward by verbs and nouns and should not be packed with adjectives; they must respond to the child's sense of play since the activity of the young takes the form of play. The most important requirement of all, however, is that children's poetry "must have the skill, the virtuosity, the technical soundness of poetry for adults. A bad poem could never be good for children." Children's poets, moreover, "must not only adapt writing to the needs of the young but must also bring children within reach of adult perceptions and thoughts."

James Stephens has perhaps said in his poem "I Am Writer" what all poets writing for the young have wished to say:

> I am writer,
> And do know
> Nothing that is false,
> Or true:
>
> Have only care
> To take it so,
> And make it sing,
> And make it new:
>
> And make it new,
> And make it sing,
> When, if it's pleasing
> Unto you,
>
> Say, I've done
> A useful thing
> —As your servant
> Ought to do.

[1969]

A PRIMER
OF SENSIBILITY
(Walter de la Mare)

THIS ANTHOLOGY,[1] famous since its original publication in 1923, has about it, J. B. Priestley has said, "something of the golden spacious air of childhood, something a thousand leagues removed from the atmosphere of most anthologies of this kind, and one realizes that this is not merely the result of good taste, a sense of what is fitting, and so on, but of something much rarer, an imagination of an unusual kind, one that is infinitely wider and more sensitive than a child's, and yet, in one sense, still a child's imagination." These lines from "The Goat Paths" of James Stephens, which is included, might serve as an epigraph for the volume:

> I would think until I found
> Something I can never find,
> Something lying on the ground
> In the bottom of my mind.

[1] *Come Hither: A Collection of Rhymes and Poems for the Young of All Ages,* edited by Walter de la Mare, with decorations by Warren Chappell. (New York: Alfred A. Knopf).

96

It is the unfindable, yet found, things with which Walter de la Mare is here concerned, first in the poems themselves, and then in the notes "about and roundabout" them. The reader, because he is young or can remember being young, is so delighted by the objects that are brought up from the depths that he does not realize until the last page of the book that he has never been told exactly what it was that was being sought, nor that what was being sought could never really be found: the delight is in the search. "The object, the eye, the memory, the insight, the spirit within," de la Mare says at one point, "these are the Five in Council." And these are the Five that working together throughout, in the poems and in the comments on them, give this book its unusual, indeed its unique, character.

Come Hither stands at an interesting point in Walter de la Mare's development as a writer. His first book, *Songs of Childhood*, was published in 1902 under the name of Walter Ramal. His second, *Henry Brocken*, a prose romance written on notepaper of the Anglo-American Oil Company where de la Mare was then employed, appeared in 1904. It is a book that falls midway between criticism and creation; and although it contains passages of real beauty, it is a failure. The bookworm, Henry Brocken, rides forth into the world of romance on his mare Rosinante; but his is, as Dylan Thomas remarked, a journey on a borrowed horse: in dealing with other people's poetry, the author oddly creates little himself. But the book is significant, for it shows de la Mare's need to be involved, as any poet must be, with other poetry while bringing life to his own. *Come Hither* is a much more mature work: in it he undertakes the same journey, but he is content to let the poems stand intact, each in its original minute or grandiose setting, while he remains in the wings as commentator and connoisseur. In this way, he brings together his gifts as prose writer and poet, critic and creator, in an effective form. The poems and rhymes he has assembled take on a new aspect by being put side by side; the literariness of the early writing is overcome, and the whole of literature here becomes properly the whole of life.

The collection opens with the section, "Morning and May"; it closes with "Evening and Dream" and "The Garden." "Morning and May" are not just the beginning of the day and the blossoming of the year, but the beginning of all time and experience; "evening and dream" are their fulfillment and their close, the end of the day, of the year, and the end of time; and beyond time, outside the full circle of experience, is the "garden." The first poem, as well as the last, is "This Is the Key"— the key of the kingdom in which there is a city, in the city, a town, and so on up to the empty bed on which rests a basket of sweet flowers. "This jingle," de la Mare says in his notes, "is one of hundreds of nursery or dandling rhymes which I found in Mr. Nahum's book. Compared with more formal poems they are like the least (and loveliest) of the wild flowers—pimpernel, eyebright, thyme, woodruff, and others even tinier, even quieter, but revealing their own private and complete little beauty if looked at closely. Who made them, how old they are; nobody knows." The key to the garden lies in the least and loveliest of flowers; the key to the world of the imagination in the least and loveliest of words.

Poetry, says Walter de la Mare in the introduction to his *Poems for Children,* is not only one of the rarest, but also one of the most curious things that men can make. Into this rare and curious realm there is for the young no better guide: he is wise but warm, careful but carefree. He is infinitely patient; he knows that children never tire of detail. There seems to be no limit to his range of interest: one moment he tells of the strange pleasure of reading a little book—and one in small print, too, (Alice Meynell's *Flower of the Mind*)—by English glowworm light, and during an eclipse of the moon; he discourses on witches and witchcraft, the names of the flowers, villages, and meadows of England, on noses, punishment in English schools through the ages, bells, graveyard inscriptions. He delights in old cookbooks ("Indeed, the next best thing to eating a good dish is to read how it is made; and somehow the old 'cookbook' writers learned to write most appetizing English.") ; and he gives us recipes for cooking lamprey and for making a lemon syllabub. Chaucer's lines on the daisy lead him off into a complete essay on the flowers in Shakespeare; and prompt him to remark that of all English poets Chaucer is the one most delighted in by his fellows. Nothing is too small to escape his eye : the byways of experience become main thoroughfares; poetry is all of life or it is nothing. "For the meaning of a poem," he writes, "is *all* the experience, thought, vision, insight, music, happiness that we can get out of it—it is all that it *does* to us."

The best children's stories are those which have the air of being told rather than written; the best children's poems are those that were meant to be heard. Never in one volume has there been such a consciously aural emphasis : here in ballads, songs, hymns, and rhymes is a record of the loveliest sounds recorded in English. No one is a better listener than Walter de la Mare. Speaking of John Lydgate's lines on Henry before Agincourt, he says that "the verse of this ancient fragment jolts, jars, and moves cumbrously as a cannon over rocky ground." And he identifies for us the birds that are laughing in Blake's green woods : "Pause an instant on the fifth word in the third stanza and you can actually *hear* the birds laughing—yaffle, blackcap, bullfinch, and jay, and the droning and the whistling and the whir-r-r." In a series of brilliant asides, which should be valuable in this day of public poetry readings, he comments on how verse should be read aloud.

And throughout these pages we hear the poet reading us his selections in a quiet, firm voice, the voice of one who is not preaching but revealing, not instructing by dark precept but by brilliant insight. For the purpose of the volume is to develop the sensibility of the young reader, to show him by simple stages that feeling, which comes first, must be cultivated if it is to grow. Nothing of John Donne is included; his poetry "awaits the mind as the body grows older, and when we have ourselves learned the experience of life with which it is concerned." But de la Mare is quick to add: "Not that the simplest poetry will then lose anything of its grace and truth and beauty—for rather it shines the more clearly, since age needs it the more." Nor are there any poems of Edward Lear or Lewis Carroll; and this may seem a curious omission in a book for the young. Nonsense constitutes an altogether different approach to the development of sensibility, however; the maze, although a fascinating area in itself, leads back into the garden proper. Walter de la Mare preferred the straightforward, simple path of lyric impulse; and his collection clearly demonstrates to the young of all ages the wisdom to which it may lead.

[1963]

WHAT IS THE USE
OF A BOOK?

"WHAT IS THE USE of a book," asks Alice in Wonderland, "without pictures or conversations?" It is by seeing and hearing that a young child experiences the world; it is through his eyes and ears that he absorbs its reflection as brought to him in books.

When we examine children's drawings, we realize that there is a reason for the distortion they display: the child is putting down what he sees. For him the universe is circumscribed by the familiar faces into which he looks. And so he draws people full-on, with huge heads drifting about like balloons or plumped down like potatoes; the body comes later. Edward Lear, the master of nonsense and one of the most original of illustrators, was aware of this when he created the Yonghy-Bonghy-Bo, whose "Head was ever so much bigger than his Body, and whose Hat was rather small." There is point to his concentration in verse and drawing on the eyes, the fingers or toes, the mouth. We have "the Pobble who has no toes," the "Dong with the luminous nose," the Old Man with "an immoderate mouth," and, above all, people who stare out at one as if their eyes were the very center of creation:

There was a Young Lady whose eyes
Were unique as to color and size;
When she opened them wide, people
*   all turned aside,*
And started away in surprise.

Lear, with insight and humor, presents his reader the world as it is in early morning, luminous and fresh, basically defined by sense perception.

To the young, sight and sound, the primary senses, are everything. The greatest children's writers have all been keenly aware of the plastic arts. If not actually painters themselves, they have had a highly developed visual sense: they know that the child must be able to see what is being said. Edward Lear was a superb watercolorist, capable of catching quickly the atmosphere of a place. Lewis Carroll, while unable to bring his own drawing to the perfection he wished, was a pioneer in photography; he put his mathematical mind to achieving through mechanical means what he could not with his own hands. Kate Greenaway's vision was such that she brought new life to old rhymes, and made the whole of language shine in the delicate clarity of her albums. Robert Louis Stevenson compiled a list of drawings he felt should properly accompany his verses.

Pictures and conversation combined give life to children's books. Sight and sound must go together; the ear as well as the eye must be trained. "Listen, Mummy!" the child says again and again; and he means what he says, he wants to be heard. But he also wants to hear and wants to listen. Beatrix Potter in *The Tale of Tom Kitten* describes three Puddle-Ducks moving down the road in these terms: "Pit pat paddle pat! Pit pat waddle pat!" The other day I read that story to my three-year-old son; he was delighted, and when we finished the book he started off merrily around the room, singing: "Diddle-duck! Diddle-duck!"

He was not only seeing but hearing the duck's movements, the word *duck* itself had taken on meaning. Every children's masterpiece reflects this awareness of the importance of sound. The old fairy tales are filled with rhythmical incantations; the names of the characters themselves have an individual and distinctive lilt.

What besides a basic visual and aural appeal must a good children's book possess? Whether written in verse or prose, it cannot be static, it must have movement. In the world of the young things happen, and they happen many times over, and from morning until night. Edward Lear knew that children want motion: the characters he depicts are all hopping, sailing, riding, flying, no one is ever still. And certainly, by his sudden and subtle changes of meter, he makes the child aware of movement. The action he describes is not only vivid but violent. People in his limericks are always falling into rivers, getting trapped in boxes, being baked or stewed. Nor is there an absence of violence in Lewis Carroll. From the moment of her fall, Alice enters a topsy-turvy world in which it is the rule of the day, reaching its mad climax in the words of the Queen: "Off with their heads!" All this, in our world of real violence, sounds like anything but proper fare for a child. However, as in all great children's literature, there is nothing dangerous in it whatsoever because things are made to happen as they happen in the child's world: for no reason and with no result. They happen as they do at the circus, the child's dream come to life. "Off with her head!" shouts the Queen; but Alice's retaliation is immediate: "You're nothing but a pack of cards!" And indeed the cards come flying down upon her, not cards but the dead leaves her sister is brushing from her face. Alice awakens from her dream, safe on the bank, as every child knew she would be from the beginning.

Children, in their books, like to have a great deal going on, and they like to hear it spoken of in words that have flavor. They grow impatient with what is insipid and tasteless. The air in the workroom of their writer should be charged with pepper: there should be spice in his images, wit in his words.

Sound, color, movement, these are the ingredients of the good book. And many volumes published every year have them: they read well, are filled with action and illustrated with lavish and exciting color. What most of them lack is something much more difficult to put one's finger on, but which shines forth from every classic. One might call it an atmosphere in which the child knows he is secure, a charged air he breathes as if for the first time, a landscape opening out infinite and fresh before him: soft rolling hills leading up to the mountains and down to the sea. No child has to be told what this atmosphere is: he senses it at once. He knows that he can put out his hand to touch familiar objects and have them respond to his touch; he can hear what is being said and understand it; he can speak and be answered. This atmosphere, one might say, emanates from the earth itself. It is there in a book like Kenneth Grahame's *The Wind in the Willows*, which its author describes as concerning "Life as it might fairly be supposed to be regarded by some of the wise, small things 'that glide in grasses and rubble of woody wreck.' " It is always the voices of the "wise, small things" that put the young at ease; and how keen the writer must be to hear them and to record them convincingly: what skill it takes to write of "the feeble mouse, the homely hen!" Behind all children's classics is a presence the child can identify with and believe in. A. A. Milne recognized the fact when he wrote, in regard to his verses, that it is not always clear who is saying them: "Is it the Author, that strange but uninteresting person, or is it Christopher Robin, or some other boy or girl, or Nurse or Hoo? . . . If you are not quite sure, then it is probably Hoo." We do not, however, require the ensuing description of Hoo: the writer's touch is sure, the presence recognizable, the reader knows where he is.

[1957]

104

"SO THEY SMASHED
THAT OLD MAN..."
(Edward Lear)

RECENTLY, when friends of mine were to depart on an ocean voyage with their children, aged three, seven, and ten, I presented them all with a copy of *The Complete Nonsense Book* of Edward Lear. Surely no book is better calculated to dispel the moments of tedium, disorientation, and malaise that we experience at sea, when the last bit of land dips out of sight, when familiar objects are stored away in our minds, and the roll of the ship provides us with rhythms to which we must somehow respond. Since the publication of his first book of nonsense in 1846, Edward Lear has meant home and hearth to English-speaking children everywhere: he has offered them a room that is never locked, a world accessible to all who need not be reminded that life can be pleasant and gay. My friends' children delighted in the poems of Lear as children always will. One of the limericks appealed to them instantly— and I like to picture them there, beating it out as they pounded up and down the deck:

> There was an Old Man with a gong,
> Who bumped at it all the day long;
> But they called out, "O law! you're a horrid old bore!"
> So they smashed that Old Man with a gong.

"So they *smashed* that Old Man . . ." How children love to come down on the word *smashed* as they must in the last line. Nonsensical the limerick certainly is, and violent, too; unhealthful, it is not. It is clean, wonderful fun, and reveals its author's profound understanding of the child's world.

The song, the sound—that is always the best part of a poem for children. The sense will follow.

> The Owl and the Pussycat went to sea
> In a beautiful pea-green boat:
> They took some honey, and plenty of money
> Wrapped up in a five-pound note.

Evoked in such clear-ringing vowel sounds, the journey is at once moonlit and magical. What can the Owl do but sing?

> The Owl looked up to the stars above,
> And sang to a small guitar . . .

The scene is set in miniature perfection, the "pea-green boat," the "small guitar," with the sea on every side and the whole wide world stretching before the travelers. How can such a voyage end but in happiness and dancing?

> And hand in hand, on the edge of the sand
> They danced by the light of the moon,
> The moon,
> The moon,
> They danced by the light of the moon.

Edward Lear runs more than once what he calls appropriately that "pea-green gamut," and no writer for children has ever approached him when he does.

Lear himself always remained something of a child; being a painter and a poet, he could remember vividly what childhood is like and could speak to children in their own language. He could invent, as they do, words that suggest far more than they mean—"ombliferous," "borascible"—words that delight with their sound. Because with sound he was always ahead of sense, he leapt ahead as children do, but he left no doubt that the sense would follow. Words have meaning but their meaning is multiple, a fact that we as adults, bound by our dictionary distinctions, can easily forget. When the Co-operative Cauliflower advances "in a somewhat plumdomphious manner" toward the setting sun, supported by his Waterwagtails and his "two superincumbent confidential cucumbers," the children contemplate him "with mingled affection and disgust," as well they might. Things are multitudinous and mingled, they are preposterous and parallel, but they are never blurred.

Lear remembers that in the child's world things *happen:* they happen not once but many times over and in rapid succession. In that world, the child's arrow, like that of Zeno, never reaches its mark because it must traverse a series of moments in time, and each moment is eternal. The child wants the assurance of things happening; every minute must be replete with action. Darkness and fear settle down only when his unconscious mind is unable to summon up a series of actions and events to hold them off; when he cannot, his defenses are down, terror moves in, and he becomes its real and tangible victim. The objects, animals, and characters in that delightful sequence of Lear's verse, *Teapots and Quails*, are in continual motion: they sail, jig, drive, hop, fly, roll, poke, and jump. Everyone in Lear's nonsense drawings, as in his verse, is moving: people are falling, running, throwing out their two hands behind them or in front, one foot is always in the air. People swing from ropes, hop into trees, fly, ride—no one is still. When characters do remain in place, they become, by the very fact, ridiculous:

> There was an old man of Hong Kong,
> Who never did anything wrong;
> He lay on his back, with his head in a sack,
> That innocuous old man of Hong Kong.

And again:

> There was an Old Man of the Coast,
> Who placidly sat on a post;

Even he cannot sit there unmoved forever:

> But when it was cold he relinquished his hold,
> And called for some hot buttered toast.

Household objects are unhappy only because they must stay put. And so what do they do about it? Like the table and the chair, the poker and the tongs, they go for a walk or a ride.

Things are in motion, things are happening, and violent things indeed. A man leaves the door ajar and some very large rats come in to devour his clothes; an old woman threatens to burn her grandchild; men fall into the river, the sea, the broth; a man locks his wife in a box; a wife bakes her husband in a stew; a man tumbles from his horse and is split asunder; another fans off his niece's head. All this removed from its context and the gusto given it by rhythm and rhyme sounds terrifying. But there is nothing alarming or wrong or dangerous in it simply because everything is made to happen in the way children expect it to: unconditioned by logic and unimpeded by moral consequence. The delight is in the happening—as it is at the circus, where the air is filled with marvels and where the child imagines that he tames the roaring lion and flies with the aerialist on the trapeze.

To the young, seeing and hearing are everything. Edward Lear, in his serious work, was a fine watercolorist, able to catch with speed and precision the contours of landscape, and—what is more difficult—to give an impression of its attendant atmosphere. His nonsense drawings are full of movement; with his bold line he suggests an entire scene in the tilt of a head or the inclination of a body. To the child on the threshold of experience the sense organs are overwhelmingly important, and Lear remembers this in his nonsense pictures; it is for a purpose that he exaggerates the eyes and ears, the fingers and toes, the mouth. The world he presents is upside-down, top-heavy, topsy-turvy as it is in a dream—or at a carnival. It is also inside-out: the poems and stories present the happenings of an inner world, justified and illumined by human emotion.

So they smashed that Old Man with a gong. The lines reverberate in the memory as Edward Lear intended; and the limerick, when recited, is followed by a familiar sound, which is that of children laughing. Was there ever one more wonderful at any time and in any land?

[1959]

THE SNARK
(Lewis Carroll)

"AFTER Shakespeare, there is no English author," Derek Hudson has said, "more deserving of study by a foreigner intent on exploring English character and English humor than Lewis Carroll." To that I would add that there is no work by him that would give that foreigner a better introduction to the Victorian era than the longest, maddest, if not most successful, poem he wrote, "The Hunting of the Snark." Published in 1876, "The Snark" meant more than even its author was willing to admit, for with it he had opened a door that most Victorians preferred to keep closed. The poem pretended to mean nothing, but what it clearly said was that existence is meaningless and the search for meaning vain. "For the Snark *was* a Boojum, you see."

In "Alice," Lewis Carroll took a happy excursion into the dark. The rabbit hole opens out into a frightening world, but Alice, representing the innocent and nascent logical mind, is able to cope with her nightmarish surroundings because she knows, as does every child who reads the book, that logic will triumph. When things go too far she brushes them aside—a house of cards—and awakens to find her sister brushing the leaves from her face; the journey has been a pleasant one. "The Snark" is another sort of dream, a nightmare in broad daylight. Subtitled "An Agony, in Eight Fits," each Fit takes the reader closer to the abyss, the terror of darkness, in which the Baker, on sighting the Snark, will "softly and suddenly" vanish away.

Andrew Lang, one of the first reviewers of the poem, pointed out that the reader sees the characters "in themselves, he does not see them in the eyes of the child, who, as in 'Alice', takes them as natural persons in a world not understood." Indeed, the "Snark" is not a children's poem at all. Although some of the word play, awkward as much of it is, may catch a child's fancy, it is doubtful that any child would be much taken with the whole of the poem. (There is the exception of that little girl who used to recite it on carriage rides; what a terror *she* must have been!)

Not only is none of the characters a child, but none seems to have the remotest connection with a child's world. Here the Butcher, the Baker, the Candlestick-maker of nursery rhymes are all transformed into Victorian business men. There is a Barrister, a Broker, a Butcher. The only character who has anything to do with games is not a player but a scorekeeper—the Billiard-marker. The only animal is the Beaver, the busiest of all animals, who, while engaged in making lace, keeps one eye on the Butcher, who kills only Beavers.

In the company of children, the Rev. Charles Dodgson (Lewis Carroll) felt at ease and completely lost his stammer. Here, however, he has left his little ladies behind; and the poem is a stammering from beginning to end. The name of every character begins with a *b:* the Bellman tinkles his *bell;* the map is *blank;* the Bandersnatch grabs the Banker even though he proffers a check made out to the *bearer;* the Snark has a fondness for *bathing-machines*, and is, of course, a *Boojum*. When

111

the Baker vanishes, not a *button* is found. No poet has done so much with *b's*, and no other may want to try.

In this poem about the failure of belief, the poet stresses the failure of language itself. The "Alice" books sparkle on every page with the richness and infinite variety of words; "The Snark" speaks always of their inadequacy. The Banker is struck dumb, and rattles a set of bones, having become a minstrel-show blackface. The Baker, the poet, cannot remember his own name; he can only bake a wedding cake, but there are no ingredients for it on board the ship. When he vanishes, it is in the midst of "his laughter and glee," and in the midst of "the word he was trying to say."

Lewis Carroll may be admitting that he can no longer play the game and create the delightful nonsense of "Jabberwocky." But because he put so much of his mature genius into "The Snark," it is, as Martin Gardner points out, "a poem about being and nonbeing, an existential poem, a poem of existential agony."

In this edition,[1] Mr. Gardner, who gave us "The Annotated Alice," follows "The Snark" down to the present—from the bathing-machine to the bomb. "Atomic energy," he writes, "is a Snark that comes in various shapes and sizes. A certain number of intercontinental missiles—the U. S. Air Force has one it calls the Snark—with thermonuclear warheads can glide gently down on the just and unjust, and the whole of humanity may never be met with again."

[1962]

---

1 *The Annotated Snark: The full text of Lewis Carroll's "The Hunting of the Snark,"* with introduction and notes by Martin Gardner and illustrated by Henry Holiday (New York: Simon & Schuster).

A TENT OF GREEN
(*Elizabeth Madox Roberts*)

A WRITER must be rarely gifted to remember and to love the child that he was and to communicate that memory and affection convincingly to both young and old. We do not want adults to be children—and there is nothing more painful than to watch the writers of some children's books trying to be—but we do welcome the artist who can remember exactly without coyness, depreciation, or self-indulgence, what he was like as a child and what he saw with a child's eyes. In England Walter de la Mare was such a one; in America we are fortunate to have had another in this century, a mature and distinguished novelist who set down in verse the early years of her life with the candor and directness characteristic of great art. I refer to Elizabeth Madox Roberts (1881–1941), whose volume of poems *Under the Tree* is an appropriate answer to those editors and critics who look disparagingly on anything "slight." This book has no weight, and yet it looms large. It has the frailty of a leaf, but the strength of the tree for which it speaks. In the poem "On the Hill," Miss Roberts describes a girl who has gone with her brothers to pick strawberries; she pauses for a moment on a high place to look out over the town, on her own house, on the poplar tree beside it; and she says:

> And over and over I tried to see
> Some of us walking under the tree,
>
> And the children playing everywhere,
> And how it looks when I am there.

With a spirited imaginative recall she tells us throughout the book exactly how it was: the town and the people in it, the church, the woods around, the fields and streams. Elizabeth Madox Roberts, who grew up in the Kentucky mountains, was interested in the speech of Kentucky people, in its peculiar rhythms and archaic charm. And coming from a region somewhat between North and South, East, and West, she seems in these poems to draw, with the quiet assurance of American humor, on the experiences of us all.

Under the Tree, originally published in 1922, has been reprinted many times since. It is now available in an enlarged edition, published by the Viking Press and fittingly illustrated with woodcuts by F. D. Bedford. Having won the respect of parents and teachers and the affection of children, the book is assured of a long life; and while certain of the poems may be found in many anthologies of children's literature, the volume should be read in its entirety.

The fifty-nine poems in *Under the Tree* are written for the most part in quatrains and couplets. The language from beginning to end is simple almost to the point of flatness; the rhymes are everywhere direct and unforced. Everything is presented in the speech of a sensitive intelligent child who seems to be trying to communicate her own experience and to understand that experience in the process of communication. The manner is straightforward and unadorned; often the lines seem to fall away in the stanzas; shorter at times than strict meter would allow, they suggest a child pausing and reaching out for words, as in "Strange Tree":

> It looked at me with all its limbs;
> It looked at me with all its bark.
> The yellow wrinkles on its sides
> Were bent and dark.

or taken aback by the very shimmer of mystery, as in "Firefly":

> A little light is going by,
> Is going up to see the sky,
> A little light with wings.
>
> I never could have thought of it,
> To have a little bug all lit
> And made to go on wings.

The child in these poems appears to be rushing ahead to tell of things of major importance to herself whether they interest the adult listener or not:

> And it was Sunday everywhere,
> And Father pinned a rose on me
> And said he guessed he'd better take
> Me down to see Miss Kate-Marie.
>
> And when I went it all turned out
> To be a Sunday school, and there
> Miss Kate-Marie was very good
> And let me stand beside her chair.

The many lines beginning with "And" give the sense not only of the child's intentness but also the breathlessness of her speech. They give further the impression of things continuing as they do in the world of the young—event following close upon event, object heaped on object. Connections for the child, as Miss Roberts was quick to realize, are more frequently marked by "and" than by "but" or "because." A crescent moon is sighted above a tree:

> And Dick said, "Look what I have found!"
> And when we saw we danced around,
> And made our feet just tip the ground.

The opening words of each line make the reader feel that the children's feet are indeed already in the air, the curve of their delighted bodies following the curve of the moon.

Youthful stress on distinction as well as continuity is wittily and neatly presented in "The People":

> The ants are walking under the ground,
> And the pigeons are flying over the steeple,
> And in between are the people.

Some of the poems in this book have the air of being about nothing at all, so slight is the subject: the child weeps because there are so many stars in the sky or pauses in the rain under a snowball bush; she enumerates the things seen in her pillow at night or composes a tune to accompany the beating of her heart:

> *The men are sailing home from Troy,*
> *And all the lamps are lit.*
>
> *The men are sailing home from Troy,*
> *And all the lamps are lit.*

In another poem she listens to the "talking sound" of the water as it asks over and over:

> "And do you think? And do you think?"

She does think; and she thinks always with her feelings. It is often said that only in British children's books are children presented as being alone, removed from the world of adults; the heroine of *Under the Tree* is an exception to the general gregarious character of most American literary children. She is a lonely child, pictured against a vast beautiful landscape, at times

116

gentle and at others terrifying. One is struck by the vision outward from the core of nature in "The Butterbean Tent," which
should be quoted in its entirety:

> All through the garden I went and went,
> And I walked in under the butterbean tent.
>
> The poles leaned up like a good tepee
> And made a nice little house for me.
>
> I had a hard brown clod for a seat,
> And all outside was a cool green street.
>
> A little green worm and a butterfly
> And a cricketlike thing that could hop went by.
>
> Hidden away there were flocks and flocks
> Of bugs that could go like little clocks.
>
> Such a good day it was when I spent
> A long, long while in the butterbean tent.

The child, sheltered by a tent of green and living things, looks
out upon green. It is the presentation of nature renewing itself,
of innocence giving way fully and beautifully before experience
that makes *Under the Tree* one of the rare children's books that
can be read and enjoyed by both parents and children. In *Alice's
Adventures in Wonderland,* another of the books in that cate-
gory, we witness, as Alice works her way through problem and
puzzle, the development of thought; here we contemplate the
growth of feeling.

In a later volume of poems, *Song in the Meadow* (1940),
Elizabeth Madox Roberts explores for adult readers, as she does
in her novels, the distant universe of legend and history that lies
behind the songs and ballads of her native state. In *Under the
Tree* she brings us that meadow close-up, golden and fresh in
miniature, alive with the sights and sounds of things observed

and perfectly remembered. In it she succeeded in accomplishing what she had hoped to in art—"to bring the physical world before the mind with a greater closeness, a richer immediacy than before, so that the mind rushes out to the very edges of sense." And the result is, as she said it would be, that the mind then "turns about and sees itself mirrored within itself."

[1962]

THE MOON OR MIT

FOR PUBLISHERS of children's books 1959 was an all-time record boom year. According to *Publishers Weekly*, 1,647 juveniles were brought out, or over 10 percent of all books published. The figure would be cause for rejoicing if it indicated that there is an unprecedented interest in children's books, and that we are on our way to developing a literate young America. However, not only is the total minute in proportion to the population of the country, but also at least half of these volumes are not what literate Americans would consider books at all; they are merchandise. Having become big business, children's books are now made to fit in between the greeting card counter and the toy department; and they have taken on more and more the characteristics of both areas: they are brightly packaged; they are intended for fun and little else.

The big news in children's book publishing last year was the success of the new *I—Can't—Read—And—I—Don't—Care—It's—Fun* books, all carefully put together around basic vocabulary lists to give kids the impression that because they could recognize a few words repeated *ad nauseam* they were reading. Instead of considering the emphasis on a minimal vocabulary a national disgrace, educators and librarians hailed the books as the answer to their prayers. "This is what we have all been waiting for!" exclaimed one librarian. Apparently it was; for it was one further step along the way toward books without words. *The Cat in the Hat* was not bad—Dr. Seuss does have a gift for nonsense and an ear for the lilt that delights children and he has written entertaining books—but neither was it particularly good; no one took the trouble to point out that the verse was poor, and the drawings remarkably banal. But the kids naturally welcomed *The Cat in the Hat* as a national hero; the humor, poor as it was, was a relief from their usual dull fare. Then too they must take what they can get; and the book was readily available. Dr. Seuss, who began his career in advertising (*Quick, Henry—the Flit!* of my childhood days) recognized a good thing, and immediately initiated a whole series of beginner's books, recruiting his writers and illustrators largely from Madison Avenue. The TV world of dancing toothpaste and talking thermometers is now within covers; and looking through hundreds of current juveniles, as I have been doing for weeks, can be pretty depressing. Among the new offerings are the true story of the squirrel space monkey, Miss Baker, and the account of the sons of two candidates for the job of being the first man rocketed into space. There are books about bees, clocks, trade winds, rope, seashells, electromagnetic waves, and atomic submarines. There are others on how to tell left from right, how to tell colors ("a mouse is *never* red"), how to visit the doctor. One books describes a "silly centipede who wants to buy fifty pairs of shoes because she believes they will make her look pretty"; another, a factual one, is designed "to give young men the help they have always needed in understanding young women"; another concerns the "rather bewildering first year of a teen-age marriage." Perhaps it is significant, in all this bizarre assembly, that the winner of the Newbery Medal, awarded

120

annually by the American Library Association for the most distinguished contribution to children's literature, should be a film producer, Joseph Krumgold, for his book *Onion John* whose central character inhabits a dump.

Onion John is told in the words of a teen-ager in Serenity, New Jersey, named Andrew Rusch, Jr. Andy cannot make up his mind whether to go to the moon or MIT (his father apparently wants him to do both) until through the influence of a lovable but unpredictable character named Onion John, who eats onions, collects bathtubs, and speaks an unidentifiable language (probably Russian) understandable only to Andy, and who wishes to fumigate the town of its do-goodism from his vantage point on the dump, he decides to stick with his father in the hardware business. A good part of the book is just as silly as it sounds; but Mr. Krumgold, who is a maker of documentary films, has a good eye and a dramatic sense. The book is inferior to his . . . *And Now, Miguel,* which also won a Newbery Medal; but it does contain some memorable scenes.

The older writers of children's books never had any difficulty bridging fantasy and reality; they *were* writers and they knew that the imagination will triumph. The wings that take the children soaring through the air in E. Nesbit's *Five Children and It* are as real as those of any bird; and the children are still, after sixty years, as real as those around the corner. *Five Children and It* was reissued last year as one of ten classics published by the Looking Glass Library in uniform, well-designed, and clearly printed volumes, paper on boards. This extension of the quality-paperback principle to children's books is the idea of Jason Epstein, the young editor who launched the well-known Anchor paperbacks. The Library proposes to make a great variety of children's classics available, to reprint the text exactly without any of the watering-down that has marked most juvenile reprint series, and to use the original drawings wherever feasible. What a treat it is to have, along with such perennial favorites as *The Blue Fairy Book* of Andrew Lang and *The*

Peterkin Papers of Lucretia Peabody Hale, the little-known *Men and Gods* by Rex Warner, the perfect volume for those avid for the Greek myths, told, and at times translated directly, from Ovid by an excellent writer who is not impeded by a vocabulary count-down.

The consulting editors of the Looking Glass Library are not school-of-education pundits and child psychologists but writers of great distinction and varied interests, W. H. Auden, Phyllis McGinley, and Edmund Wilson. Five new titles have now been added to the ten originally published: *The Phoenix and the Carpet* by E. Nesbit, *The Princess and Curdie* by George MacDonald, *The Red Fairy Book* by Andrew Lang, *Otto of the Silver Hand* by Howard Pyle, and a new collection, *The Looking Glass Book of Stories*, edited by Hart Day Leavitt, who has chosen the stories from favorites of his students at Phillips Andover Academy. By moving children's books back thirty or forty years, the Looking Glass Library has moved them ahead; and the editors intend in time to publish new books of similar quality. The volumes have not yet reached supermarket distribution; but it will be a happy day if they do.

Another fortunate event in the juvenile field is the launching by the editors of *American Heritage* of the American Heritage Junior Library. The first two items in the series are *The Story of Yankee Whaling* by Irwin Shapiro, in consultation with Edouard A. Stackpole, curator of the Marine Historical Association of Mystic, Connecticut, and *Indians of the Plains* by Eugene Rachlis, in consultation with John C. Ewers, assistant director, Museum of History and Technology, The Smithsonian Institution, Washington, D. C. The volumes are straight history, excellently written, and each is illustrated with 150 pictures (at least half of them in color), including period paintings, maps, and rare drawings; the layout is magnificent and every page a delight. The books are expensive, but not for the wealth of material they contain; they provide a rare imaginative experience, a journey into history, and a visit to a museum in the company of the most enlightened and interesting of guides. Beside them, on junior's shelf, I would, if possible, place another large and handsome book, *People and Places* by Margaret Mead, which also contains a study of the Plains Indians, along with others of the Eskimo, the Balinese, the Minoans of Crete, and the Ashanti of West Africa.

Golden Press, which is distributing the American Heritage volumes, is also publishing the *Tintin* picture adventure books, already celebrated throughout the world in their original French. To the four previously published, *King Ottokar's Scepter*, *The Crab with the Golden Claws*, *The Secret of the Unicorn*, *Red Rackham's Treasure* have now been added *Destination Moon* and *Explorers on the Moon*. *Tintin* adds new and undreamt-of dimensions to the unpromising form of the comic strip, which one would have thought had been finished off by Disney and his crew. Tintin is an intrepid boy reporter, tall enough to look as if he had just outgrown the plus-fours that he wears night and day. Tintin's round face, pink cheeks, and unwavering topknot of gold hair and his raised eyebrows give him a look of perpetual amazement, that is echoed by the open and slightly elongated face—and raised eyebrows—of his dog Snowy (in French "Milou"). The two bob along over the pages to carry the adventures forward at a pace unequaled since the days of flickering silent films. Tintin has all the answers and all the merit badges, but he somehow avoids seeming insipid, perhaps because he represents like Alice the force of innocent but effective reason working its way through a nightmare world. While the boxes supply all the ins-and-outs and ups-and-downs of violent action—and it is amazing what variety there is in the drawing and color—the dialogue in the balloons is all in legible print on straight lines.

These are books not to be skimmed through with the untrained eye, but books that are to be read. There is no attempt to simplify the vocabulary for the young reader; a good part of the humor and invention is verbal as well as visual. The invective of Captain Haddock, Tintin's nautical pal, is as good as any that has appeared in children's books for years.

Two new collections of poetry attempt to bring back some of the verbal magic that is on its way out. *The Barnes Book of Nursery Verse*, edited by Barbara Ireson, is the best collection of rhymes and verses for small children that I have ever encountered. Mrs. Ireson has done an amazing job of research in bringing together old nursery rhymes with new verses from everywhere. But she has been careful to make this collection more than a grab bag of sweets; she knows that taste can operate just as effectively in choosing verse for beginners as for experienced readers. Originally published in England, the book is gaily illustrated by George Adamson in the best tradition of wry and witty understatement. If Mrs. Ireson's collection replaces those chosen by leaden-eared psychologists with an insistence on the psychological necessity of finding just the right inane poem about Flag Day and Thanksgiving, she will have done a real service for children.

William Cole is rapidly becoming the leading anthologist of children's poetry; and his new anthology, *Poems of Magic and Spells*, one of his best, builds a strong bridge between fantasy and reality that may be crossed and recrossed. His magic universe does not exclude the modern scene, as evidenced by his including the little-known and terrifyingly beautiful poem, "The Wheelgoround" of Robert Clairmont. Nor does it omit humor. Mr. Cole does not want his readers to meditate on ghosts and graveyards without the occasional comic relief of gargoyles.

Some of the shimmer of magic is occasionally allowed to remain on tales from abroad. The current interest in Japan has filtered down to the children's market; we are offered various volumes, all the way from the art of origami to an account of the romance of Prince Akihito. *The Very Special Badgers, A Tale of Magic from Japan* by Claus Stamm, illustrated by Kazue

Mizumura, *is* special. The American child may well miss the significance that the badger has in Japan, but no matter: the mystery only adds to the charm, and the occasional awkwardness of the English wording does not detract from the story's impact. The pictures are delightful; the book is a fine one to hold and to hear. *The Blue Boat* by William Mayne, which comes to us from England, is written in the E. Nesbit tradition that gives fantastic extension to everyday happenings. It is a reminder that vitality in a children's book, as Kenneth Grahame said, is the test, and that "whatever its components, mere truth is not necessarily one of them."

[1960]

THE BOBBSEY TWINS
AT AN ORGY

R EADING IS FOR children the beginning of the world—
the world expanding in every direction, all the fact
and fantasy of life—and how disheartening it is to
see limits placed upon this world by the masses of bad books
that pour off the presses year after year. W. H. Auden speaks in
one poem of the "novels by co-eds" that "rain down on our
defenseless heads," but that downpour is nothing beside the
avalanche of dull, insipid, tastelessly illustrated, expensive children's books that sweeps down every spring and fall. These volumes are also written by co-eds as well as by fourth-rate
teachers, frustrated and fussy librarians, itchy children's book
editors, and hearty scoutmasters.

Some of the worst drivel is intended for the teen-age
market. *Donna Parker in Hollywood*, which sells in drugstores,
begins thus: " 'So this is California!' Donna thought. Pools,
studios, celebrities, blue skies! And, for a girl on her first trip
west, more excitement, more fun than seemed possible. From
the moment the handsome boy sat down beside her in the plane,

Donna knew this trip was going to be *special.*" (And, one is tempted to add, a good many years and a good many husbands later Donna woke up to realize that this special excitement was not life.) If the anguished parent thinks that by paying more he can provide his daughter with something better, he is frequently mistaken. The carriage-trade version, expensively bound and illustrated, is probably entitled *Nancy at Newport*. The imaginative fare for boys is just as bad; one book advertised this season relates the adventures of a horse that played outfield, but that one I have not examined. In the hope of finding the diet improved for younger readers, I looked at *Our New Baby's ABC* by Beman Lord (pictures by Velmy Ilsley) which is designed for children two years old and up. It tells in alphabetical form about the "new baby at our house," all the way from A for Applesauce to Z for Zwieback. The text, together with the cute illustrations executed by a former fashion illustrator, is enough to make any self-respecting baby rush to turn on *Gunsmoke*.

Television and comic books, with their gaudy monsters and their creaking but action-filled plots, are the natural outlet for the child who knows that horror and violence are very much a part of this world, and who does not find them in the fiction offered at the bookstore or library. With factual and scientific books he makes out better; most of the imagination expended in the production of children's books goes into them; they are often extremely well written and full of insight. (The books in the American Heritage series are good examples.) It is ironic, however, that in the Soviet Union, where such stress is put on science, reading begins with selections from the greatest poets, and fairy tales are revered. Most Russian beginners' books are in verse, and the modern Soviet children's poet is honored in a way quite unimaginable in this country where no literary prize for children's literature—and there have been many over the years—has, to my knowledge, ever been given for poetry.

The publication of children's books thrives on an ever-increasing array of untalented writers and illustrators. At a recent meeting of the Authors Guild, it was pointed out that sales of juvenile books have increased 225 percent in the past ten years; that the publisher of children's books has the advantage of a huge institutional market; and that he makes three-fourths of his sales from his back list. He also makes a larger profit from the money he puts into children's books for the simple reason that he pays out less in royalties to the writer of juveniles than he does to the writer of adult books. And so the level of mediocrity is successfully maintained by what amounts at times to a large supply of slave labor.

One of the chief reasons for the fact that the children's writer receives so little of the profit being made is the virtual tyranny of the illustrator. Ten years ago, with beginners' books, publishers looked for a good text and then went out and found an illustrator to do appropriate pictures for it. Today, not only do the illustrations often come first but they so overshadow the text that frequently even a good text is wholly lost. It is now standard procedure for many publishers not to accept a text until an illustrator approves of it and agrees to take it over. And take it over he usually does: the sort of collaboration that once existed between writer and illustrator is rare today, and the visual element predominates. The result is the beginner's nonbook—a package of gaudy illustrations often done by those who make their living in advertising—and every year the package becomes more expensive. Parents in the end are responsible for continuing the situation: instead of picking up a book and examining the text, they let themselves be dazzled by its façade. Anyone who has watched a small child examine the *Oxford Book of Nursery Rhymes* knows that his eye is enchanted by the simplest black-and-white woodcut when the detail is exquisitely executed.

A recent book by Maurice Sendak, *Where The Wild Things Are*, which was the winner of the 1964 Caldecott Award for the most distinguished picture book of the year, demonstrates some of the problems of illustration. Mr. Sendak is without a doubt one of the finest illustrators of children's books, but he is not a writer. The text of this volume, which the University of Chicago Graduate Library School found to have a "lovely lyric quality," is absolutely lacking in the rhythmic flow that a single page of Beatrix Potter possesses. There is simply no verbal wildness; the creatures that Mr. Sendak has so brilliantly drawn, hanging from trees in a fantastic wilderness, seem to exist in a state of suspension. Fantasy, true fantasy, demands its verbal advocates.

For all the continuing emphasis on illustration, an interesting development in children's books has taken place in recent years. A decade ago it was almost impossible to find a publisher for a collection of children's poems; while A. A. Milne's volumes continued to prosper, few publishers felt there was any market for a book by a new, native poet. That situation has changed, and poetry is now acceptable. Little of what is published and praised is in any true sense poetry, but of late publishers have attempted to enlist the support of real poets. Sometimes the results are unfortunate (not all good poets can necessarily write for children) ; frequently they have been encouraging.

Among poets who have produced work of merit are Theodore Roethke, John Ciardi, Richard Wilbur, and Randall Jarrell. Mr. Jarrell's *The Bat-Poet* (pictures by Maurice Sendak) has been hailed as a masterpiece, and if it is not quite that, it is well worth attention. *The Bat-Poet* concerns a "little light brown bat, the color of coffee with cream in it," who finds that he cannot sleep by day; he begins to discover the daylight world and the creatures who inhabit it—the squirrels and chipmunks, the cardinals, blue jays, and chickadees. As he listens to the mockingbird, he tries to make up a song, to imitate other creatures. Only the chipmunk will listen to his efforts. His fellow bats, who have deserted the porch for the barn, cannot understand his poems at all. *The Bat-Poet* is in essence about imitation—about poetry; it has some fine imaginative detail and the mood is warm and welcoming. Here is the cardinal feeding his young : "The father

129

was such a beautiful clear bright red, with his tall crest the wind rippled like fur, that it didn't seem right for him to be so harried and useful and hard-working: it was like seeing a general in a red uniform washing hundreds and hundreds of dishes." Yet for all its delicate precision, the book lacks the dramatic element that great children's books always possess. Nothing really happens in *The Bat-Poet*, and no character emerges distinctly as a character. There is nothing very batty about the bat and the style of the bat's poems has little of the airiness of a flickering, fluttering creature. Still, Mr. Jarrell's book contains a mystery and magic rarely met with today, and these qualities are also present in Maurice Sendak's carefully detailed illustrations. (Mr. Sendak is here far more lyrical—and wild—than in his own *Where The Wild Things Are*.)

Another of the best books by a poet to appear is *Loudmouse* by Richard Wilbur. The Modern Masters series, of which it was part, was under the general editorship of Louis Untermeyer, whose plan was to have writers who had not written specifically for children before compose books for beginners; Robert Graves, Shirley Jackson, William Saroyan, and others contributed. As so often happens with a project of this sort, the series was reviewed en bloc, and reviewers passed over some of the best individual titles. *The Horn Book*, whose influence with children's libraries is considerable, simply dismissed the entire thing as unworthy of attention because the text of the volumes had been based on a word list. The idea of such a list is anathema to any writer, and it is certainly the wrong approach for children who should be encouraged from the very beginning to stretch their muscles. But none of the best writers—and certainly the group is uneven—evidence a sense of constriction because of any list; writing for the young is not for serious writers an act of prostitution. A gifted and experienced poet like Richard Wilbur is capable of writing simply, without being condescending.

Edward Blishen, editor of the *Oxford Book of Poetry for Children*, has this to say in his introduction: "A poem simple in language and form can contain a difficult idea : a big poem with long words can say something quite straightforward." And the same thing applies everywhere; parents should remember this in looking for books at any age level.

A last word about the *Oxford Book*. Anthologies of poetry always receive more notice than individual volumes and it is regrettable that a collection as fine as the Oxford should contain superb poems by British poets and nothing by Americans except for "Casey Jones" and "The Purple Cow" of Gelett Burgess. (The author of the latter is given, incredibly, as "Anon.") But the illustrations are magnificent and, more important, thoroughly integrated with the text—a tribute to the fact that children still look for the words, the great words, their heritage.

[1964]

THE TRULY
HANDICAPPED

THOSE READERS who think that John Hersey is exaggerating had better look around them. Barry Rudd, the hero of *The Child Buyer*,[1] is a potential genius; but he is considered by most of his teachers a questionable and dangerous deviate from the norm. He appears on the talent chart of exceptional children put together by his school's Director of Guidance, who is working for an "in-service credit in play therapy," only because he scores poorly in "followership," which leads the director to suspect that he might be that dangerous thing, a leader.

A special feature of the December 1958 issue of the *National Educational Association Journal* was concerned with "exceptional children"—"for teachers who face the challenge of teaching exceptional children in the regular classroom." Among the pamphlets listed in this issue that may be ordered from the Council for Exceptional Children of the National Education Association are "Child Therapy," "Classroom Teachers

[1] John Hersey, *The Child Buyer* (New York: Alfred A. Knopf).

132

Can Help Maladjusted Children," "Teaching Driver Education to Mentally Retarded Adolescents," and one entitled "What Is Special About Special Education?" which consists of a "series of reprints from *Exceptional Children* on blind, mentally handicapped, deaf, hard-of-hearing, gifted, crippled, partially seeing, and speech-defective children." Thus, the gifted child in the public school is considered one of the truly handicapped, one who falls midway between the dumb and the lame. Some of the writers in this same journal are quick to add, however, that not every physically handicapped child is necessarily mentally gifted; in other words, doubly handicapped. Natural intelligence is handicap enough. And how in our schools is it to be dealt with?

The answer given in *The Child Buyer* is—as it is in our education journals—special classes, acceleration, enrichment. On the latter solution, Professor Walter R. Barbe of the University of Chattanooga deserves to be heard. Writing in *School and Society* for 10 May 1958, he says: "The fact that this term is so difficult to define and the lack of any agreement on what the term should really include explain the reason for the objection to enrichment programs. The regular classroom teacher is usually quite busy locating materials for the average child, and the question arises whether she will have time to locate material for the gifted child."

The question does indeed arise; and when it does, the answer given is that of Miss Millicent Parmlee Henley, State Supervisor for Exceptional Children, in *The Child Buyer*. You run into trouble, Miss Henley says, about "these extreme deviates at the upper end of the bell curve" by *"singling them out."* "The kind of thing Dr. Gozar has done in the lab work with this boy. I came right out and said this in my lecture. We talk about the defense of democracy—how undemocratic can you get? Why shouldn't the next child get the extra help—the slow learner? The extremely gifted child should not be removed from the common-learning situation. He's the last one who needs extra attention."

Anyone who thinks that this is not the reply given every day of the week should consult the *NEA Journal* on "homogeneous" and "heterogeneous grouping." Only recently, under pressure from the criticisms of Admiral Rickover and others, has Dr. Charles E. Bish, director of the NEA project on the Academically Talented Student, decided that "a school climate in which high achievement receives high respect strengthens individual pupil growth and promotes a higher level of aspiration, as well as better spiritual and moral values," a fairly obvious, if wretchedly worded, conclusion that it apparently took the project long months to reach.

The Child Buyer is a savage attack on modern education and on the ends that it serves, and hence ultimately on the morality of a society that either neglects education entirely or else in a crisis thinks of intelligence as a marketable commodity, to be literally bought up for industry and the industrial state to use for whatever insane purpose they may choose. In machine-made America, Mr. Hersey points out, many people seem to think that because the machine pays for education, the educated, especially the gifted who supposedly benefit most from it, must be willing to dedicate themselves to the machine, must, indeed, allow their minds to become machines. Thus the machine-mind will be able to perfect the machine so that it may in turn train more machine-minds. The justification for all this? As the Child Buyer in Mr. Hersey's novel puts it, national defense, or, under present conditions, man's "best defense" and his "greatest need" —"to leave the earth." I summarize rather badly because I think it should be clear that Mr. Hersey is attacking not only the present deplorable state of education in this country but also the major remedies that have been proposed for it, remedies that grow out of a complete misconception of the role of intelligence in a free society.

Because education in this country has tried to make itself a science, which it cannot possibly be (Mr. Hersey is wonderful in his command of the pseudo-scientific gobbledegook of the educationists), it is corrupt, and can only be corrupted further by offering up its best intelligence, which it is unable to locate or to serve in the first place, on the altar of science. No one at the end of the committee hearings in Mr. Hersey's novel remains untouched by corruption; all are willing, for one reason or another, to sell out.

Perhaps John Hersey's novel or philosophical dialogue or treatise on genius and the uses to which it is put—whatever you want to call it—is not entirely successful as a work of art. It may be impossible to satirize those who caricature themselves so readily to begin with, as most educationists do; and one thinks at once of Sybille Bedford's *The Trial of Doctor Adams* as a similar book far more skillfully constructed around a framework of fact. But all the same Mr. Hersey makes his point; and because he has been willing to meet head-on one of the most important problems of our time with such force and intelligence he deserves high praise.

[1960]

IV

A POET
LOOKS
AT POLITICS

VI

MY POETIC CAREER
IN VERMONT POLITICS

W HEN Robert Frost accepted the official designation of Poet Laureate of Vermont in 1961 at
Stowe, he recited a quatrain written especially
for the occasion:

ON BEING CHOSEN POET OF VERMONT

Breathes there a bard who isn't moved
When he finds his verse is understood
And not entirely disapproved
By his country and his neighborhood?

Vermont is also my neighborhood although I have lived there
only fifteen years to Mr. Frost's fifty. A joint resolution of the
Vermont General Assembly early in 1961 stated that whereas
Mr. Frost was well-known as a poet and whereas he had made his
home in Vermont for many years, he should be declared its official Poet Laureate. What the resolution did not say was that
whereas he had received almost every literary award that a poet

139

can receive in the world, just *barely* enough time had gone by for him to be duly recognized by Vermont. I personally have not been chosen Poet Laureate, but I was chosen as Representative from the town of Pownal to the Vermont House of Representatives. I am one of 46 Democratic members of that body out of a total of 246. In the election of final officers of the 1961 session, I was elected Official Poet (there was no residence requirement, no opposition, and, I might add, no honorarium).

You may ask what a poet is doing in politics, and I must say that I sometimes wonder myself.[1] Shortly after the election when I was in Seattle on a lecture tour, I was introduced at the University of Washington by my friend, the poet Léonie Adams. She said in her introduction that we have had poets in this country who have done a variety of other things besides write poetry. We have had a successful businessman, Wallace Stevens; we have had another, Dr. William Carlos Williams, a prominent physician; and now we have—and she paused—a poet who is also a politician. It sounded as if what she meant was : "Now at last we have a real *crook*." I took her to task afterwards about this, saying that there had been many poets involved in one way or another in politics. William Butler Yeats, was, after all, a member of the Irish Senate. "Yes," she said, "but that was in Ireland and that's different." And I said, "But this is in Vermont, and what makes you think that's not different, too?"

How different it is I was soon to learn. I have no personal knowledge of other state legislatures. My observations are based solely on my experience in the Vermont General Assembly, but since I participated in the longest session—seven months—in the history of the state, I had ample time to observe what was

---

[1] I no longer do, since I have now withdrawn. This report on the Vermont legislature was written before the election last fall of Philip H. Hoff, my former seatmate in the house, as the first Democratic governor in 109 years. Although I worked hard campaigning for the governor, I did not run again myself. Even with this revolutionary change in the front office, the legislature has changed but little, and what I have to say of it here is just as true today. (And perhaps still true now, eight years later, after the U.S. Supreme Court's decision on reapportionment and after Governor Hoff's three terms and subsequent defeat for the U.S. Senate.)

going on, as well as what was not going on, and time to verify my conclusions. Legislatures, by their very nature, have a way of copying one another. Since Vermont has one of the largest legislatures anywhere in existence and since it has changed imperceptibly since the eighteenth century, a close look at it may throw some light on the legislative process in general, leading us on the one hand to marvel at the nature of democracy and on the other creating in us some serious concern about how we manage to govern ourselves at all.

A word about the make-up of the Vermont House of Representatives. According to the constitution, every town in the state has a representative; there are 246 towns and 246 representatives. To understand exactly what this means, one must realize that the total population of the state is 390,000, somewhat less than that of the city of Rochester, New York. When I went to Montpelier, I thought that coming from a town of some 1,500 people I would naturally be representing a small community. When I discovered that 60 percent of the towns represented have populations of less than a thousand, I was aware that my constituency was not as meager as I thought. Next to me in the House sat Mr. Hoff, representing Burlington, Vermont's only real city, with a population of 35,000. Behind us, and slightly to the right, sat Miss Eddy of Stratton, representing twenty-four people. Each of us, of course, had but one vote.

The League of Women Voters had recently conducted a statewide campaign to try to have legislation introduced to define what constitutes a town. The reaction to this campaign, which seemed to me in every way sensible, was on the part of the legislators one of supreme indifference; they could naturally not be interested in voting themselves out of office. This reaction was best summed up by the President Pro Tem of the Senate, Asa Bloomer of Rutland, who remarked that the ladies of the league, rather than interest themselves in the complications of legislation, would do better to stay at home, look after their children, and protect them from the onslaught of pornographic literature.

The 1961 session was remarkable in many ways: it was the longest, but also the youngest, in history. The average age of the members of the House was fifty-nine. Of 246 members over half, 132, were over sixty; 65 were between the ages of fifty and sixty; 32 between the ages of forty and fifty; 15 between the ages of thirty and forty; 2 under the age of thirty. The youngest member was the member from Shaftsbury, who was twenty-four, affectionately known to many of his colleagues as Cornwallis because of the fact that he frequently appeared on the floor wearing a defiant red blazer. Since Vermont has a greater percentage of elderly people than almost any other state in the union, it is natural that the age of its legislators should be high. I do not wish in any way to attack the elderly: many of the young fogies, of which Cornwallis did not happen to be one, did more to prevent the enactment of sensible legislation than some of their older colleagues.

The constitution gives no age requirement for representatives; it says only that they shall be the persons in each town "most noted for wisdom and virtue." (No such requirement exists for the Senate; apparently you can be a renegade and be elected Senator as long as you are over thirty.) Since Vermont towns have always given the widest interpretation to the term "town" it is only natural perhaps that they should give an equally wide interpretation to the term "wisdom." If we are to believe the testimony of some legislators both past and present, wisdom has not always necessarily meant literacy. It has been said that in many of the small towns, the standard procedure over the years has been to take one of its older citizens who had been on town relief, buy him a suit of clothes, and send him up to Montpelier, where the state could look after him and keep him warm. Some of my fellow legislators swear that in the 1959 session there was one elderly gentleman who appeared daily wearing an antiquated sailor outfit until several members of the house decided that the dignity of the chamber required them to chip in and buy him a proper suit. The members of the 1961 session appeared on the whole particularly well groomed; and the added number of women legislators, more than there had ever been, may have had something to do with the fastidiousness of the male attire. I noted only one point of sartorial interest: some of the gentlemen had a predilection for extremely broad and bright neckties that sometimes flashed across the room during debate with the full effulgence of diplomatic sashes.

I look up to my elders; and I found it often restful and reassuring to gaze out on the white and nodding heads that gave the chamber an appearance not unlike that of a wintry Vermont slope. There was only one moment when age impressed itself on me in a sudden and somewhat terrifying manner. One afternoon in the committee room upstairs in the State House, the education committee on which I served was meeting as it usually did from one until five o'clock. In the middle of the afternoon, the door was suddenly flung open and in stepped a man of great age; he had white hair that fell down to his shoulders, a wild and rolling eye; and he wore several layers of clothing of indeterminate age and dimension. He moved forward slowly into the room, leaning on a long and heavy wooden staff that reached above his head. Our chairman shouted at him and asked him to identify himself. He said only that he came from Ryegate. The chairman said that we would not be getting to the problem of Ryegate that afternoon; would he care to return? He apparently heard nothing that was said, but sat down unconvinced, and waited. After ten minutes, he again rose, leaned on his staff, and he and the chairman went through the same exchange. This time he decided that he had had enough; he strode slowly back to the door, rested on his staff, and eyeing us wildly, lectured us for the next fifteen minutes on the causes of the Korean conflict. After his departure, we discovered that he had been for many years the member from the town of Ryegate, and that he had come over to Montpelier to be sure that there would be none of this newfangled nonsense about a union or regional school in his bailiwick.

Early in the session I was impressed by the fact that not all the legislators present were aware of what was going on. At the opening of the session the newly elected speaker allows those members who have been reelected to take their same seats. Then he asks that the infirm, the lame, those who have difficulty with hearing and sight come into the chamber and occupy whichever seats they wish down in the well of the House. Those who are left remain outside until their names are picked from a hat. I had met and chatted with one of the members from the southern part of the state (which I soon discovered was always referred to in Montpelier as "The Banana Belt"). He and I had chosen two seats that we thought were reasonably accessible, and we planned to take them if they remained. We had both read that morning in the Burlington *Free Press* of a section of the chamber that is known as "Sleepy Hollow." Here some of the older members are supposed to have slept undisturbed for years. The *Free Press*, however, did not give the location or the composition of Sleepy Hollow; and naturally we were curious.

Our names were drawn for seats, and mine came up before that of my friend. When I went in, I was fortunate in being spotted by some of my Democratic colleagues, and hustled into the one remaining seat in a section to the right of the speaker that turned out to be the main Democratic pew. My friend was less successful; he took a seat up in the back in the central section of the House between two elderly members. He turned to one and then the other immediately and put the question that was on our minds: "Where is Sleepy Hollow?" Both of his seatmates answered: "Ain't never heard of it." When the seats had all been assigned and the governor came in to make his inaugural address, my friend looked to the right and to the left and saw his companions snoring peacefully away, as they continued to do

144

for the next seven months. He had settled down in the middle of Sleepy Hollow.

Like many another novice in politics, I soon discovered that it is extremely important to know how to begin a speech. Conclusions are not so important because, if people know you at all, they probably know what you are going to say anyway; but it is important to startle them into attention. Certain openings have the approval of seasoned politicians. One is simply: "I *will* say this," followed by a long pause. If you open in this manner, you can go on to say absolutely anything because you have made it clear that you are a person of great importance and that you have something of great importance to say. You yourself may not be at all sure what is coming next, and in your heart of hearts you may be willing to admit that it is not very much; but in any case you have prepared your listener: "I *will* say this."

Another opening is the self-abnegating one that, if properly used, can be completely disarming. In the Vermont house we often heard the classical beginning: "I haven't very much to say, but . . ." One of the prominent women members, a robust sandy-haired young lady, who was introduced to us early in the session by the chairman of the Ways and Means Committee as unaccountably the "raven-haired beauty of Waitsfield," has a political philosophy somewhat to the right of that of Mr. Welch of the John Birch Society. The member from Waitsfield—and, according to the rules, we refer to every member in this fashion, and never by his or her name—began a number of her speeches by saying: "I don't want to be a stinker, but . . ."

Another effective way of getting a point across is by saying two different things at once and saying them emphatically. One legislator, for example, frequently answered interrogation by: "Actually it is, and actually it isn't . . ." This tends to trap your hearer into a mood of total acquiescence and then you can get away with murder.

You can also make your point by not saying anything at

all, giving the impression that you know better than to open your mouth, or, if you do, that you are your own best listener. One day on the floor one member was interrogating another. A third member rose to request that the member answering the interrogation speak a little louder because he wasn't being heard. The speaker pointed out that the member could not possibly speak any louder because he wasn't speaking at all. He was maintaining a respectful and awe-inspiring silence that suggested that he knew better than to be trapped into any answer. This reticence is in the tradition of Calvin Coolidge, who never used one word if he could convey his meaning with fewer; and there are many young Cal Coolidges—or "callow Coolidges," as one Montpelier reporter termed them—intent on perpetuating this tradition.

Mumbling, which is a middle ground, can also be effective. In this case, in reporting a bill you do not allow any words other than an occasional preposition to be heard, and this only to remind your listeners you are still talking. Occasionally some member will in exasperation, or just because he is tired of sitting, get up and request that you use the microphone. But the important thing to remember when you come down into the well of the House to use the mike is that you continue to mumble into it. The House will then take to private conversation, correspondence, reading of newspapers, exchange of racing tips; and an hour later when the speaker puts the question to a vote, the members under the impression that they are voting for adjournment will all shout a resounding "Aye!"

Anyone who believes the myth that Vermonters are tight-lipped by nature would do well to attend a session of our General Assembly. The oratory is constant; it flows, to use a phrase of Cyril Connolly's, like a "steady stream of brackish water"; it even branches at times into clear and lucid pools. I myself have been eloquent on a number of occasions. I spoke with great fervor, for example, against the weakening of the union school law, against the publication of the names of people on relief rolls in towns, against the retention of the death penalty; I spoke equally

146

fervently *for* reapportionment as voted by the Senate, for the abolition of the poll tax as a voting requirement, for the enactment of fair-employment-practices legislation. Something of the measure of my effectiveness as an orator is indicated by the fact that all the bills I spoke for were defeated and all those I opposed were passed. My only consolation lies in the fact that some of those I opposed, while passed in the House, were overwhelmingly defeated in the Senate.

For example, I was one of twenty-nine members who stood to oppose placing a bounty on coyotes. (The introducer of the bill confused everybody at first because he pronounced the name of the animal as *Kye-at*, leading some of us to suppose that he was referring to some kind of Alaskan boat.) My reasons for opposing the bill were simple: I could not see that we had much evidence that there are any coyotes in Vermont; and even if there are, there was no need to place a bounty on them since they would be shot anyway; and one could foresee the possibility of coyote ears being smuggled over the border from New York State; and the likelihood of the elimination of a good many dogs. When the twenty-nine of us stood up to oppose the bill, the rest of the House howled like coyotes; but in this instance we had the last howl when the bill went down to defeat in the Senate. The press on this particular occasion stated that Mr. Smith of Pownal had risen to speak in favor of the bill because he felt that the wolves in Vermont should be kept from our doors. What I had said was that I thought that Vermont—and it is rare indeed for anyone to refer simply to *Vermont;* it is always *the State of Vermont*—should concentrate on keeping the wolf from the door rather than chasing nonexistent wolves in our woods. (One of the interesting aspects of political life for the writer is to see how his words and actions can be transformed by the press into pure fiction.)

My ability as an orator was such that frequently my friends, if they had a bill they especially wanted to get through, would come to me beforehand and plead with me *not* to speak in favor of it. I had been speaking so often that my Democratic seatmates threatened to hold me down by brute force. I agreed that I had perhaps been overdoing things. The next morning when we arrived in our seats there was spread out before us a detailed road map of the state. The reporter of the bill, which had to do with the construction of a section of highway, was an opponent of mine. He spoke for about half an hour explaining the measure in detail. At the conclusion of his speech, before my seatmates could grab me, I leaped to my feet. I could not resist pointing out that the number of the highway on the bill did not exist on the map. My remark brought a complete halt to the proceedings. The Speaker called the reporter to the rostrum, and after a lengthy conference, it was discovered that the bill, which had been studied in committee for well over a month and reported twice on the floor, was incorrectly worded; if we had passed it, we would have been voting money to improve a nonexistent highway. My seatmates decided after this that I did serve at least as a kind of corrective.

My oratorical ineffectiveness may be explained by the fact that I have not really mastered the political metaphor. I have been hampered, I find, by my feeling for poetic metaphor, which is an entirely different thing. An example of the type of political metaphor I have in mind I take from one of our governor's addresses. "We must," he said, "either hang in suspension or move ahead." That seemed to me a very difficult and tenuous choice.

The following passage is taken from a few speeches delivered in the course of an hour. I have not dressed it up; it is verbatim. Most of it was spoken by a member known by the name given him by the President Pro Tem of the Senate—Diogenes. Diogenes was a tall imposing figure, a basso profundo, and when he spoke, the chamber shook to the deep rumble of his inanities. Diogenes though had courage, and he sometimes came out with things that a man of less imagination would have shied away from. He once even dared use the word "socialism" without its attendant epithet of "creeping." Here is the passage from the debate; remember that it must be read with the proper bass and inflection: "Vermont farmers, let us not bury our head in the sand, and cut our throat. . . . This bill is a punch in the nose to every business on the Connecticut River. . . . We must stand on our own feet and paddle our own canoe. . . . The member from Glover has spoken the correct truth." The correct truth as opposed, of course, to the incorrect one. To appreciate the atmosphere that engenders such political metaphors, one must remember that the temperature of the Vermont House ranges in the winter months between eighty-five and one hundred degrees; there is never a shortage of hot air.

Plagued by all this prose over a seven-month period, I found it at times necessary and helpful to break into therapeutic verse. The first occasion arose when a bill had been introduced to make the Morgan horse the official state animal. This was a nonpartisan measure; members of both parties rushed to sign it and identify themselves to the folks back home as friends of the Morgan. When the bill was in the General Committee, various other animals were proposed—the porcupine, the goat, the catamount, the cow. But it was decided in the end that the Morgan horse was the most acceptable.

The cow has always been prominent in Vermont. There have always been more cows than people; and most of them vote, since our representation is, in effect, based on acreage. The towns were all laid out in neat geometrical six-square-mile areas; and as with old farms, the stone walls surrounding have remained, even though the population may have shifted. (The State Department of Agriculture has recently declared that there are now slightly more people than cows, but this unprecedented change may be due merely to the notorious discrepancies in the reports of the town listers.) The cow, in any event, was *out* for a number of reasons. For one thing, it already appears on the state seal, on which it is depicted in a field with a pine tree and mountains in the background. There has been a dispute for over a century as to which way the cow should face. It is usually shown moving toward some sheaves of grain. It was pointed out that it would be a moronic farmer who would put his cow out when harvesting his grain. This problem was solved for a while by having the cow move in the opposite direction, away from the grain. But then that really did not seem satisfactory. So one artist put a river between the cow and the grain. Anyway, the cow was out, although when the House passed the bill and it went to the Senate, one Senator tried eloquently but unsuccessfully to promote the cow again.

It was reported on the floor that it was important for Vermont to claim the Morgan horse as its state animal immediately, because Massachusetts wanted it for its own. Mr. Morgan was from Springfield, Massachusetts, but he had bred the Morgan in Vermont. Not mentioned was the fact that the University of Vermont owns a Morgan Horse Farm, which has been losing money and that the designation of the animal was essential to the farm's survival. The reporter of the bill, the youngest member of the House, the twenty-four-year-old redcoat Cornwallis, suggested that I might comment on it before third reading. Vermont in 1960 voted by referendum to allow pari-mutuel betting in the state. (Previously it had been a little green island surrounded by racetracks, but the attraction of green folding money proved too much even for Vermont integrity.) Cornwallis thought that since I came from a town that might have the first track in the state (as indeed it now has), I should speak on the subject of the Morgan horse—the little horse that Robert Frost has made famous in poetry—even though I personally had opposed pari-mutuel betting.

I agreed to speak, and on the third reading of the bill read:

A MINOR ODE TO THE MORGAN HORSE

I may not incline
To the porcupine,

And I may be averse
To what is much worse:
The bear
That is rare,
The goat
That's remote,
The sheep, from which year after year
   you must remove the coat,
The catamount
That does not amount to that amount,
The cow
That somehow
We, as a human minority, cannot allow;
And although, as one of the Democratic minority,
   I should, alas,
Far prefer the jackass,
I must—until a state animal can choose
   its own state—
Not hesitate
To vote, of course,
For the Morgan horse.

My ode was taken up by the Associated Press, and appeared in newspapers in various parts of the country; but unfortunately the teletype operator who transmitted it must have thought that every poem must end at the bottom of a page. In any case, when he came to the bottom of the page, he stopped—which meant stopping with the word "hesitate" and omitting the final lines, "To vote, of course/For the Morgan horse." The result was that friends of mine in Colorado wrote to inquire anxiously if Vermont reticence had begun to affect me mentally, since it did seem strange that I should compose an ode to a horse without even an indirect reference to that animal.

I wrote poems on other occasions as well: On St. Patrick's Day I answered in skeltonics a challenge from the Irish of the

Senate, composed by Senator Lefevre and addressed to the Irish in the House. Not all my pieces were read on the floor; some during the long debates made the rounds of the Chamber in the hands of the nine- and ten-year-old page boys, whose lightning efficiency made it possible to carry on conversations and to coordinate the threads of debate in a way that no telephone operators could possibly have facilitated. The page boys are remarkably alert and quick; some of them slow down later, however, when they grow up and become governors and legislators.

There was no end of doggerel—odes, lyrics, limericks— that got written by many hands during the session and recited in the corridors of the statehouse or in the private sanctuaries of smoke-filled hotel rooms. But none of Montpelier's versifiers ever equaled the Governor (F. Ray Keyser, Jr.) when, at the New England Music Festival at Rutland, he recited a short poem of his own devising. The Rutland *Herald* at the time commented: "Opinion in Rutland was that it is Calliope (the muse of epic poetry and eloquence) with whom Governor Keyser consulted. His poem bore no title, although members of the audience had several private suggestions, ranging from 'Textile Tango' to 'Ode for Insomnia.' " The poem went:

> These two clean sheets
> Between I lie
> Have come from unknown lands
> From unknown hands.
> And somewhere they were spun
> By the engine's silent hum.
> It feels so good to sleep—
> Thanks for a world, and two clean sheets.

Such a clear and clean example of poetic abandon, if not poetic license, could not go unanswered by His Excellency's loyal opposition. I composed a shorter version of "Textile Tango" with the subtitle "On Being Chosen":

These two clean sheets
Between I lie;
They elected me their Governor—Why?
They elected me their Governor—Why?

Vermont suffers from what I would call "Big House psychology." This is something familiar in the South. Many Southerners grow up thinking that there is a big house somewhere in the family, to which they can later return; people will be there to look after them; they will be taken care of. As the years go by, however, and they grow more mature, they realize that if any such house existed it has diminished in size. They may even be willing to admit that it never really existed at all.

Some such thinking surely characterizes Vermont, for it is living up to an image of itself that is largely false. Vermont is a small, poor state (*Business Week* reported recently that it has the second-lowest personal income rate in the country; only Alaska's is lower. It should be remembered also that Vermont has the third-highest tax rate per capita of any state.) It is poor, but it has illusions of grandeur. How else explain how we can afford, how we can tolerate, some of the things we do? How else explain our House of Representatives except by "Big House psychology"? Larger and richer states have long ago made some attempt to reapportion their houses; but still we allow the state to be run by our small towns. What we have in Vermont is not just the struggle between rural and urban populations. What we have is not a rural dictatorship but a rural aristocracy. Being in the Vermont House was for me like a journey back into the eighteenth century, when one had to own land to vote. Our representation is, in essence, based not on population but on acreage. The Vermont House is our House of Lords. Ours is a benevolent aristocracy; our small towns tell us they will be perfectly happy as long as their way is paid. They dislike any state control, but as long as they control the state and the state pays most of the bills (and those bills are, of course, paid by those other acres on which there are at least as many people as cows), they will be happy; that is, as long as they are taken care of and do not have to face reality.

A Vermont legislator is paid during the session seventy dollars a week; in addition, he is reimbursed for one round trip to Montpelier, and for another round trip home for Town Meeting in March. For anyone who had to go 135 miles up and back every week—and there were a number of us who did—this was not enough even to cover our basic expenses. The 1961 session voted not to raise its own pay (that would look bad to the folks back home), but it also voted not to raise the pay of the next session. What is feared naturally is that if the pay is raised even slightly, legislators might be attracted to the office who could not afford this leisurely pace; and the Big House might have to go. What is feared also, on the other hand, is that if any real effort is made to decrease the length of the session, the same type of legislator might be voted in and he would immediately raise his pay, thereby becoming a professional and thus endangering the cherished amateur standing of the rural aristocrat.

Everything in Vermont government is the reverse of what one would normally expect: our Senate is our representational body—our House of Commons; it was added in 1836 for the purpose of eliminating the inequities already present in the lower chamber. The Senate consists of thirty members elected from the counties according to population, and the constitution guarantees each county at least one; it is to be reapportioned every ten years on the basis of each new census. It was not, however, reapportioned ten years ago and it was not reapportioned this time. The Senate did vote to reapportion itself, but the House refused to concur. The basic reason for this was that it would have added two senators to Chittenden County, which includes the city of Burlington and is strongly Democratic.

The Senate is our liberal body, and it is amazing how much sensible legislation it has been able to get through over the years;

154

but I could give examples of a few zany items that it tried to pass this time. The Senate functions in accordance with the principles of democracy; the people elect the Senators and they get the kind of legislation they ask for. I think of the Vermont General Assembly as an iceberg with the one-eighth representational part, the Senate, represented in full view; the seven-eighths, the non-representational House, hidden lethally below the surface. Or I think of it as resembling, to use a lighter image, one of those Happy Hooligan dolls that we used to have as children, with a weighted base so that the body when you touched it would fall away and then spring back into position, always giving the sense of getting nowhere fast.

I have given some examples of the Happy Hooligan type of legislation that kept us so long in session. Of deer-damage bills there seemed to be no end. On the question of whether or not to allow fishing by single line through the ice at Dog Pond I had no opinion, nor on the regulation of muskrat in Addison County. Fortunately I didn't have to in the end because, to its great credit, the 1961 session decided finally to turn over these questions to the Fish and Game Commission with the passage of the Omnibus Fish and Game Bill, a measure that had first been introduced over a decade ago.

We did, however, have the problem of the gores; specifically, Avery's Gore and Buel's Gore. When Vermont towns were surveyed and laid out in their six-square-mile segments, naturally because of the curvature of the earth sometimes little left-over parcels of land remained where the rectangles met. This is just as in dressmaking when a little triangular piece of cloth, a gore, is left in cutting. Vermont has a number of gores, and nobody has been able to decide what to do about them. Almost nobody lives in them, they're not worth anything, but they're there, and you don't want to upset what's there. One woman legislator pointed out that her county had a great many gores, and she felt that they were a wonderful tourist attraction, simply because they didn't exist anywhere else. Gores, in any case, are certainly bores. We had Avery's Gore. The problem there was whether Avery's Gore should be annexed to the town of Montgomery or to the town of Bakersfield. The debate was unending. At one point, one of my fellow legislators was tempted to rise and move that the towns of Montgomery, Bakersfield, Enosburg, and Belvidere, all contiguous to the gore, be annexed to Avery's Gore. But he knew better than to attempt such consolidation.

We also had, as many sessions before us have had, the ban on the nonreturnable beer bottle. I thought that I was equipped to understand English, but during the debate on this question—and it was the longest of the seven-month period—I was not always sure. The nonreturnable beer bottle is a beer bottle that you cannot return; so what do you do with it? You throw it away. And where do you throw it? You throw it on a Vermont hillside; and what happens to it then? It is eaten by a cow. We were treated in public hearings to endless photographs of cow's intestines, showing how the creatures did not particularly relish this diet of brown beer glass. We were also given interminable statistics on the number of tractor tires slashed by this lethal sweep of glass over the green hills. The effect of listening to all this is that one trembles even to contemplate holding a glass in one's hand, much less pouring anything into it. And this is just the effect desired by the sponsors of the bill, which always passes the House and then is defeated by the Senate. This is a measure directed against the makers and sellers of beer, a Prohibitionist bill backed by the Farm Bureau. We have few outside lobbies in Montpelier; they're all built right into the legislature.

One final example of Happy Hooliganism, House Bill 388, provided that no motor vehicle registered in Vermont, manufactured or assembled after 1 January 1962, could operate on the highways unless equipped with these safety devices:

(1) A convex front bumper extending six inches beyond the most forward part of the body mounted with a

156

spring recoil mechanism on two parallel four-inch tubular steel frames, all capable of withstanding a fifteen-ton impact.

(2) A concave rear bumper extending six inches beyond the rearmost part of the body mounted with a spring recoil mechanism on two parallel four-inch tubular steel frames, all capable of withstanding a fifteen-ton impact.

(3) A three-inch tubular steel side bumper mounted in the area of the rocker panel on each side of the vehicle running the full length of the rocker panel and to within ten inches of the first rear wheels on any truck. Such bumper to be mounted in a manner so as to be capable of withstanding a fifteen-ton impact.

(4) The bumpers provided for in subdivision (1), (2), and (3) shall be mounted seventeen inches from center of bumper to road surface under normal operating load conditions.

(5) The front and rear bumpers shall have eight-inch-wide convex and concave surfaces.

(6) Hinged front seat backs triggered for quick foot release enabling safer impact against other vehicles, trees, utility poles, rocks, abutments, etc.

(7) All such equipment to be subject to the approval of the commissioner of motor vehicles.

The bill further provided that railroad locomotives could not operate in this state after 1 January 1962, unless the lead locomotive "is equipped with a car pickup wedge of such design as may be required by the commissioner of public service," and that the commissioner "shall take into consideration the design of side bumpers as required by Section 1 of this title, the size and design of motor vehicles most apt to come in contact with the wedge, and the impact forces most likely resulting from contact."

It is not difficult to understand why this was known as the

Rubber Baby Buggy Bumper Bill, and why the Irish poet Padraic Colum, to whom I showed it, said he thought it a document that would have delighted his friend James Joyce. Nor is it difficult to understand furthermore why the bill was killed in committee (the Governor was, after all, trying to attract industry to the state, and this was clearly not the way to do it), and finally why we felt that we could, in the end, dispense with the mock session, which had always been the customary terminal frivolity.

A poet must always begin with the particular, and I have tried to give the look and feel of what it is like to be on the inside, in even a small way, of the Vermont lawmaking process. Katherine Anne Porter remarked some years ago that she had no doubt whatever that man would get to the moon, and that he probably would get there before he devised an adequate garbage-disposal system for the city of New York. Colonel Glenn and his associates may well be looking down on us before Vermont has amended its governmental ways. And yet since most of what I have described took place, reapportionment has in part occurred (thanks to the State Supreme Court, which now has before it a suit questioning the reapportionment of the House as well as the Senate), and there are signs of hope. Avery's Gore and the non-returnable beer bottle may yet return, but perhaps a few more years of debate will uncover a solution.

[1964]

A MARCH
THAT WENT SOMEWHERE

W HATEVER ELSE it meant or may come to mean,
the March on Washington was a lesson in courage and dignity for the entire world. "We are
here to demand what we should not have to demand," the
marchers said again and again; and the shame that every American must have felt in the fact of their having to ask for what
was rightfully theirs was balanced by the pride he could feel in
their doing so with such eloquence and dignity. Here before the
world was the American dream in action.

For all its superficial resemblance to a huge Sunday School
picnic, there was indeed something dreamlike about the whole
affair. The occasion, with the background of all the planning
that had gone into it, was itself a dream come true. This was
the note sounded early in the program by Josephine Baker, who
had flown in from Paris. No one had asked her to come, she said
in a voice that seemed, like that of so many speakers that afternoon, on the verge of breaking into song; but she knew that she
had to come. In her blue Free French uniform, wearing her

French decorations, she looked out on the huge throng ("all salt and pepper mixed in together, just as you should be"), and said that this was the greatest day in her long life: "You are on the eve of complete victory." And then, at the end of the afternoon, Dr. Martin Luther King spoke for all the marchers when he outlined the great triumph of liberty that he envisaged. "I have a dream," he said, and the long catalogue of what he saw in his dream went right to the hearts of his hearers. "This is the faith that I go back to the South with," he concluded, "with this faith we shall be able to hew out of the mountain of despair a stone of hope." This was what the marchers had come to have expressed for them publicly before the Lincoln Memorial, before the Houses of Congress, the country and the world.

All those who had worked so hard and long, who had hoped and prayed for the success of this event, were rewarded in every way—by the massive turnout, by the weather, by the impact of the speeches. For in the back of everyone's mind had been the fear that this dream might easily end up a nightmare. We arrived at Silver Spring, Maryland, the evening before the march, and my wife and I left our Vermont bus to take a taxi into Washington to spend the night. The friends with whom we stayed told us of some of the rumors that had been making the rounds of Washington: Arsenals had been broken into, it was said, and arms secretly distributed. This story had been circulated by a Negro woman working with them in one of the government offices. There was, they were certain, absolutely no truth to it; it was simply an expression of her fear, which had become virtually psychopathic.

I thought of James Baldwin's observation (I had been reading his essays on the way down in the bus) that the mere fact of being a Negro in this country had led thousands of his people to the edge of paranoia. (We got back to our bus to find that the only violence of the previous night had come from white teenagers, whom we had seen earlier in the parking lot; they had ripped off the March on Washington signs.) This same fear, which was in the back of all our minds, had been brought home to us when we stopped for lunch in a restaurant on the New York Thruway. A woman, discovering the significance of the buttons we were wearing, asked with a puzzled and terrified look on her face, "But aren't you afraid?" Would something somehow go wrong?

Nothing did; and it was clear from the beginning that nothing would. Coming into Washington surely at no time in history has been quite like what it was on the morning of the March. We left Silver Spring after 8 A.M. and moved along streets that seemed completely deserted—like the streets in a De Sica film—everything waiting, everyone in the shadows. Before long we came quietly and easily in behind other buses; and a white-helmeted cop motioned us over to the curb. Then we saw the beginning of the formation. Here were other buses— tens of them lined up; and in minutes when others had arrived, we pulled in behind the police escort and were on our way.

This was the first period of waiting of the whole day, and waiting was all part of the schedule; but then we thought of how little we had had to wait—in comparison with those in the bus in front of us from Dayton, Ohio, or those others we were to see later who had come from across the country. Moving into the city in the early morning was an eerie feeling—Washington in the cool clear air had the appearance of a stage set awaiting its actors.

The driver switched on the radio; and we listened to the concerned and apprehensive voices of the announcers as they moved from the railroad station to the Monument and back. The tone of their voices, as they tried to summon up excitement, made one all the more apprehensive. They were pointing out that since several trains had apparently been canceled and since none of the trains had had as many people as scheduled, there would be far fewer people than the hundred thousand estimated, and therefore the March would not only be nonviolent, it would be almost nonexistent.

It took us little time to see that what was going out over the airways had little to do with the reality of the situation. Our bus moved into its assigned place in front of the Pan-American Union, and as it did we could see bus after bus moving in, and in a matter of minutes, the buses one could count in tens one could count only in hundreds. The vacuum of the city was being filled quickly, quietly, all according to schedule. Groups were descending from their buses and assembling on the grass; there was no sense of rush but one of readiness, no sense of anxiety but one of quiet anticipation.

And so when we did move off with the other groups, we found the area beneath the Washington Monument already packed with people; the singers were singing on the platform, and we went to the corner under the Headquarters sign and picked up our instructions, our programs; and then we realized that we were on our own. (It was at this point that we ran into another Vermont group—we had spotted the Barre, Vermont, placards—it was like greeting our oldest friends.) And as soon as we merged with the crowd, we were sure that everything was all right—we had lost our identity, but to something much larger than any of us. This was a mingling of all groups from all parts of the country, of all colors and all creeds; it *was* exciting to look out at the banners from Kansas City, from Detroit, from Danville, from Birmingham—and a huge oilcloth one from Clarksdale, Mississippi. And when we were a part of it, we realized at once that this was no mob, no Times Square stampede.

It may have seemed at first like a picnic or a Sunday School outing or a holiday rally; but what was absent was what made all the difference. This is the only time in my life that I have ever been part of a rally of any kind where one did not feel the presence of Madison Avenue. Nobody was selling anything with the exception of the official programs or flags for the parade—no dolls, no toys, no gimmicks. It was a simple matter; nobody had

162

to be sold anything; everybody was here because he wanted to be here, and because he wanted this to be what it was—a massive display of purpose and rectitude. Even the Hollywood and TV personalities, who are certainly the last ones to speak of anything but themselves, rose to the occasion with singular modesty. (Ledger Smith *had* roller-skated all the way from Chicago; and he was greeted on the platform, as well he should have been. He was advertising himself certainly, but he was not introduced as representing any special brand of roller skates; he was there because he *chose* to be.)

As we stood, sat, walked, and waited there by the Washington Monument, it became clearer every minute as more and more groups poured into the area, that these marchers had a deep intensity. This seemed reflected even in the clothes they had chosen to wear. Everyone was dressed quietly and tastefully. Since this was a march for jobs as well as freedom, it was part of the intention of the organizers to have included as many unemployed as possible. And they were there; but no one was badly or embarrassingly dressed or overdressed. No one was drawing undue attention to himself because each felt that the whole thing was so much bigger than himself. All was polite, subdued, understated. "I have never been so proud of my people," an elderly Negro woman was heard to remark. And perhaps, in a sense, this was the greatest outpouring of pride that this country has ever witnessed. And the pride was reflected on the faces that one saw on all sides, faces shaped by suffering, molded by character, faces that needed no Madison Avenue masks to hide or distort them.

We moved off down Constitution Avenue toward the Lincoln Memorial shortly after eleven, a little before schedule (this was the only slight show of impatience that I noticed during the entire day—it all happened so quickly that the leaders of the March had to rush to get themselves in front of the marchers). It was at this point that we realized what this was all about: Here state lines, town lines, lost all significance. This was what we had been waiting to do; but there were no bands, no fanfare.

163

Suddenly all the rivers were pouring into the sea, and the sea was moving, marching, or rather shuffling, since the March went so slowly, down toward the Lincoln Memorial. By the time we got there, we could see that the entire area in front of the Memorial all the way down to the reflecting pool was filled with people, and groups of weary marchers sat dangling their feet in the pool.

The program—as is inevitable on any such occasion—was too long; but people listened all the same; and even those out of range of the loudspeakers seemed not to want to keep the others from hearing. The two words that predominated throughout the afternoon were "freedom" and "now." There was a feeling of urgency certainly, but one of triumph as well; for time after time, the speakers said that this was only the beginning. And what a beginning! Walter Reuther spoke for all the white members of the audience—and a third of us were white—when he said that he was there because not just Negro Americans but all Americans were involved.

As the program unfolded—a massive display of talent and intelligence, giving new meaning to old words—there was not absent, for all the reverence of the crowd, a quiet undercurrent of humor. It was not the rowdy humor of the ball park or the carnival; but it was there all the same—one of America's truly enduring characteristics. As I wandered back in the crowd toward the end of the afternoon, there in the middle of the walk on folding chairs sat two middle-aged and middle-class Negro gentlemen. One of them held in his lap the back of a sign on which he appeared to be writing; the other was addressing the throng that fanned out quietly around them. "Give this man your name," he said, "if you are from Pennsylvania, and tomorrow morning you will wake up rich and free."

Everyone knew that a good many mornings would pass before he would wake up, in Pennsylvania or Mississippi, either one or the other; but still in the back of his mind were the words of Martin Luther King, "I have a dream . . ." and of the song, "Deep in my heart I do believe."

"We shall overcome," we sang throughout that day; and in the face of such spirit that can rise above injustice, intolerance, and even murder, who is to say that they—that we—shall not?

[1963]

V

THE PITTSBURGH POETS:

The *Spectra* Hoax

ONE

I N AUTUMN of the year 1916, magazine editors and
reviewers of poetry found on their desks a new and
quite unobtrusive-looking volume of verse of some
sixty-odd pages. It was bound discreetly in gray with a design
of two superimposed triangles, black on white on the front cover
and white on black on the back, and bore the title *Spectra* in
large black letters and below it, in smaller letters, the words
"New Poems." Under the interlacing triangles were the rather
odd and previously unknown names of the two authors, Emanuel Morgan and Anne Knish. On the title page was the subtitle,
A Book of Poetic Experiments; the New York publisher was
Mitchell Kennerley. There was no dust jacket, and no biographical information on the authors. Such a modest volume might
have been expected to pass unnoticed; but in literary circles it
proved, on the contrary, to be something of a bombshell.

In her preface Anne Knish outlined the purpose of the
book. "This volume," she wrote in a direct and matter-of-fact
way, "is the first compilation of the recent experiments in

Spectra. It is the aim of the Spectric group to push the possibilities of poetic expression into a new region—to attain a fresh brilliance of impression by a method not so wholly different from the methods of Futurist Painting." And to get at the nature of the so-called Spectric technique, she launched immediately into an explanation of the term "Spectric":

> In the first place, it speaks, to the mind, of that process of diffraction by which are disarticulated the several colored and other rays of which light is composed. It indicates our feeling that the theme of a poem is to be regarded as a prism, upon which the colorless white light of infinite existence falls and is broken up into glowing, beautiful, and intelligible hues. In its second sense, the term Spectric relates to the reflex vibrations of physical sight, and suggests the luminous appearance which is seen after the exposure of the eye to intense light, and, by analogy, the after-colors of the poet's initial vision. In its third sense, Spectric connotes the overtones, adumbrations, or spectres which for the poet haunt all objects both of the seen and unseen world,—those shadowy projections, sometimes grotesque, which, hovering around the real, give to the real its full ideal significance and its poetic worth. These spectres are the manifold spell and true essence of objects—like the magic that would inevitably encircle a mirror from the hand of Helen of Troy.

Miss Knish, who seemed knowledgeable and intensely devoted to her subject, went on to define in daring and all-inclusive terms the effect of the Spectric poem on its reader: "The insubstantiality of the poet's spectres should touch with a tremulous vibrancy of ultimate fact the reader's sense of the immediate theme."

Immediacy appeared to be the keynote of Spectric theory. In describing a landscape, the Spectrist would not attempt a map, but would "put down those winged emotions, those fantastic analogies, which the real scene awakens in his own mind." Thus he would find, in Miss Knish's words, "the vividest of all modes of communication, as the touch of hands quickens a mere exchange of names." And if the Spectrists were all-embracing, they were down to earth in the sense that to their "reflected experiences" adhered "often a tinge of humor." Like the great Oriental artists, in contrast to Occidental ones, they did not fear the flash of humor in serious works.

Although Miss Knish's preface began in a somewhat high-flown manner, it ended with a certain modesty; for she declared that the Spectric method was still in its infancy; and, reminding the reader of the book's subtitle, she pointed out that the poems it contained were only experimental efforts "toward the desired end." It was with Emanuel Morgan that the theory originated, and in his experiments in the volume he employed only regular rhymed stanzas for "the best expression of his genius," whereas Anne Knish, who, in this preface at least, seemed to have taken on the voice of authority for the movement, used only free verse. The Spectric manner might well employ either one or the other. But if Miss Knish, in conclusion, was reticent to the extent of saying that the Spectrists did not really claim to be the inventors of their method, she was firm in maintaining that they were the first to use it consciously and consistently and to formulate its possibilities "by means of elaborate experiment," and that, in so far as she and Mr. Morgan could discover, there were few recent poets writing in English who could be described "in a sure sense" as Spectrists.

Not all readers of poetry, however keen their interest, could follow Anne Knish's Spectric adumbrations (one reviewer indeed found the preface as "brilliant as a rainy midnight in the country"); but there was no doubt about the fact that before many months had passed the Spectrists had arrived. A reviewer in the *New Republic* of 18 November 1916, who as it turned out had good reason to know whereof he spoke, put it succinctly:

171

"There is a new school of poets, a new term to reckon with, a new theory to comprehend, a new manner to notice, a new humor to enjoy. It is the Spectric school; composed, as far as the present publication goes, of a man, the cornerstone, and a woman, the keystone—Emanuel Morgan and Anne Knish." At a time when "schools" were springing up everywhere like daisies in a field or crabgrass on a lawn, here was a new group that had rooted out all the rest. The Vorticists, the Imagists, the Futurists, the Chorists now were passé; the Spectrists had moved into the front ranks of the avant-garde. Edgar Lee Masters, in a letter to Emanuel Morgan dated 1 December 1916, wrote that he thought highly of *Spectra*, "an idea capable of great development along creative lines," and that Spectrism was "at the core of things and imagism at the surface." Other poets and critics of note were equally impressed: John Gould Fletcher spoke of the Spectrists' "vividly memorable lines"; William Marion Reedy in *Reedy's Mirror* hailed them in glowing terms. Eunice Tietjens, associate editor of *Poetry*, wrote of *Spectra* to Mr. Morgan on 9 May 1917: "It is a real delight!" Headlines in newspapers throughout the country ushered them in; and soon the word "Spectra" was on every tongue. Not everybody liked this newest of poetry; but then that was to be expected—not everybody liked poetry anyway. Still, the Spectrists were facts, as Don Marquis pointed out in the New York *Evening Sun* of 26 December 1916. "Are you hep to the Spectric Group?" he wrote. "Have you a little Spectrist in Your Home?" Apparently, for better or worse, almost everyone had.

Who were these experimenters, and what did they offer that made them such a poetic rallying point? As around the leaders of any new movement, whether in politics or poetry, a certain mystery gathered. They seemed, as was natural with such passionate poets, to speak through their works; and not very much was known of their background. What was unusual to begin with was that so esoteric a group should emerge from Pittsburgh, a city that had not exactly been identified with the mainstream of

172

American literature. Readers soon learned from newspapers and magazines that Emanuel Morgan, with whom the theory originated, had returned to his native city after twenty years in Paris. His primary interest had always been painting until his friend Remy de Gourmont had turned him to literature; he had only recently begun to publish verse. Anne Knish, who had also lived in recent years in Pittsburgh, had been born in Budapest. She was the author of numerous critical reviews in European periodicals, and of one volume of poems in Russian bearing the Latin title *Via Aurea*. It was rumored that Anne Knish was strikingly beautiful and excessively temperamental; and when shortly afterwards another young and hitherto unknown poet, Elijah Hay, a "briefless barrister," joined the group, Mr. Hay and Mr. Morgan were reported at knife point over the tempestuous Knish.

Whether or not the Spectric poems exactly followed the theory did not seem to matter—they were certainly lively enough. Anne Knish's emotional nature was evident in her work: indeed, some of her poems (the writers, disdaining titles, printed them as Opus this and Opus that with noticeable gaps between the Opus numbers) seemed scratched into the paper with talons rather than pen:

> Skeptical cat,
> Calm your eyes, and come to me.
> For long ago, in some palmèd forest,
> I too felt claws curling
> Within my fingers . . .

And in *Opus 131* she was equally feral:

> I must have firebrands!
> I must have leaves!
> I must have sea-deeps!

Emanuel Morgan, also, was not without his exclamatory moments (*Opus 104*) :

> How terrible to entertain a lunatic!
> To keep his earnestness from coming close!

Even at the sight of so common a dish as frogs' legs, he could feel imperial (*Opus 9*) :

> When frogs' legs on a plate are brought to me
> As though I were divinity in France,
> I feel as God would feel were He to see
> Imperial Russians dance.

Here were poets to whom intensity was all-important. It was clear that they would make no compromises in their art; they would not lower their standards to win readers. On that score, Anne Knish was unequivocal in her *Opus 40:*

> I have not written, reader,
> That you may read. . . .
> They sit in rows in the bare schoolroom
> Reading.
> Throwing rocks at windows is better,
> And oh the tortoiseshell cat with the can tied on!
> I would rather be a can-tier
> Than a writer for readers.

Emanuel Morgan in his *Opus 79*, the final poem of *Spectra*, apparently wanted to remain with his readers only in an anonymous, pervasive, and even somewhat deadly fashion:

> Smell me, a dead fish . . .
> Taste me, a rotten tree. . . .
> Someday touch me, all you wish,
> In the wide sea.

The "cornerstone" and the "keystone" of *Spectra*, to judge by their manner of expression in both prose and verse, were not out to court "poetry lovers." They were convinced, moreover, that they would be around for some time.

Of that not everyone was so sure. Although Amy Lowell is said to have enthusiastically recommended the volume to a group of apprentice poets at Harvard, she appeared to be on the whole unimpressed. Certainly as the "fair Trotsky" of the Imagist revolution, as H. L. Mencken termed her, she was scarcely ready to welcome competition; and it is reasonable to assume that she had her doubts. The Boston *Christian Register* of 12 April 1917, echoed her sentiments: "In the preface to this extraordinary volume in which the spectric method is outlined we find very little that is attractive to us." The reviewer in the St. Louis *Post-Dispatch* of 7 April 1917, wrote: "They have a theory of poetry all their own, but the stuff in the volume does not seem to be poetic. It is mostly a conglomeration of stuff thrown together so that stars and cheese, and female limbs and green shadows and similar combinations are catalogued in one bit called opus number so and so. Well, for those who like this sort of thing this is the sort of thing they like." The New York *Herald* of 29 December 1916, referred to Spectric poetry as "daughter of Futurist poetry, a granddaughter of *vers libre*, and no relation at all to real poetry." Quoting Mr. Morgan's *Opus 40:*

> Two cocktails round a smile,
>   A grapefruit after grace,
> Flowers in an aisle
>   . . . Were your face.
>
> A strap in a streetcar,
>   A sea-fan on the sand,
> A beer on a bar
>   . . . Were your hand.
>
> The pillar of a porch,
>   The tapering of an egg,
> The pine of a torch
>   . . . Were your leg.—

175

Sun on the Hellespont,
White swimmers in the bowl
Of the baptismal font
Are your soul.

the Detroit *News Tribune* of 18 January 1917, asked: "Are we justified in saying that the poetic and the very spectric likeness of a hand to a beer has never before been revealed to the public? And almost anyone would love to have a leg like a porch support."

"Gibberish," the Los Angeles *Graphic* said of the same lines, "written for one purpose only—to attract attention." Of *Opus 40* Mrs. Marguerite Wilkinson, a well-known critic, wrote in the Richmond *Journal* of 9 December 1916: "Five years ago we would have called this bizarre. Today we read it with the feelings of the unsophisticated wanderer in art galleries and studios, who says, safely enough, when he can think of nothing else, 'How interesting! Such a soul . . . hand . . . face . . . such a leg!' " In the Chicago *Evening Post* of 9 March 1917, Miss Susan Wilbur, who said that she really thought that Emanuel Morgan and Anne Knish had concocted the preface to pull one's leg, declared that she preferred Mr. Morgan's work to Miss Knish's because of its humor; and she also quoted *Opus 40* as an example of something to "out-Carroll Lewis Carroll." On the other hand, Miss Wilbur felt that Anne Knish had added quite a number of color words such as "amber" and "indigo" to modern poetic diction, and that she gave very well the "illusion of that tangled sense imagery which goes to make up consciousness."

But whatever doubts were raised and whatever hesitations expressed, Mr. Morgan's humor and Miss Knish's tangle of sense imagery had made their point and were to gain more and more adherents during the course of the next year and a half. The Philadelphia *Public Ledger* of 24 March 1917 was of the opinion that the Spectrists would not "disturb the world of verse in America or set any river on fire, unless it be the Monongahela when it is covered with oil scum"; but the sentiment slightly to the north, in Newark, New Jersey, was quite different. There Thomas Raymond, Republican nominee for mayor, decided to avoid political issues and to limit his campaigning to readings of *Spectra* and Walter Pater; he won the election, and at his inaugural party read selections from the volume, with special attention to the work of Anne Knish. Letters poured into Pittsburgh requesting the advice and opinion of Morgan and Knish on a variety of subjects; little magazines asked for the latest Spectric products. Harriet Monroe accepted several new poems of Emanuel Morgan for publication in *Poetry*, thereby giving him the seal of approval of the official organ of the American poetic renaissance. In a letter to Mr. Morgan dated 4 January 1917, Miss Monroe wrote: "I like *Opus 102*, but a tiny poem or two would not be enough to give the flavor. If I could have about two pages the reader would have a chance to get it." Mr. Morgan complied with her request, and to *Opus 102* were added *Opera 107, 108, 64*, and *116;* he suggested "Blind Glimpses" as an appropriate title for the group. *Reedy's Mirror*, which had welcomed Spectrism from the start, also opened its pages to Mr. Morgan; the *Little Review* had its readers illuminated by the latest rays from the spectrum with the publication in its issue of July 1917 of Mr. Morgan's *Opus 96*. One of the most influential and advanced of the little magazines was *Others*, edited from New York by Alfred Kreymborg and backed by Walter Conrad Arensberg, one of the first great patrons of modern art. As the successor of the *Globe*, which had sponsored the first appearance in February 1914, of *Des Imagistes, An Anthology*, it had published in 1915, in successive issues, "Peter Quince at the Clavier" by Wallace Stevens and "Portrait of a Lady" by T. S. Eliot. *Others*, whose motto was "The old expressions are with us always and there are always others," had brought out a special issue in October 1915 of dance poems of the Choric School. It was only natural then that it should devote a special issue in January 1917 to the Spectric School: the Spectric poems might not involve the dance, but they were certainly filled with action and with "other" expressions. The Spectric *Others* opened with *Opus 344* of Anne Knish, the opus number apparently indicating the extent of Miss Knish's feverish poetic activity since her original publication. The number included, besides new work of Morgan's, poems of another Spectrist, Elijah Hay (bearing titles such as "Nightmare after Talking with Womanly Women" and "Spectrum of Mrs. X" rather than opus numbers); it concluded with a "Prism on the Present State of Poetry" in which Morgan, Hay, and Knish spoke alternately, followed by a voice proclaiming with utter finality: *There shall be ashes.*

Perhaps because of the forthright, "damn-the-torpedoes" quality of their poetry in contrast to the veiled and wishy-washy nature of that of some of their contemporaries, the three writers received letters of unusual candor from correspondents of all sorts. "Dear Mr. Morgan, please tell me—am I a Spectrist?" wrote a Harvard undergraduate, enclosing examples of his work. To one such correspondent, Emanuel Morgan wrote: "In our own convenient terms, Spectrism belongs to its time in that it intends the poem or spectrum, by means of laughter or other illumination, to send an enchanted X-ray through the skin to the lungs and liver and heart of life." A number of young men, apparently impressed by such whiplash lines as "Madam, you intrigue me," addressed Elijah Hay in the most intimate terms. Among Mr. Hay's correspondents was the poet Dr. William Carlos Williams, who apropos of the Spectric issue wrote that he preferred Morgan, Hay, and Knish in that order. "The woman as usual," said Dr. Williams, "gets all the theory and—as usual—takes it seriously whereas the male knows it's only a joke—serious as it is. A. K.'s things suffer from too much theory. Morgan is well represented, you are uneven—good and bad, A. K. has some fine passages."

A critical symposium entitled *The Young Idea, An Anthology of Opinion concerning the Spirit and Aims of Contemporary Literature*, edited by Lloyd Morris and published early in 1917 by Duffield, paid special attention to the Spectrists. Morris divided the poets and prose writers, to whom he had sent a questionnaire on the current direction of American literature ("In a word, where does our literature stand today, and whither is it going?"), into two groups—the Empiricists and the Romanticists. The Romantic group included, along with the Imagists such as John Gould Fletcher and Amy Lowell, the Idealists such as William Rose Benét, Joyce Kilmer, and Ridgely Torrence, the Pessimists such as Floyd Dell and Don Marquis, the Traditionalists such as E. A. Robinson, the two Spectrists, Emanuel Morgan and Anne Knish. While Imagism and Spectrism were both programs of revolt in the field of expression, Morris maintained in his introduction, they were diametrically opposed. "The Spectrists thus seem, in a measure," he wrote, "to be chiefly interested in blurring and encircling with a haze of symbols the image which the Imagists, in their poems, are anxious to convey with photographic precision." A number of the contributors in the various categories touched on the Spectrists. Arthur Davison Ficke, listed among the Empiricists, pointed out that the "eccentricities and absurdities" of the new schools were no worse than the "banalities and sentimentalities" of the old ones; and, as time would show, he was right to add that "in fact, the vigorous shock that some of these aberrations have administered to the moribund body of poetry is distinctly galvanizing." Another of the Empiricists, Witter Bynner, was equally right in saying, "The pattern of the so-called 'schools' of poetry will do no harm, I think; for they will freshen and diversify technique. But they are a side show. And the three rings in the main tent are beauty, vigor, and common sense." Emanuel Morgan limited himself in his contribution to the symposium to stressing the Spectric characteristic of humor; Anne Knish, although she began with some diffidence ("I do not know if I have a right to speak on this subject; for American poets will resent perhaps the criticism of one whose native tongue is the Russian and who has written only one English book. Yet since you ask me, I will answer, with humility, as to poetry only."), went on at great length in an awkward Old World manner. With a degree of annoyance and a certain *hauteur*, she concluded: "We who are of the Spectric School of poets have tried, contradicting no ancient truth, to give fresh interpretation to Classic gospels. If our aesthetic dogma be sound, the other poets will before long become aware. But these are in American poetry days only of beginning; and I think those people know nothing of European literary history who speak so much of 'new, new, new.' "

As the fame of *Spectra* spread, its directing forces, Miss Knish and Mr. Morgan, became increasingly mysterious. Few people had actually seen them: reporters, critics, and aspiring poets called at their Pittsburgh addresses only to find that the two had just left for New York; those who tracked them down in New York discovered to their dismay that they had moved on to Chicago. True, Alfred Kreymborg had been heard to refer publicly and "with a real gleam in his eye" to Miss Knish's extraordinary beauty. But although many people had been in correspondence with them, few had ever laid eyes on the pair, or, for that matter, on the gifted Mr. Hay. Rumors began to circulate at literary gatherings and on college campuses that Miss Knish and Messrs. Morgan and Hay might be spectral as well as Spectric, that they might indeed be three-thirds of a ghost and not exist at all.

A writer who had referred frequently to the Spectric school in the course of his lectures throughout the country was Witter Bynner, the young poet who had won praise for widely published poems since the appearance of *An Ode to Harvard* (1907) —in later editions called *Young Harvard*—and who was not identified with any particular "school." In an address before the Fortnightly Club at Chicago in May 1916, he said: "Most of this schismatic poetry is nothing but rot. How one can take up his time with it is beyond me." He did, however, see a ray of hope in the Spectrists, samples of whose work had apparently already reached him before publication. Quoting Emanuel Morgan's *Opus 62*, which begins:

> Three little creatures gloomed across the floor
> And stood profound in front of me,
> And one was Faith, and one was Hope,
> And one was Charity.

he went on: "Now of course this sort of stuff isn't quite so hopeless as some of the other, but what does it mean? A few may see intelligence in it." Bynner was asking similar questions about the Spectrists nearly two years later, on 26 April 1918 in a speech before the Twentieth Century Club at Detroit. He was challenged midway in his lecture, to his utter amazement, by a young man who asked simply and directly, "Is it not true, Mr. Bynner, that you are Emanuel Morgan and that Arthur Davison Ficke is Anne Knish?" Bynner's answer was just as straightforward; it was "Yes." "A direct and large lie was too much for me," Bynner explained later. Then and there, to the vast amusement of the audience, he related in detail for the first time the true story of *Spectra*. "Brush off the dusty form of Mr. Barnum's Cardiff giant, and put it away forever," said the Detroit *News* a few days later; "there is now revealed a greater hoax than this." *Spectra* is indeed one of the greatest literary hoaxes ever perpetrated in America; and the story that Bynner had to tell was an incredible one.

TWO

IN February 1916, on the way to visit his friend and fellow poet, Arthur Davison Ficke, who was then living with his first wife Evelyn Blunt Ficke at Davenport, Iowa, Witter Bynner stopped off at Chicago. While there he attended a performance of the Diaghilev Ballets Russes in the company of Laird Bell and Howard Vincent O'Brien. During the intermission, after a performance of *Le Spectre de la Rose,* danced by Massine, Bynner discussed with his friends the absurdity of some of the recent "schools." There were the Imagists and the Vorticists, of course, but had they heard, he asked— glancing up from his program with one of the booming laughs that became proverbial among his friends—of the *Spectrists,* the new poets who had just appeared in Pittsburgh; *they* were the ones to watch. Bynner, who had just come from Pittsburgh and who had been thinking what a good idea it would be to found a new school himself and to have some ·'fun with the extremists and with those of the critics who were overanxious to be in the van," found himself, with this chance but inspired conversational gambit, faced with a virtual *fait accompli*. The possibilities of the words "spectral" or "spectric" flashed over him in a moment; and he remembered them when en route to Davenport the following day. He composed the first three poems on the train, and on arriving at Davenport, set forth to Arthur Davison Ficke and his wife his plan for a burlesque. Ficke, who was just as irritated as Bynner by the "schools" of the moment and who also thoroughly enjoyed a good joke, entered immediately into the spirit of the occasion. The Spectrists that evening came into being: the first problem, before producing more Spectric poems, was to settle on the names of the writers. Names "of a foreign tinge" were wanted "as making the school more impressive to mere Americans." Bynner's choice was, he recalls, "lumberingly poetic—the first part of it being a suggestion of 'I hear Emmanuel Singing' and the second a sound reflecting the German word *morgen*—so that the rather misty idea was 'morning song.' " He visualized Morgan as a middle-aged gentleman with a long, square-cut beard. Arthur Davison Ficke, remembering having seen in the culinary columns of some Sunday newspaper a recipe for the then little-known Jewish pastries called knishes, decided on "Anne Knish." Aware of the humorous Yiddish-vaudeville sound of the word although not perhaps of its full Yiddish meaning, he saw Miss—or Mrs. (she was probably divorced)—Knish as a Hungarian lady who, through wide experiences, had kept an open mind and a pure soul. The personalities of the mythical writers became more clearly outlined in proportion to the "spectra" or "spectrics" produced; and these were written at a fast clip. In fact, so absorbed did the poets become in their productions that the constant composition and recitation of Spectric verse became too much for Mrs. Ficke. She ordered the pair out of the house until they had finished their manuscript. They retired to a hotel across the river in Moline, Illinois, where, as Arthur Davison Ficke put it, from ten quarts of excellent Scotch in ten days they extracted the whole of Spectric philosophy.

"The method of composition," Bynner wrote in a later account of the incident, "was simple. Sometimes we would start with an idea, sometimes with only a phrase, but the procedure was to let all reins go, to give the idea or the phrase complete head, to take whatever road or field or fence it chose. In other words it was a sort of runaway poetry, the poet seated in the wagon but the reins flung aside." One of these runaway episodes is related by Arthur Davison Ficke in an unpublished essay. One day at luncheon Witter Bynner purposely slipped off his chair and fell noisily to the floor, his motive being, says Ficke, the "commendable one of startling the attending waitress into violent hysterics." When order had been restored and as much as possible of the cheese soufflé removed from the dining room floor, the hostess remarked sadly but patiently, "How terrible to entertain a lunatic!" Bynner, "with a shriek of voluptuous and joyous recognition," dashed immediately to the study, where in the person of Emanuel Morgan he wrote down his renowned "Madagascar" (*Opus 104*):

> How terrible to entertain a lunatic!
> To keep his earnestness from coming close!
>
> A Madagascar land-crab once
> Lifted blue claws at me
> And rattled long black eyes
> That would have got me
> Had I not been gay.

There must have been many other such occasions during the period of composition. The poets seized on everything that was in the air; and the air was filled with spectres, which were all channeled into appropriate "spectra." The opus numbers in the book itself are in the true sequence of composition, although spaced farther apart than they should be in reality because much of what was put down had eventually to be discarded. (In view

184

of the nonsense they got away with in the end, perhaps they need not have been so careful at the time about eliminating those efforts which seemed "too wild for inclusion.") Some of the results looked so good, Bynner says, that then and there they "signed, sealed, and filed a solemn document swearing that the whole performance had been done as a joke." Ficke adds that "it was only Bynner's opportune departure, this third day of March, that prevented us from becoming seriously interested in further and genuine experiments, and thus perishing at the hands of the monster which we had created."

Little did they realize how soon their two-headed beast would descend on the unsuspecting public. They had three copies of the manuscript bound, one each for themselves and one to send to the publisher Mitchell Kennerley, who had published both poets under their own names. Kennerley, to their great astonishment, accepted it at once for publication, apparently (as Bynner remembered it) as a bona fide manuscript; and when informed of the real identity of the authors, agreed to keep the secret.

Arthur Davison Ficke enjoyed drawing with ruler and compass; and it was he who was responsible for the design of the superimposed triangles, black on white and white on black, on the front and back covers of the book. "It is fortunate for Kennerley, Bynner, and myself," he said, "that the guardians of morality in These United States never detected the obscene significance of the design I made—for, as anyone can readily see, I dared to depict, twice over, the 'Loves of the Triangles' in all their unashamed nakedness. It is probably the most scandalous and indictable design known to the Western World. China has produced more shocking ones, but not America." (Ficke was clearly having fun relating his own parody to one of the most famous in literary history. In 1798 the *Anti-Jacobin* published *The Loves of the Triangles*, a parody by Canning, Frere, and Ellis of *The Loves of the Plants* by Erasmus Darwin. The verse of the poet-physician, grandfather of the great Charles, did not survive this witty onslaught.) He intended his drawings to serve merely as suggestions for the publisher; but Mitchell Kennerley proceeded to photograph his rough sketches and reproduce them exactly.

It was Ficke, too, who was solely responsible for Anne Knish's much discussed preface. Witter Bynner, with his Welsh and English antecedents, Ficke contended, would have been quite incapable of such a concoction; only someone descended as he was on one side from a long line of German professors could produce so "pretentious a farrago of semi-sensible, almost-intelligible doctrine." Witter Bynner satisfied himself with a suggestion here and there and with the presumptuous dedication to Remy de Gourmont, indicating that Morgan had been his friend and disciple. "I did strike out a few passages which seemed to me too obvious nonsense," he says, "but, reading emanations in later years of aesthetic theory and code, I realize that we could have gone all out."

The two poets decided on Pittsburgh as the home of Mr. Morgan and Miss Knish because they believed that there would be less danger of the secret being ferreted out there, "since interest in schools of poetry is not the big thing in the life of the average Pittsurgher." "But we had to do something," Bynner recalled at that period, "about the letters that came to the poets, so we gave as Emanuel Morgan's address, the address of a lady in Pittsburgh whom I know—a lady who hates everything that savors of Vorticism or Imagism!—and she, poor thing, was promptly deluged with letters about Spectrism." The lady in question, Helen Esquerré, wife of Edmond Esquerré, professor of chemistry at the Carnegie Institute of Technology, was not very taken with the idea of the hoax, since she felt that it was a waste of Witter Bynner's time and gifts; but she proved a loyal accomplice throughout the affair, and there were moments when she seemed rather to have enjoyed it all herself. At the time of Emanuel Morgan's first acceptance by Harriet Monroe, she telephoned her husband's colleague, the essayist and poet Haniel

Long, the news. Long, who had also just had some poems accepted by Miss Monroe and who also had little sympathy for Bynner's stunt, was sadly disillusioned as to the editor's critical faculties. When Harriet Monroe asked for biographical information on Emanuel Morgan, Mrs. Esquerré, seizing on Long's suggestion that she make him work in a glass factory, wrote that Mr. Morgan, a graduate of the École Normale (which was safely far away), was interested in the manufacture of pure crystal. (*Not*, Mrs. Esquerré asked Bynner please to observe, of *glass*.)

There were moments in Mrs. Esquerré's Spectric correspondence when she felt that she had come dangerously close to letting the cat out of the bag by her diction or script. Harriet Monroe, in November 1917, wrote to Emanuel Morgan saying that it was his handwriting more than anything else that "has forced me to think of you as a perfectly nice lady." But she accepted (in Mrs. Esquerré's hand) Morgan's categoric denial of the charge. Then the complimentary copies of the special Spectric issue of *Others*, which were sent to the Spectric poets (at Mrs. Esquerré's address) by Dr. William Carlos Williams in March 1917, by Wells Fargo, never arrived. Inquiries made of Wells Fargo and of Dr. Williams brought no results, and apparently the productions of the poets, while being acclaimed elsewhere, were adrift in their native city.

The Pittsburgh poets had no difficulty making their own way in the world, but Bynner and Ficke soon found that they had ample opportunity to help the mythical Morgan and Knish establish themselves in the literary firmament. In the summer of 1916, before the book's publication, Herbert Croly, the founder of the *New Republic*, and Philip Littell, its literary editor, were dining in Cornish, New Hampshire, at the house of Homer Saint-Gaudens, where Bynner was then living. When the two men noticed the proofs of *Spectra* lying on his worktable, Bynner feared that the end had come. He recovered himself in time to say, however, that this was an advance copy of a book sent to him for comment and that the publisher evidently had great confidence in it. One can imagine Bynner saying, as he often did publicly later, that the Spectrists were, alas, just another of the schools; but that they did perhaps offer a "ray of hope." Both Croly and Littell, delighted to have happened on something so new and vigorous as *Spectra*, urged Bynner to review the volume for the *New Republic*. Naturally the latter took pleasure in complying with the request, and even greater pleasure in collecting the fifteen dollars he was paid for his article. Bynner prepared the way for the enlargement of the school ("I suppose we shall soon be hearing the names of other members of the spectric edifice"), and had fun at the expense of the preface ("This theory is as heavily presented by Anne Knish as if she were the graduate of some German university. Perhaps her birth in Hungary accounts for the effect."). He outlined the little that was known of the poets personally, and remarked that they saw fit to number their works confusingly "Opus" this and "Opus" that. "It may be that the Spectrists are offering us," he wrote, "a means toward the creation or understanding of the essential magic of poetry. Their attempt, at any rate, goes deeper than the attempts of any of the other latterday schools in that it cuts under mere technique. . . . Perhaps a wider experience of life and of media has made the Spectrists' ability in English verse more flexible and more potent than that of the other poets we may compare with them. Certainly their theory demands an art not stopping short with direct notation by the senses, but reaching connotation of all kinds. And they are ambitious, without being too solemn!" He concluded with a masterful understatement: "But whether or not there be meaning or magic in the book, I can promise that there is amusement in it and that it takes a challenging place among current literary impressionistic phenomena."

Mitchell Kennerley, besides heading his own publishing house, also published the *Forum*, in which Ficke and Bynner had frequently appeared under their own names; and he suggested early in 1916 that Knish and Morgan prepare the way for their volume with an article on the Spectrists. This they did with an essay entitled "The Spectric School of Poetry," which appeared in the June number. "I'm nearly prostrated by the sight of the *Forum*," Arthur Ficke wrote to Witter Bynner when he saw the piece in print. "Somehow the thing looks so much madder than I'd supposed. It's so terrible, the essay, that I grow a little sick at my stomach thinking of it. It's just like W. H. Wright's normal style. Oh dear, Oh dear!" (Ficke was, of course, thinking of Willard Huntington Wright, otherwise known as S. S. Van Dine.) Referring to the Anne Knish preface, parts of which they quoted, they had written: "The Imagists, suicidally advertised by a concerted reciprocal chorus of poet-reviewers, might once have been capable of employing this very theory in a tentative way. The time is past, however, when the Spectrists can hope for cooperation in this quarter: and the latest of the modern movements in poetry must be content to go its own way after the fashion of 'the spear that knows no brother.' "

Go its way the new movement did, and with a success that neither Ficke nor Bynner had ever envisaged; the spectres that they had loosed upon the air were to haunt them on more than one public occasion. Mrs. Corinne Roosevelt Robinson, the sister of Theodore Roosevelt, herself a versifier and an active member of the Poetry Society of America, frequently gave literary luncheons at her house in New York. At one of these gatherings, Witter Bynner had met Roosevelt; the president had shown an interest in his poetry, as in that of Edwin Arlington Robinson and other contemporary poets, and had later, at the suggestion of Maurice Francis Egan, then ambassador to Denmark, offered the poet the post of consul at Venice. Because of his inability to speak Italian, Witter Bynner had had to decline the offer. At a later luncheon, attended by John Jay Chapman, Edgar Lee Masters, and William Marion Reedy, Mrs. Robinson brought up the subject of *Spectra* and, producing a copy, asked Witter Bynner to read selections from it. While Reedy (who had already been informed of the true identity of the authors) and

Edgar Lee Masters (who had not) vied with one another in praise of the poems, Bynner strained every muscle to keep a straight face. He had been free to smile earlier, however, when, as Emanuel Morgan, he had received in a letter Edgar Lee Masters' effusive commendation of *Spectra:* "You have an idea in the sense that places do have an essence, everything has a noumena [*sic*] back of its appearance and it is this that poetry should discover. Any poetry that correlates gets over; and poetry that only gets the image and separates that from all other images loses much of the spirit and meaning. Hence to me Spectrism if you must name it is at the core of things and imagism at the surface." (Witter Bynner and Arthur Ficke threw dice to decide who was to retain possession of the Masters letter; Bynner won three times in succession, and it was his to keep.) Both the perpetrators of the hoax must have nodded their heads with a certain mournful satisfaction also when they received Lloyd Morris' letter requesting both Miss Knish and Mr. Morgan to contribute to the symposium in *The Young Idea:* "May I not call your attention to the importance of your individual opinion to the investigation as a whole, and respectfully urge you to favor me with it?"

It had originally been the plan to enlarge the school as the hoax gained momentum; indeed, it was necessary to do so in view of Anne Knish's hints that there were others to be heard from. But Spectric verse proved to be more difficult to produce than one might have imagined; and the poets had to be sure that those they approached would be sealed to silence. It was Witter Bynner's recollection that Edwin Arlington Robinson made several unsuccessful attempts, and that Edna St. Vincent Millay, when let in on the secret, declined to be a disciple. George Sterling, the San Francisco poet, volunteered to join up under the name of Yvonne Roux, a nineteen-year-old French girl born in Texas but "safely out of there." Sterling assumed, however, that ribaldry was the keynote of the school, and his efforts at naughtiness fell flat. The Spectrists decided that the "spontaneities" of

Yvonne Roux went too far and would surely give them away; this is "Spontaneity 19":

> My aunt says she is
> Forty:
> She is
> Fifty-one.
> Once she was good-looking.
> She must have had
> Chances for many indiscretions.
> Now she hates modern
> poetry.
> And the audible amours of cats.
> Now she stands at the window,
> With her parched lips,
> And satin-backed hands,
> Hating our rooster and
> his successes.

"Spontaneity 77" was even more "spontaneous":

> I want so many things!
> Why are you not
> A millionaire?
> But there are some things
> your money
> Could not buy:
> I want to strangle my
> sister,
> Leisurely.
> I want to be the author
> of a book called
> "Pubic Plays."
> I want to make the minister
> Eat a fig-leaf salad.

I want a tongue a yard long
That I may clean myself
Like a cat.
The Niagaras in my heart
are soundless,
Finding no bottom.

These were a far cry from Sterling's usual stately Swinburnian productions; and clearly they would not do. Bynner also wrote his friend Rose O'Neill, the inventor of the Kewpie doll, to ask her assistance. Although Miss O'Neill felt that the Spectric poems "hit you almost every time with a curious inner magic," she was herself unable to produce any.

With the deadline for the Spectric issue of *Others* only a few days off, the two poets, having failed in their search for disciples, found themselves together again at Davenport, Iowa; and they retired once more across the river to Moline, Illinois, this time to the home of Marjorie Allen Seiffert, a well-known poet of the Chicago school. Harriet Monroe in her autobiography remembers Mrs. Seiffert as a "round-faced, red-cheeked beauty," who belonged to "a supersophisticated little 'smart set' group" in the tri-cities of Moline, Rock Island, and Davenport, people whose grandfathers had made their fortunes in the manufacture of "the first steel plows and other agricultural aids." "Their dinners were superlative for food and service," wrote Miss Monroe, "and for a quick fencing of witty talk among intimates intellectually up to date." When at such a dinner the perpetrators of the hoax explained their predicament to Mrs. Seiffert, she tried immediately and failed as the others had; and the gentlemen then resorted to force "part jolly, part desperate." "We had told our tale to her in her bedroom, where she was making further efforts to be Spectric," Bynner remembered later, "and into it we locked her, determined that not until she had become Spectric should she emerge." While the party downstairs enjoyed cocktails and part of dinner, Mrs. Seiffert labored "almost angrily" until from a succession of manuscripts that she thrust under the door, Witter Bynner and Arthur Ficke selected a number they considered worthy of inclusion. She chose the name Elijah Hay almost as soon as she was released from her imprisonment; and the verses she had written appeared with scarcely any change in the Spectric *Others*.

With a cousin acting as scribe and go-between, Mrs. Seiffert—as Mr. Hay—carried on a correspondence over a period of months with Dr. William Carlos Williams, Alfred Kreymborg, and others. When Dr. Williams wrote saying that he preferred Morgan and Hay to Knish because she took the whole matter too seriously, Mrs. Seiffert forwarded the letter to Witter Bynner with the comment: "The cream of the whole thing is that Arthur, who especially scorns the whole business, is criticized as taking it too seriously! And what a wonderful argument for the feminist cause that we poor women cannot take our verses in a lighter vein!" As their correspondence progressed, Dr. Williams' frank and open manner with Elijah Hay became at times too much for Mrs. Seiffert. "How unfortunate that men use such unladylike expressions in their letters to each other!" she wrote Bynner. She wondered also if Dr. Williams had not begun to suspect something. In any case, the exchange of letters appears to have developed a real bond between Mrs. Seiffert and Dr. Williams; when they met, even before the exposure of the hoax, they appear to have delighted in each other's company.

As the cause gained ground, the Spectrists often had the pleasure of being presented to themselves. Alfred Kreymborg, announcing personally to Witter Bynner that he had persuaded the Spectrists to compile an issue of *Others*, assured him that the school was genuine since friends of his were acquainted with both the founders, and that Anne Knish was, of course, a devastating beauty. The poems in *Others* were even more extreme than those in *Spectra*, and were "designed to give the secret away to the knowing, but the Spectric vogue had taken too firm a hold." Indeed, the hoax might well have continued months longer had it not been for America's entry into World War I; but it soon became impossible to joke about anything, even about the state of American letters.

Arthur Ficke's Spectric monster, undismayed by the Atlantic, followed him to France and surprised him there in what constitutes one of the truly surrealistic consequences of the hoax. Ficke, a judge advocate wearing the uniform of a United States Army captain and "trembling with awe," breakfasted one morning in Paris with a brigadier general of the regular army, whom he had known slightly during peacetime. Their conversation turned to literary matters, and the general brought up the subject of *Spectra*. He asked Ficke if he supposed the book to be genuine or just a hoax. Arthur Ficke answered that, although many people whose opinions he respected took the volume seriously, he himself had always been inclined to suspect that it was fake. The general congratulated him smilingly on his astuteness, and said firmly that he was quite right. Asked how he could be so sure, the general replied all the more firmly, "Because I myself am Anne Knish." Naturally Ficke then plied him with questions about the whole affair and begged him to reveal the identity of Emanuel Morgan, but the general declared that he was under oath not to do so. Arthur Ficke understandably described this encounter as one of "the most deliriously happy hours I have ever spent."

By autumn of 1917 word had begun to get around in the literary world that the Spectrists might not be all they seemed. "Alice Henderson [of *Poetry*] is wiser than mere surmise could make her," Marjorie Allen Seiffert wrote to Witter Bynner on 2 October, "who told—do you think?" If it was not entirely clear by early 1918 who had told, it soon became evident that the game was almost up. The poets themselves began to tire of the masquerade; Arthur Ficke wrote from France that his mind was "quite out of key with such fooling," and Marjorie Allen Seiffert confessed that she would like to dust her skirts of "the Hayseed clinging thereto." As the cracks in the

Spectric edifice increased, the poets began to point accusing fingers at one another. Marjorie Seiffert confessed to Witter Bynner in February 1918 that she had told Alfred Kreymborg that she was Elijah Hay "for business reasons," but that he had no reason to suspect either Ficke or Bynner. Mrs. Seiffert, who had, as Elijah Hay, written a poem entitled "To A.K., a Nurse in France," was convinced that Alfred Kreymborg believed, because of the identity of the initials, that it was addressed to him. She was tempted, she said, to accuse *him* of being Anne Knish; but in the end she refrained from doing so. Moreover, Mrs. Seiffert contended, suspicion had naturally attached itself to Witter Bynner because he was "so crazy about the delightful myth" that he would "introduce Spectra into the most unlikely conversations."

Witter Bynner is the first to admit that he did carry the whole thing dangerously far; and as the initiator of the scheme, it is natural that he should have done so. He promoted the new school in his reviews, conversations, interviews, and lectures. Mrs. Cyrus Hall McCormick on 25 April 1916 wrote to him from Chicago that the Fortnightly Club sponsoring his lecture there was most eager to hear him speak on the Spectrists; even someone so well informed as Mrs. William Vaughn Moody did not know who they were. But Bynner not only promoted the school himself; he spurred other lecturers, the popular Mrs. Ralph Waldo Trine among them, to unfurl the Spectric banner throughout the country. He had, moreover, introduced the Newark judge, Thomas Raymond, whom he had met in New York at one of Julia Ellsworth Ford's evenings, to *Spectra;* and Raymond had made it known to a vast audience in Newark in the course of his successful campaign for mayor. Bynner was later somewhat embarrassed to admit that he even played salesman for the volume among his friends, on at least one occasion urging it on a group of young businessmen with the words, "This book of verse is to poetry what Cubism is to painting." He also had in readiness, should suspicion be directed his way, a letter dated 24 October 1917, addressed to Emanuel Morgan requesting the latter to use it in any way he wished. "I find myself in a curious position," it stated, "partly of amusement and partly of irritation because of a rumor apparently started as a joke by Arthur Davison Ficke, the poet, a great friend of mine, *viz. that I am you.* Not content with that, he seems to have wished on me a dual personality; for according to a letter received today from a friend who lives in his town, I am not only you, but Anne Knish, too." He had also ready an article by Emanuel Morgan on the work of Witter Bynner, since such reciprocal praise would seem only natural; but he had no occasion to make use of either document. When faced with his direct accuser on the evening of 26 April 1918, he knew that he had done with laughing up his sleeve.

How the end came about is, perhaps fittingly, not much clearer than Spectric theory itself. While Witter Bynner had kept the secret from his own stepsister, Ruth Wellington, until May 1918, he had dropped hints and made allusions to the truth everywhere he had been. Arthur Ficke had told a number of his neighbors at Davenport and friends in Chicago. Among them was Maurice Browne, the British theatrical producer, whom Mrs. Seiffert characterized as an "arch gossip." It is Witter Bynner's belief that Browne, having spread the word through Chicago, where he headed the Little Theatre, was responsible for the truth reaching the accuser in Detroit's Twentieth Century Club. It seems more likely, however, that the news came from the University of Wisconsin.

According to Dr. Horace M. Kallen, at the time of *Spectra* there was at the University of Wisconsin at Madison, where he was then an instructor in the Department of Psychology and Philosophy, a group of male undergraduates interested in literature who called themselves the Stranglers; their female counterpart was a group called the Furies. The *Wisconsin Literary Magazine* was the joint product of these groups. Witter Bynner, not long after the appearance of *Spectra*, came to Madison on one of his regular lecture tours. He spoke to the Stranglers on the subject of current American poetry and quoted freely from *Spectra*. Dr. Kallen's suspicions were aroused, he says, by the fact that *Spectra* "hovered between being contrived and being on the loose"—like the work of someone who was drunk but not too drunk to know what he was doing. He also had made mental note of the fact that Witter Bynner and Arthur Ficke had been among the first to write on *Spectra*. After the lecture, in private, Dr. Kallen asked Witter Bynner directly if he and Ficke were not Morgan and Knish. Witter Bynner did not answer Yes, but the way he said No led Dr. Kallen to conclude that his suspicions were justified. It was as if he had been "taking the Fifth Amendment," Horace Kallen says. (Witter Bynner, however, remembered no such early confrontation, but believed that Dr. Kallen was present at the Detroit lecture. Whether the question was put at Madison in private or not, it is clear that the hoax was not publicly exposed until April 1918; and it seems probable that the young challenger did come from the University of Wisconsin.)

The Spectrists had, in any case, been popular with Wisconsin undergraduates, who had invented, as a take-off on *them*, the school of Ultra-Violet poetry, which they introduced in the January 1917 issue of the *Wisconsin Literary Magazine*. As a preface to the works of Manual Organ and Nanne Pish, Ernest L. Meyer had written:

It will be observed that the basic principle of the new school is the association of ideas ordinarily unassociated. To the unimaginative, this savors of insanity; but the psychologist recognizes the phenomenon, while the poet goes a step farther and sees in it the highest manifestation of inspiration. One man, says the poet, sees a tomcat on a back fence and thinks of brickbats and shotguns, which is banality and matter-of-fact prose; another man sees the same cat and immediately associates it with false teeth and a lawn party in Chicago, which is genius and Ultra-Violet poetry.

The article on the school was duly reprinted by *Reedy's Mirror;* but it was some time before the eyes of the Ultra-Violet poets (in reality, the Wisconsin Stranglers and Furies) were sharp enough to detect that they were, in fact, parodying a parody. Whatever else, they were certainly enjoying themselves:

MANUAL ORGAN

BLOSSOM *34*

I wished for her smiling lips.
She wanted my golden curls.
I was a banker's son.
But she was just "one of those girls."

Oh, I wish I were a gnat's tail!

NANNE PISH

BLOSSOM *56*

For me, one day, the earth bloomed bright,
And flowers spread their perfume,
I had a job.

And for a day
I bore the brimming growlers
And speared the juicy Frankforts;
And then—
I quit.

Why has cheese a rind?

Parodying the parodists is even further removed from reality than criticizing the critics; and when the whole affair had gone this far it was time that it stop. It was with a distinct sigh of relief that Arthur Ficke wrote to Witter Bynner from France: "I see by the papers that you have removed the last lingering bit of the cat's tail from the leaky bag, and that it has made a first-class Roman holiday."

Newspaper columns across the country dealt even more fully with *Spectra* now that the true identities of the writers had been revealed. Naturally the reviewers and critics who had not been taken in, or who had spoken of the Spectrists with caution, were among the first to announce how right they had been; those who had been deceived tried to cover up their steps as gracefully as possible. *The New York Times* in its literary section took pride in announcing, in a summary of the hoax, that it had not reviewed the book in the first place. *The New York Times Magazine* of 2 June 1918, however, published a long article by Thomas Ybarra, much later the author of *Young Man of Caracas*, on *Spectra* with photographs of Ficke and Bynner, who would, it maintained, take their places beside the great literary hoaxers of all time.

The Poetry Society of America in its Bulletin for May 1918 remarked that the reviewers who had attempted to make sense out of the introduction to *Spectra* would have the hardest score to wipe out. Lloyd Morris, who in *The Young Idea* seemed of all critics the most impressed by Spectric theory, claimed in a letter to Witter Bynner to have been informed of the suspected identities of the Spectrists when reading final proof of his book and to have gone ahead "with full knowledge." "I don't deny that *Spectra* baffled me entirely and pleased me greatly," he wrote. "Why should it not have? And why should I have treated it differently after knowing who wrote it than I did before?"

The St. Louis *Post-Dispatch* had said of the original publication that "for those who like this sort of thing this is the sort of thing they like," thereby quoting without realizing it a remark that originated with Max Beerbohm and that was later attributed to the Greeks, a miniature hoax in itself. It now called the book one in which there was neither rhyme nor reason. "The verse," its reviewer wrote, "was not unlike the gibberish of a maniac, who had been given a strong drink. It was a huge joke on the part of the two poets, and as they had rightly anticipated, a number of literary critics hailed the new volume with delight. Here was something new—the authentic voice of genius! The two had written as crazy verse as they possibly could, and behold! It had been taken seriously." Many of the magazine editors who had warmly welcomed *Spectra* were now noticeably silent. Miss Harriet Monroe, who had accepted five poems of Emanuel Morgan's and one of Elijah Hay's for publication in *Poetry*, now refused to print them. Witter Bynner took Miss Monroe to task for not daring to stand by her critical judgment, saying in effect that if the poems were good they were good under whatever name they appeared. "Emanuel Morgan wishes to continue as the person he has become," he wrote, "a person quite distinct from W. B. and enjoying himself in a manner not altogether foreseen by W. B. In other words, he has got away from me and refuses to be called back." (Miss Monroe's refusal to print the Morgan poems reminds one of a remark attributed to Cyril Connolly, when, as editor of *Horizon*, he was approached by a hurt author who had waited long months in vain for the appearance in print of an accepted contribution. Mr. Connolly silenced the eager young man by brutally declaring that while his material may have been good enough to accept, it was certainly not good enough to print.) Miss Monroe speaks of the *Spectra* affair briefly in her autobiography, referring to one Emanuel Morgan poem "waiting guiltily for publication" and quoting from Bynner's protesting letter. "And who has been stringing whom?" she wrote to him at the time. "But you sure had the nerve—to boost that precious trio in your lectures." She left it to her associate editor, Alice Corbin Henderson, who in 1917 had helped her edit an anthology of the "new" poetry, to comment publicly on the hoax. In an editorial in *Poetry*, Mrs. Henderson, without any reference to the Morgan poems then in the magazine's files, wrote with a certain air of self-justification and injured pride :

Mr. Bynner and Mr. Ficke must have had some amusement
out of the joke, if it was as successful as it is said to have been
—which seems incredible. If the joke proves anything at all,
it is simply that critics are an unselective lot, particularly
in the presence of the "new poetry," or "new art," about
which there is a fair amount of uncertainty and which it is
better to praise slightly than damn utterly—for one might
find oneself running after the bandwagon! But would the
result have been any different if one had put forth a book,
say, of *Prisms and Prunes*—very charming rhymed jingles,
the words making apparent sense, syntax observed, but
with nothing underneath? Certainly not. For this happens
every day. People who actually do not exist are often
praised for writing verse of which they furnish the mere
echo; the originals being found tucked away on the library
shelves. . . . What satisfaction is to be had I wonder from
thus baiting the public? Only the satisfaction of knowing
that it is possible to do so—which is, after all, axiomatic.

To this Emanuel Morgan replied in a letter published in a later
issue of *Poetry* under the heading "A Spectral Ghost": "Our
intent in publishing the book was not to question the use of free
verse and not 'to bait the public,' but to satirize fussy pretence;
and if we have in any degree focussed laughter on pomp and cir-
cumstance among poets we shall have had enough satisfaction
in our fun."

Miss Jane Heap of the *Little Review* was less restrained in
her comment than Mrs. Henderson; she came out swinging.
"Early last June," she wrote in an editorial, "the Spectrics sent
in a fat bunch of poems to the *Little Review* (unsolicited). One
poem, Opus 96, by E. Morgan, appeared in our July number.
The others were returned with an Andersonian note. Poor
M. C. A. [Margaret C. Anderson, editor of the magazine] was
so taken by storm that she 'published with eclat' in the same
issue an ecstatic eulogy of the 'new school':

> Banish
> Anne Knish
> Set the dog on
> Emanuel Morgan."

And to show how such "artist-editors" as Ezra Pound were "completely astounded by the new 'virile' school," she went on to quote a letter he had written on 10 August 1917:

> Morgan's "spectric" business is a little late. People intending to be "schools" should have "done it first."
> Or rather they should base their school on something having to do with their art, not on a vague aesthetic theory. His manifesto advances no proposition affecting his own medium, i.e., words, rhythm, etc., only some twaddle about ultra-violets. Jejune. There is no difference between his free verse and any other free verse.
> After all Imagisme had three definite propositions about writing, and also a few "don'ts". And it differed from the neo-celtic-twilightists, etc., who preceded it. Morgan is only another Imagist imitator with a different preface from Amy's.

Miss Heap passed over the fact that Margaret Anderson had indeed asked Emanuel Morgan to submit other poems; and Ezra Pound, missing the humor of the whole thing, failed to see that the target of the Spectric attack was Amy Lowell rather than himself. Miss Heap concluded, "I confess to a deep ignorance of the nature of the hoax. If a man changes his name and writes better stuff, why does that make the public so ridiculous? . . . I can't do much for names, myself: a frog by any other name can hop as far and no farther."

Amy Lowell had still to be heard from; her response was eagerly awaited by Bynner and Ficke. Before the publication of the book, in March 1916, Arthur Ficke had sent Miss Lowell the manuscript of his article, "Modern Tendencies in Poetry," which was published later in the September *North American Review*. In the piece he mentioned the Spectrists in a list of contemporary schools; Amy Lowell replied that she had never heard of them. When the June 1916 issue of the *Forum* appeared with "The Spectric School of Poetry" by Anne Knish and Emanuel Morgan, Miss Lowell did take note of their existence and sent the article to John Gould Fletcher; Fletcher's reply was that it was all rubbish. Both Fletcher and Miss Lowell seem to have changed their minds when the book itself was published: Fletcher spoke of the Spectrists' "vividly memorable lines" and Miss Lowell made favorable mention of them to Harvard undergraduates. Emanuel Morgan in his words on the Imagists in the *New Republic* of 18 November 1916, however, went much too far. While he found the Imagist insistence "on natural cadence and clear-driven expression salutary," he went on to say that they would "not count so much themselves as in their jacking-up of the technique of the poets through whom vibrate richer matters than the tickling of a leaf on a windowpane or the flickering of water in a bathtub." The latter reference was clearly to Amy Lowell's much-quoted polyphonic prose poem "Bath," which had appeared in the anthology *Some Imagists Poets 1916*:

> The day is fresh-washed and fair, and there is a smell of tulips and narcissus in the air.
> The sunshine pours in at the bathroom window and bores through the water in the bathtub in lathes and planes of greenish white. It cleaves the water into flaws like a jewel, and cracks it to bright light.
> Little spots of sunshine lie on the surface of the water and dance, dance,

and their reflections wobble deliciously
over the ceiling; a stir of my finger sets
them whirring, reeling. I move a foot
and the planes of light in the water jar.
I lie back and laugh, and let the green-
white water, the sun-flawed beryl
water, flow over me. The day is almost
too bright to bear, the green water
covers me from the too bright day. I
will lie here awhile and play with the
water and the sun spots.

The sky is blue and high. A crow
flaps by the window, and there is a
whiff of tulips and narcissus in the air.

Bynner had already had occasion to evoke publicly the picture of
the hefty Miss Lowell in her tub. The Chicago *Tribune* had
said on 5 May 1916 that in a talk at Chicago he "walked un-
blushingly in on Miss Amy Lowell's 'Bath' and criticized that
lady severely for using the dictionary as a Saturday night tub."
She found other direct references to herself in Mr. Morgan's
article; and when the presentation copy of *Spectra* arrived, she
did not acknowledge it. Early in 1917 when Amy Lowell was in
New York to deliver a series of lectures on modern poets at the
Brooklyn Institute of Arts and Sciences, she met Witter Bynner
at a party given by Jessie Rittenhouse. Bynner launched into a
friendly discussion of the New Poetry and asked her her opinion of the Spectrists (the Spectric issue of *Others* had just appeared). "Bynner," she said, "I think they are charlatans." It
was on this note that her letter to Bynner dated 5 June 1918
opened.

Dear Emanuel:

You certainly did well with "Spectra." [She had just
read the exposé of the hoax in *The New York Times Book*

Review.] And how glad I am that I always said it was charlatanism! I verily believe that you began to respect me
from the very moment that you asked me what I thought
of it, and I told you that I thought the authors were insincere. Of course, I had no idea it was a genial hoax. I simply
thought that Miss Knish and Mr. Morgan were trying to
gain notoriety out of a singularity in which they themselves
did not in the least believe, and perhaps you will remember
that I never acknowledged the presentation copy which you
so kindly sent me.

But I must say that I think you sailed a bit close to the
wind in your review in *The New Republic* where you said:
[Here Miss Lowell quoted extensively from the review,
ending with the passage, "If I have overestimated the importance of *Spectra*, it is because of my constant hope, that
out of these various succeeding 'schools' something better
may develop than an aesthetic dalliance of eyeglass and blue
stocking." This last phrase, because of the pince-nez she
wore, she interpreted as a personal reference.]

Was this quite "cricket"?

Perhaps you thought you had a right to treat us in
that way, believing us to be insincere also. But, dear me, that
is all past, isn't it! And now I understand the reason for
Ficke's sending me one of his beautiful Japanese prints
after my first lecture in Chicago, inscribed, "With the
admiration of the enemy." This was his *amende honorable*,
and yours, I take it, was your defence of "Guns as Keys" at
the Poetry Society last year, for which I am most grateful.
In what terms should a lady acknowledge a gentleman's
admission that perhaps he made a mistake in trying to cut
her throat?

Still, your stiletto has not quite lost its keenness, since
in this interview in the *Times,* I notice that you again refer
to us as a part of the dubious company of "Gists" and

"Cists." ("Ah, Saul, Saul, it is hard for thee to kick against thy pricks!")

It is very "sporting" of you to attempt the dual personality plea; but how will it affect the dear public, so ignorant, and so fearful of being made a fool of? And how will it affect your serious lectures? But that is for you to decide, and please believe that although the specific instance of your early hostility is news to me, the general attitude certainly is not; and that, barring this return on your track which your present remarks seem to indicate, I freely forgive you, even to the extent of sending you my new book as soon as it comes out, and I trust you will like it.

The hoax was a bit of fun, but the way you pushed the hoax—ah, well, permit me to quote from the immortal Emanuel:

Asparagus is feathery and tall
And the hose lies rotting by the garden wall.

The only question is whose hose.

Sincerely yours,

Miss Lowell was clearly relieved that the New Poetry, in her eyes the "most national" thing that America had to offer, along with skyscrapers and ice water, was still hers to command: Ezra Pound she had already dismissed and there *was* no Emanuel Morgan. While she continued a friendly correspondence for some time with Witter Bynner, she never really forgave him; he became her "official enemy." When the Ayscough-Lowell correspondence was published in 1946, Witter Bynner realized for the first time the full extent of her bitterness toward him. She did not forgive, and she did not forget; *Spectra* apparently haunted her for some time. In September 1922, she published anonymously *A Critical Fable*, patterned on her cousin James Russell Lowell's *A Fable for Critics*. It was intended as a kind of light "peripatetic, poetic 'Who's Who,' " but much of it is little better than doggerel. Miss Lowell tried to spread the rumor that Leonard Bacon had really written it. She even went so far as to write to a relative of his that he must be lying if he denied it. Conrad Aiken accused her of being the author, and remarked, when she refused to confess, "Well, since you persist that you didn't write it, I can say what I really think of it. I think it's damn rotten!" When Louis Untermeyer wrote to say that he suspected her, she replied that she suspected him. Despite a somewhat unfavorable self-portrait, based on the contemporary image of her as a public figure, "bronco-bursting with rainbows," few people were deceived. Her attempt to have the book placed on the recommended reading list for women's clubs prepared by the *Bookman Magazine* (she acted as chairman of the journal's poetry committee) also failed. The truth was soon out; and she turned to the more serious matter of her biography of Keats. Her own hoax had been less successful than *Spectra*.

Others in the Spectric audience also spoke up after the exposé. The Harvard undergraduate who had asked Emanuel Morgan whether or not he was a Spectrist now wrote to Witter Bynner a letter that began: "You infernal humbug . . ." (It should be noted, however, that this young poet, Royall S. Snow, had written in the first place to Emanuel Morgan at the suggestion of Witter Bynner.) The answer of most editors was not that the result would have been the same whatever the writers had presented, but rather that the hoax worked because Witter Bynner and Arthur Davison Ficke had written better than they knew and that the joke was not on the editors nor on the public but on themselves. "The disclosure would be a good joke on the public," commented *Reedy's Mirror* of 24 May 1918, "were it not for the fact that the burlesque poetry is more successful than the authors' serious work. To make matters worse, Emanuel Morgan continues to write after being exposed as somebody else—talk about a Frankenstein monster!" Alfred Kreymborg maintained —and he repeated the judgment later in his critical work *Our*

Singing Strength—that the Spectrist poems of Emanuel Morgan and Anne Knish were superior to anything that Bynner and Ficke had published under their own names. The publication of additional poems by Elijah Hay and Emanuel Morgan in the December 1918 issue of *Others* seemed to bear out his belief that the Spectrists had every right to exist, no matter what they called themselves.

Bynner and Ficke were ready to admit that, to some extent, the joke was on themselves. Shortly after the disclosure, Witter Bynner commented sadly that he could not get rid of Emanuel Morgan. "I find now that I write like him without the slightest effort—I don't know where he leaves off and I begin. He's a boomerang! Why, Ficke and I never attracted half the attention with our serious bona fide work that we did with this piece of fooling. Just as he was leaving for France Ficke said to me—and there was a distinct note of grief in his voice: 'Do you know, some of my best work is in *Spectra*.' " And much later, reviewing the whole episode, he said that some people still thought that Ficke and he had written better as Knish and Morgan and added, "Once in a while we think so ourselves." To this, Arthur Davison Ficke's unpublished retort was, "This is inaccurate; we never think that, as applied to *our own poetry;* but we thoroughly think it about *each other's.*"

Naturally those who found Knish and Morgan superior to Ficke and Bynner lost no time in finding reasons, psychological as well as literary. Arthur J. Eddy, in a letter to *Reedy's Mirror*, wrote that anyone familiar with Freudian psychology would realize that the writers had revealed the *"real* Bynner" and the *"real* Ficke because they had let themselves go and had not permitted, in Freudian terms, the "conscious censor" to intervene. The two were betrayed as "more human, more natural, more hail-fellow-well-met than their serious verse indicated them to be; and by conventional standards their serious verse is good—good but *conscious*, while their burlesques are the gleeful outpourings of their unrestrained, boyish selves. Their burlesques are their own while their serious verse is largely *literature*—traditional."

Indeed, whatever their first intention had been, the writers did learn something from their "experiments" about the nature of poetic composition. Of *Spectra* Marjorie Allen Seiffert wrote later to Vincent Starrett, "It was basically a joke, but subbasically it loosened up our styles, injected a lively sense of irony into our poetry, and did us all a lot of good; or so it seems to me." And later in a letter to me she has said, "I look back upon *Spectra* as a delightful mousetrap, carefully designed by Hal Bynner and Arthur Ficke to catch the 'Neos' and in which they themselves were neatly caught. Some of their best writing was spectric from that time on." William Carlos Williams, also recalling the episode, wrote to me, "As far as I remember I was completely taken in by the hoax and while not subscribing in every case to the excellence of the poems admired them as a whole quite sincerely. Marjorie Allen Seiffert especially became my friend. . . . I have always thought that the forcing of the mind, the making it take some artificial hurdles, purely invented, got it into a mode which is the essence of poetic invention itself—pure fantasy itself which is the essence of *A Midsummer Night's Dream*—or any poetic invention. Many of us never achieve such an escape from this world."

The career of Emanuel Morgan, after his exposure, provides a curious footnote. Although he published *The Beloved Stranger* (as *Songs of the Unknown Lover*) in *Reedy's Mirror* 1918 and later in book form in 1919 under his own name, Witter Bynner wrote it "as Emanuel Morgan." There was irony in the fact that the introduction to this volume was written by William Marion Reedy, one of the first to express enthusiasm for Morgan. The book contains a number of genuinely beautiful lyrics that reflect the freedom Bynner had attained under the Morgan mask. In one, "Self-Portrait," omitted from the published sequence but quoted by William Marion Reedy in his preface, Emanuel Morgan, as Witter Bynner's Doppelgänger, is revealed in a kind of shadowy and humorous self-denial:

> I saw myself sitting at the next table,
> But only in profile;
> The mettle of color was there
> On the cheekbone,
> And the little crepe moustache
> Though not black enough,
> And the lower lip
> Drooping like a rope in water,
> And the nose curving to ruin like the Chinese wall
> With its little dark gates of old life . . .
>
> But when the full face turned,
> I knew again
> That there was no such person.

Humor is not absent from *Pins for Wings*, published by the Sunwise Turn in New York in 1920, the only subsequent volume to appear under the name of Emanuel Morgan. Here the "spectra" of many of Morgan's contemporaries are recorded with true "spectric" accuracy; many of the "pins," which hold the wings to the board, seem sparklingly pointed:

GERTRUDE STEIN

Wings rotting
under water

CONRAD AIKEN

phosphorescent
plumbing

ROBINSON JEFFERS

Aimée Semple McPherson
in a thunderstorm

H. D.

the Winged Victory
hopping

Thereafter Emanuel Morgan remained silent until 1927, when
a group of his posthumous poems appeared in the anthology
American Caravan with the accompanying announcement that
on hearing that Anne Knish had died of an obscure disease at
Budapest, Emanuel Morgan had committed suicide at a Pittsburgh sanitarium. In a concluding "Fragment" we are given
what were apparently his final words:

> Whether I be a mountain to climb
> Or a puddle to look into—
> Look,
> Take your time.

Copies of *Spectra* have been for many years collectors'
items. Recalling the hoax in an article in the *Saturday Review*
of 7 October 1939, Leonard Bacon said that it was truly magnificent and the best thing that ever came out of the Imagist
movement. In a letter to the magazine Arthur Davison Ficke
then wrote: "We all thought the thing rather a lark at the time;
and if the passage of two decades has tarnished the lark's wings
a bit, let us not forget that everybody concerned regarded the
episode as of a degree of unimportance which is somewhat belied
by later discussion of it." He seemed with this to be forgetting
what he had said some years earlier:

When we invented the Spectric School, both of us were
genuinely indignant at the charlatanism of some of the

new "schools" of poetry; and it was with the most deadly intentions that we made our attempt to render their "schools" patently ridiculous. We had great fun doing it—but back of the fun was an intensity of malice which Bynner does not explain. We who devoted our whole lives to poetry were angry and indignant on seeing apes and mountebanks prancing in the Temple. We had learned quite well that poetry is not as easy as that.

The statements are not, I think, really contradictory. It would be wrong to exaggerate the importance of *Spectra*, for that would be to deny its basic nature: it was indeed a lark, but the poets all the same did make their point.

THREE

EVERYBODY loves a hoax except, of course, the people who are hoaxed, and no one seems to want it to come to an end once it has started; like the old-fashioned movie serial, it has always to be continued. The story of *Spectra* should end here; but true to classical form, it must end where it began, and so it does. Very soon after the hoax broke in 1918, Witter Bynner, then a member of the English department at the University of California at Berkeley, received a letter from Candor, New York. It read:

My dear Mr. Bynner: I venture to write you to express my profound admiration of your book *Grenstone Poems*. Although knowing as I do that you must move in the best literary circles, you probably will not care much for homage of one you have never met. I got your book out of the free library at Owego and read it all through that night and I like it very much though I do not understand it all. It gives you such a picture of life. Now, Mr. Bynner, what I want

213

to say is this: I write some and I feel I write different from most. When my mother was married she had the poems of Whittier and Willis and I knew them almost by heart. But when I read your book I saw how different it was. I did not think they were writing such good poetry today.

There is no one here who I can show my poems to. All my friends would laugh and their [*sic*] not the kind of poems to show the preacher because sometimes I fear I am not as strong in my faith as I should. Not that I am wicked, though my poems may sound that way which I know you will understand. I always hoped someday I would get to the city for the schooling I need. But I felt I had to stay on the farm and help out my folks.

And now I am drafted and have to leave next week. This seems to cut off all that my life has been. Before I go I would like to have the opinion of someone I feel knows what poetry is on my poems which enclosed please find. Please say what you think because I know they are not as elegant as they would be if I put more time on them but I feel I should write about what I know.

The letter, signed by a certain Earl Roppel, contained a sheaf of poems. The first one, entitled "Moon Light," was accompanied by the note, "This is one I wrote after reading your book":

> Last night when I was in our surrey,
>   Driving home with my best girl,
> I saw the moon run down the fence-row
>   Like a fat squirrel.

Another commented on the impact of the war on his pastoral existence:

> The Germans murder sailor lads
>   On the seas.
> But here I only hear the birds
>   In the trees.

214

Today when I came to the house
   From the sowing
My little sister said to me,
   "Are you going?"

And last night when I sat with Lucy
   In the yard,
She said the same. But does she know
   It is so hard.

To this Mr. Roppel had added: "Of course, Lucy isn't a real name." "Memories" was a cameo portrait of the poet's mother:

I think of my mother
As moving toward the kitchen door,
The dirty water circling in her dishpan.
Yet I find she possessed
A book with flower-stained leaves.

And then there was a picture of himself after the long day of farm toil:

At night I sit beside the stove,
   So tired I cannot see.
But at my plowing all the day
   The great thoughts come to me.

They say that men have dreampt [*sic*] strange dreams
   In mansions in the city,
And I am not so rich as they,
   Nor am I half so witty.

Yet all the day in the hot sun
   Visions come crowding strong as death,
As sweet as those that Jesus had
   When he was young at Nazareth.

Bynner showed the poems to his colleagues on the University of California faculty, and they all agreed with him that they displayed a freshness and sincerity that Robert Burns himself might have admired. The prize poem of the lot was one that drew the special attention of Professor Arthur Farwell of the University Department of Music. He promptly set it to music and later had it sung in San Francisco by a chorus of three thousand trained voices. Professor Farwell was quoted at the time as saying that the work, entitled "Sunset," was the best patriotic song-poem in America:

> Flag of our country, strong and true,
>   The sky is rosy with your bars;
> But as they fade it turns to blue
>   And radiant with your stars.
>
> And as I watch the setting sun,
>   I call to God apart,
> "Give me the soul of Washington,
>   And give me Lincoln's heart."

Professor Farwell had gone ahead with his venture, rather unethically perhaps, without the author's permission, but this seemed impossible to obtain. Witter Bynner's letters to Earl Roppel in Candor were forwarded to a New York City address, from which they were returned marked "No such person." An inquiry of the library at Owego, ten miles from Candor, brought back the information that, to the best of the librarian's knowledge, no Earl Roppel had ever made use of that institution. People in the San Francisco area began to wonder about the fate of the mysterious poet. Zoë Burns wrote in the San Francisco *Bulletin:*

> Ever since I read the story and some of the work of Witter Bynner's lost poet, I've been wondering what has become of the lad who had such a freshly interesting outlook upon life from the narrow confines of a little New York hamlet and to whom the great dreams came thronging while he plowed

216

the fields. . . . And I'm wondering if the war took that fresh fine almost-girlish sweetness out of him and made him bitter as it has so many of our youths. . . . Was the heart of him smitten by the thunder of war? And the melody of his spirit silenced by its horrors? Was perchance his very life blown out like a candle in the blast?

When he looked closely at the New York address to which the letters had been forwarded, 86 Greenwich Avenue, Witter Bynner began to ask less sentimental rhetorical questions; he now suspected that all was not right with Earl Roppel. Was it possible that some of his literary colleagues were taking revenge on him for *Spectra*, and was he in turn being hoaxed? He came to think that the culprit was none other than his good friend Edna St. Vincent Millay; but it was not until 1920, when an article signed by Malcolm Cowley appeared in the *Literary Review* of the New York *Evening Post*, that the truth was finally known about Earl Roppel of Candor, New York, the "bard of the rushing Catatonk."

Malcolm Cowley related how two young poets (later identified as himself and his friend S. Foster Damon), finding themselves on the afternoon of 15 June 1918, on the banks of the Catatonk, had sat down and composed the best of Earl Roppel's poems within an hour. They conceived of the idea because they had been impressed by the success of *Spectra* and wanted to see if the hoaxer could not be hoaxed, and also because they wanted to ridicule certain common poetic abuses: "false simplicity, easy quatrains, and rhymes like 'girl' and 'squirrel,' 'roses' and 'posies,' 'bowers' and 'flowers.' " Malcolm Cowley in his account of the episode says that the following poem shows the bard of Candor "in his tenderest posture":

> The fields are full of daisies,
> And Joe-Pye weed so juicy,
> And where the yellow maize is,
> I weave a crown for Lucy

Of buttercups and violets,
Arnica and wild roses,
And Quaker-lady eyelets,
And other lovely posies.

But Lucy will not hear me.
She wants expensive flowers,
Such as do not grow near me,
But live in hothouse bowers.

Mr. Cowley had given Earl Roppel his name and invented his personality; Mr. Damon had written the patriotic lines sung by the huge choir in San Francisco. The two men had sent letters and poems from Earl Roppel not only to Witter Bynner but also to Conrad Aiken and Amy Lowell. Bynner's letter did not, because of a post-office error, reach the young men (the New York address they had given was that of Kenneth Burke, who was to handle Roppel's correspondence after Mr. Cowley and Mr. Damon had left for the war). Mr. Aiken's and Miss Lowell's did; and both of them were taken in as Bynner had been. In his reply Mr. Aiken was critical but helpful, and advised the young poet to read Keats and Tennyson. He later sent him an inscribed copy of Palgrave's *Golden Treasury*, dated 8 July 1918. Amy Lowell was even more enthusiastic than Conrad Aiken, and volunteered to get some of Earl's poems published in *Poetry*. Miss Lowell told him that in no matter what camp he was sent to he would find the books of the leading contemporary American poets (she had contributed them herself). "He has the modern spirit," she told Foster Damon, her young protégé later at dinner; "I don't know where he got it, but he has it." "She did not tell me that he had been reading her books at the Owego Free Library," Mr. Damon remarks, "nor did I tell her that one of the poems I had written was deliberately in her style." (This was probably the one that ended with the invocation: "O Venice! Masks! Stilettoes!") When Miss Lowell discovered that Earl Roppel did not exist, she thought it a fine joke. "Not impossibly," Mr. Damon comments, "because there was no publicity." When Mr. Damon was working some years later on Amy Lowell's biography, he came across Earl's letter, long since forgotten, and found it decidedly moving —until he came to the signature.

Of Earl Roppel Malcolm Cowley wrote later to Witter Bynner: "Finally—as you yourself found in burlesque—we began to put too much of ourselves into him. Requiescat." And at another time he added that when he was in Paris, Allan MacDougal showed him a letter from Witter Bynner in which he was convinced that Roppel was a hoax, and concluded with the question, *"Can it be Edna?"* Edna Millay was at the time enjoying an apéritif at a neighboring table. "The more I think of Roppel," said Mr. Cowley rather wistfully, "the more I am sorry he died before his book was published."

And so, as in a folk tale, was the trickster tricked; and what could have been more appropriate from both a literary and a democratic point of view than to have the very sophisticated Emanuel Morgan meet his match in a supposed country bumpkin? And what more classical irony could there have been than the fact that Malcolm Cowley, one of the men behind the mask, was *really* from Pittsburgh?

FOUR

MANUEL MORGAN and Anne Knish were joined in the pantheon of fictitious twentieth-century poets some time later by two charming writers with equally implausible names—Ern Malley, a young Australian garage mechanic, and Fern Gravel, a small-town Iowa girl. Malley was the creation in 1944 of two talented poets, Harold Stewart and James McAuley, in Sydney, Australia. Stewart and McAuley invented Ern Malley while serving in the Australian Army to hoax the leading Australian literary magazine, *Angry Penguins*, and its editor, Max Harris, as well as the whole modern poetic school. Mr. Harris in the Autumn 1944 issue of *Angry Penguins* devoted thirty pages to the posthumous works of Ern Malley, whom he proclaimed a giant of contemporary Australian poetry. One of his coeditors said that Malley "worked through a disciplined and restrained kind of statement into the deepest wells of human experience." The Ern Malley cult spread immediately to the United States; some of his poems were included in a selection of Australian verse made by the American poet Harry

Roskolenko, for a special issue of the magazine *Voices*. The biography of Ern Malley made even greater demands on credibility than that of either Morgan or Knish. He came out to Australia after World War I—so Max Harris reported—with his mother and sister and left school to become a garage mechanic in Sydney at the age of fourteen; at seventeen he left his job and went to live in the Melbourne slums, where he earned a few pounds as an insurance salesman and a watch repairman. When called up for military service, he was discovered to be suffering from Graves' disease, and he left a description of the terrible ravages of this disease in his last months; he died in 1943. "Knowing that he faced almost certain death before his twenty-fifth year," Mr. Harris wrote, "Malley set about his experiment. He amassed a diverse but beautifully integrated body of erudition over the three or four years, so that his poetry possesses a richness and breadth of vocabulary which is quite amazing. He threw off everything which would weaken his struggle to produce a cool, unimpassioned interpretation of the conflict between his mind and vision and the prospect of immediate death." He left Melbourne and a young girl with whom he was very much in love and composed the sixteen poems that he entitled "The Darkening Ecliptic"; they bore as an epigraph the "old proverb":

Do not speak of secret matters in a field full of little hills.

Mr. Harris praised the "quiet humor" of Ern Malley's poems, as when he speaks of

A man's inalienable right to be sad at his own funeral.

Ern Malley's biography had been composed, along with the entire manuscript of his poems, in a single afternoon by Corporal Stewart and Lieutenant McAuley. The poems were produced from a collection of books, including the *Oxford Dic-*

tionary of Quotations, which happened to be on their desks; the only principle governing the selection was that no two consecutive lines would make sense. Three lines of one poem were lifted intact from an American report on the drainage of breeding grounds of mosquitoes. Here is one complete poem, entitled "Night-Piece (Alternate Version)":

> The intemperate torch grazed
> With fire the umbrel of the dark.
> The pond-lilies could not stifle
> The green descant of frogs.
>
> We had not heeded the warning
> That the iron birds creaked.
> As we swung the park-gates
> Their beaks glinted with dew.
>
> A splash—the silver nymph
> Was a foam lake in the night.
> But though the careful winds
> Visited our trembling flesh
> They carried no echo.

The authors stated that their experiment had shown that "literary fashion can be so hypnotically powerful that it can suspend the operation of critical intelligence." The Malley poems were a montage of striking and unrelated phrases—they abound in words like "umbrel" and "descant"—chosen at random; but the authors found that, like the Spectrists, they could not help putting some sense into the nonsense.

When the Ern Malley issue of *Angry Penguins* was seized by the Australian police on the grounds of obscenity (the poet's way of expressing himself in a number of instances had been fairly forthright), the poems became a *cause célèbre* which ended ultimately on the floor of the Australian parliament. In support of his critical judgment in printing the manuscript, Max

Harris produced testimonials as to its merit from leading British literary figures, including T. S. Eliot and Sir Herbert Read. Corporal Stewart and Lieutenant McAuley, they maintained, had wrought better than they knew, and the joke was on them.

The career of Fern Gravel, the Iowa child poetess, was equally luminous and touching; and some six years were to elapse after her original publication before it was revealed that she had come into being not in the Midwest but on a beach in Tahiti. In 1940 the Prairie Press of Muscatine, Iowa, issued a volume called *Oh Millersville!* The name of the author was given as "Fern Gravel"; but an introductory note to the book revealed that this was not her real name but the pen name she had chosen when in an Iowa town that she called Millersville she scribbled out the poems in the early years of the century at the ages of nine, ten, and eleven. Although secretive about her poetry, Fern was supposed to have had an adult confidant to whom she sent her compositions as quickly as she turned them out, and who had taken the trouble to preserve them. They were being printed now with the consent of the "authoress," who, "until recently reminded, had all but forgotten that she had ever been 'inspired.' "

And inspired indeed she had been, to judge by the response of the reviewers of *Oh Millersville!*—all of whom seem to have reacted to the exclamation point of the title as to a hypodermic needle. "We have found the lost Sappho of Iowa!" exclaimed the New York *Times*. "So good that it hurts!" echoed the Washington *Post*, "Fern Gravel never dreamed that she was writing social history." *Time* was somewhat more guarded but none the less enthusiastic. "Every so often," it said in its issue of 13 January 1941, "some precocity in pigtails mesmerizes a U. S. publisher into printing her verse creations. The resultant rash on the nation's body poetic generally passes away as soon as the publisher's advertising appropriation has been spent. *Oh Millersville!* is a collection of juvenilia that no American will want to see pass away." The poems of Fern Gravel were, according to

Time, "as good examples of deadpan lyricism as have ever been printed." (With this remark it was perhaps covering itself if the work proved to be a hoax.) The Detroit *Free Press* found the book full of charming humor, excellent as history and not bad as a source book for child psychologists, and moreover as "important in its way as in a far different way was *Spoon River Anthology*." "It's rather early to be saying a book will be one of the most unusual and charming of the year," said the Philadelphia *Inquirer* early in 1941, "but here we are, out on a limb and unafraid. Long after 1942, we think, you'll remember this book with a good warm feeling and a smile."

Warmth was the quality stressed by most reviewers. "There is so warm a feeling of validity about these verses, and so accurate a sense of individual character," wrote no less a figure than poet Paul Engle in the Des Moines *Register*, "that their impact is far stronger than a simple amusement at childish simplicity." Iowa had apparently taken Fern to its heart, but New England was no less receptive. The well-known poet John Holmes wrote in the Boston *Transcript*, "The book is amazing, amusing, full of the human scene, and not to be missed, because there can't be another like it in the world." Fern Gravel seemed indeed to have fulfilled the prophecy expressed in "Before the Looking-Glass," the concluding poem of her book:

> I almost never look at myself
> Except when I am brushing my hair.
> I know, of course, that I am not pretty
> But I do not really care.
>
> I am not going to get married;
> I expect to travel,
> And people will come to hear the lectures
> Of the famous Fern Gravel.
>
> That is how I will make my living;
> I will not have any special home.

I will live in hotels in the different cities
Where only my intimate friends can come.

And I will be the authoress
Of many many books.
If I am famous for my lectures and poetry
It won't matter so much about my looks.

Oh Millersville! proved in the end to be exactly what its publisher claimed it to be, "a priceless item of Americana," but for reasons other than those expressed by its early readers. In an article entitled "Fern Gravel: A Hoax and a Confession," published in the September 1946 issue of the *Atlantic Monthly*, James Norman Hall told the truth about the Sappho of Iowa.

One of the late novelist's most vivid memories of his childhood was as a boy of five or six holding hands with other children and dancing in a ring. The song he remembered hearing the children sing was:

> Green gravel, green gravel,
> The grass is so green!
> The fairest young lady
> That ever was seen.

And the vision remained with him for years afterwards. In 1938 a friend in Tahiti lent him a copy of *Precious Bane* by Mary Webb, and in it he found the complete song:

> Green gravel, green gravel, the grass is so green!
> The fairest young lady that ever was seen.
> I'll wash you in milk, and clothe you in silk
> And write down your name with a gold pen and ink.

He then read through the whole book, and a few nights later had a dream in which he saw himself again in the Iowa town of his youth, but as a man, not as a child; the occasion was the same remembered afternoon and the children were dancing in a circle and singing as before. This time they sang, however, instead of "*green* gravel," "*Fern* Gravel." Among the children was a small girl he remembered named Fern; her face was "plain and slightly freckled, and her hair was braided in two tight pigtails . . . a solemn little thing, with large dark eyes, and she had a decisive way of stepping as though she knew at all times exactly where she was going and why; even in a singing game when she wasn't going anywhere." In the dream all the singers vanished and Hall was back again in Tahiti, and still with Fern, persistent little thing that she was. "The song is about me," she said, "and I want you to write down my name with a gold pen and ink." She added that her home was Omillersville. "O" in Tahitian means "it is"; and he concluded that she must be saying, "It is Millersville." Fern was surely thinking of Mitchellville, Iowa, a few miles from the place where Hall had grown up. "Call it *Oh Millersville!*" said Fern, "with an exclamation point! They're nearly all about Millersville." And apparently, as soon as he was wide enough awake to fetch his gold pen and ink, he wrote down the poems just as Fern dictated them, right from the opening lines:

> Millersville, oh, Millersville!
> That is my home and I like it, but still
> I wish that once in a while I could go
> To cities like Omaha and St. Jo.
> You get tired of living in such a small town
> With so few streets for walking around.
> I would like to visit some larger places
> And see many thousands of different faces
> Of people I do not know at all
> That you cannot see in a town so small.

Boredom is Fern Gravel's theme certainly:

> From one end of the town clear to the other
> Is only about half a mile.

226

We don't have any excitement
Except once in a long long while.

When anything does happen, such as a piano concert by Blind
Boone, the Negro pianist, or the suicide of Mr. Reasoner, whose
wife stayed away too long in Des Moines, or the visit of William
Jennings Bryan, Fern records it all in lines as lumbering as the
wheels of a slow Iowa freight. One of her most distinguished
efforts is her ode to Pears' soap:

Of the different kinds of soap, the one I like so well
Is Pears' soap because of its wonderful smell.
In this town only one family
Use this soap that smells so beautiful to me.
It is in the Smouses' lovely home.
Whenever Mrs. Smouse has me come
To spend the night, when Mr. Smouse is away,
I often wish I could always stay.
The first thing I do is wash my hands and face,
Their bathroom is such a wonderful place;
It is as large as my bedroom at home, almost.
I couldn't even guess what it must have cost.
The soap they use in the Commercial hotel
Is awful; it has a horrible smell.
Sometimes we have our Sunday dinner there,
And the smell of their soap I can hardly bear.
It is of different colors, blue and green,
And their roller towels are never clean.
Our soap at home is much better than theirs,
But there is not any soap in this world like Pears'.

The force of nostalgia is such that those who remembered liking
Pears' soap were ready to hail any kind of doggerel that set forth
its virtues. After Hall had made his revelation, he was attacked
by many of the readers who had given their hearts to the prairie

poetess. One woman wrote, "You are a criminal—you have destroyed Fern."

Another poet, invented by one of the enthusiastic reviewers of the work of Fern Gravel, could not, as it happened, be so easily destroyed. During the fall and winter of 1939–1940, at the time John Holmes, as poetry reviewer, was writing his praise of Fern Gravel for the Boston *Transcript*, the editor of the book pages, Howard Mumford Jones, decided that his name and that of Holmes and Charles B. Palmer, the feature writer on the paper, were appearing too frequently on the Wednesday and Saturday book pages. Another reviewer was needed, and since one could not be hired, one had to be invented. At a staff conference called to decide the subject, when none of the gentlemen had come up with a satisfactory name, Miss Margaret Clark, the staff secretary, suggested Gurney Preston, or Preston Gurney. The name caught Jones's fancy; and Miss Clark explained that it was a combination of her middle name and the middle name of the young lady who reviewed murder mysteries.

Thus Preston Gurney came into being, and during the following months he worked hard for the *Transcript*, signing columns and reviewing books; his name appeared also on the list of authors of books received. Holmes, in his weekly column, "Poetry Now," gradually made Gurney a poet, lamenting the fact that he had been so neglected in recent years and quoting his verses. Preston Gurney became a very real character in the offices of the newspaper, where a faked signed photograph of him hung on the wall.

One day when John Holmes stopped at Goodspeed's Bookshop, under the Old South Church, to pick up some books he had ordered, the clerk presented him with a greenbound volume that he said was sure to interest him. It was entitled *Poems*, and its author was Preston Gurney. Holmes thought the *Transcript* people were carrying the joke a bit far, but upon investigation he discovered that the book was authentic: there had been a Preston Gurney, a Baptist minister and a benefactor of Brown

228

University, where the literary prizes that he had established were still awarded annually, an amateur poet who had published, at Wollaston, Massachusetts, in 1901, a volume called *Briers of Wild Rose,* and whose poems were no worse than those that Holmes had attributed to him. He had the advantage, however, of not having to be invented; he had really existed.

Why bad poets should ever be invented when so many exist in the first place may be difficult to answer. John Holmes had his practical reasons; and the motive of James Norman Hall in launching the career of Fern Gravel was clearly different from that of either Bynner and Ficke or Stewart and McAuley. His story of the genesis of *Oh Millersville!* has the ring of truth to it, although the vagueness of certain details and the strong nostalgic air of the verses suggest that there were perhaps a few empty bottles in the background. The way had been prepared for Fern, in any case, by the vogue at the time for such child geniuses as Nathalia Crane and Hilda Conkling, who were real enough; and the framework of the hoax, the discovery of a grown woman's childhood effusions, was the one used earlier by J. M. Barrie in his presentation of *The Young Visiters,* by his fictitious nine-year-old genius, "Daisy Ashford." And the predilection of the public for bad poetry, whether written by a Hungarian woman named Anne Knish who had previously expressed herself only in Russian, or by a young Iowa girl named Fern Gravel who had not yet learned English, was equally strong.

FIVE

Spectra is not so much a parody of any one individual style—although certainly Amy Lowell comes in for her share of the barbs—as it is of the style of a whole period; and it is partly as a period piece that it holds our attention today. Naturally much of Spectric verse, with its intimations of free love and drunkenness, its suggestions of French heels, bobbed hair, the noise of trolley cars, and the dance of Isadora Duncan, its use of words such as "cocktail," "cigarette," and "sin," appears far less daring now than it did in its own time. And yet it holds our attention not only because it recalls an exciting period but also because it satirizes certain poetic poses that are still very much with us. It is burlesque as well as parody: some of the looniest lines went some time ago into our anthologies of light verse and there they will remain; we do not need to know all the background of the era to appreciate the best of the nonsense. Some of the verses are very funny indeed, some are not funny at all; some are good bad poetry, and some are just plain bad. The whole of Spectra, as well as the best of

230

Emanuel Morgan's verse that followed, communicates the spirit of fun that went into its composition, a spirit that would have a salutary effect on poetry in any day. How it could have been taken seriously may be difficult to see, but then Knish and Morgan had woven quite a net.

Anne Knish sets the tone of the volume with the opening poem, *Opus 50*, with its lines:

> I think I must have been born in such a forest,
> Or in the tangle of a Chinese screen.

The keynote is sounded—the piano playing, the obscure quivering of lights, the voices of the subconscious working their way through the colors of the spectrum. The tangle of the screen suggests also the combination of light and shade weaving throughout the verses—the *chinoiserie* around which the hoax is constructed. Indeed, the Oriental comes in for quite a play, especially in such verses as *Opus 118*, a delightful offhand, backhand take-off on the whole Chinese manner that was coming into vogue with the Imagists. Anne Knish emerges in the volume as the earth-woman, the sibyl uttering endless oracular proclamations. She hates housecleaning and domesticity; she loathes her husband, the "sodden thing" sleeping upstairs; she loves jade. She is repelled by everything that smacks of the bourgeois: she is not only disgusted with love, with herself, she is also disgusted with her readers. Those who live in glass houses should not throw stones, but she is ready to throw them herself at her own glass house, her spectric palace. She is prepared to pull the carpet out from under everything, even if it means herself with it. Anne Knish is, in short, the shrill and insistent poetess full of vim and venom; and she is always with us. Arthur Davison Ficke keeps his eye fixed on the type of person he is parodying; and the absurdity of the high-flown lines gives him ample opportunity for humor. Because of his own interest in the plastic arts, he has great fun with Anne Knish's vocabulary. Her use of such words as "plexus," "focus," "nimbus," and "refracting" bears out the

Spectric language of the preface; and her attempts at composing the purely "abstract" poem by merely using geometric terms is as much a take-off on the art jargon of the time as it is on the Imagists. Although Ficke uses some of Amy Lowell's language —"cathedral spires," "gargoyles," and other words that recall her *Sword Blades and Poppy Seeds* (1914)—his treatment of her is more of Amy Lowell the public figure, the Imagist dictator, who often spoke about literary matters as if (in the words of Witter Bynner) "she were addressing the foreman of a gang," than it is of Amy Lowell the poet.

Both Anne Knish and Emanuel Morgan have a decided predilection for violence throughout the book, and this in itself may partly account for its successful reception. Anne Knish evokes the soothsayer in Rome inspecting the "purple entrails of victims," and Emanuel Morgan asks that his beloved pound him with a volcano stone until "the true blood pricks through the paint." In their taste for disaster, they call to mind Julia Moore, the Sweet Singer of Michigan, who delighted in such subjects as the Chicago fire, the Ashtabula train disaster, and the yellow fever epidemic in the South. (Bill Nye said of Julia Moore that she was "worse than a Gatling gun": "I have counted twenty-one killed and nine wounded, in the small volume she has given to the public.")

Emanuel Morgan is, as he would have to be as a foil for the "tempestuous" Knish, somewhat more restrained and more lyrical: for him the heart, which "finds epics on the breast-bone of a chicken/And lyrics under the lettuce," is everything. He is "the stag with the golden horn" waiting till his day is born; and he is "beset by liking so many people." He is frustrated in love and in his expression of it, and is "blinded by the sweetness of the locust tree." His soul shines; and he thanks God that he can laugh:

> Eve laughed at Adam long ago,
> And Adam laughed at her.

He is also more in touch with the current scene, the theater and the dance, the "distance Isadoran." Laughter for him "will do for kindling." The later Morgan becomes more resigned and perhaps more quotidian; the gulls then look "more like lima beans." Morgan's poetic forte is bathos—what D. B. Wyndham Lewis in his introduction to *The Stuffed Owl* has called the most obvious and predominating trait of good Bad Verse, "that sudden slip and swoop and slither as down a well-buttered slide, from the peaks into the abyss." Bynner's part in the volume is not parody so much as burlesque of the entire romantic mode. When Emanuel Morgan does not succeed, he reads like a parody of A. E. Housman or of Witter Bynner himself; when he does, he writes delightful nonsense that exists on its own merits quite apart from anything else, as in:

> If I were only dafter
> I might be making hymns
> To the liquor of your laughter
> And the lacquer of your limbs.

or in *The Blind Pig*, written some time after the hoax:

> What if he bring us
> Another one? Can he?
> Apple-pie order, a prune for your granny!
>
> Your words are Choctaw,
> Mine Hindoostanee—
> Apple-pie order, a grin for your granny!

Emanuel Morgan's *Opus 41*, which catches all the colors of the spectrum, contains the delightful Firbankian line:

> With a beaded fern you waved away a gnat . . .

which reminds us that *Spectra* appeared in the same year as *Inclinations* of Ronald Firbank. Readers have always been attracted to the seeming profundity of what they cannot understand, whether in poetry or painting; pure nonsense has its charms for adults as for children. And so Mr. Morgan's spectric humor triumphed in its own peculiar way.

While *Spectra* was merely a joke, it did much to clear the air of the stuffiness that tends to gather about literature when it loses its sense of humor and earnest but lumbering personalities take over. Its influence was healthful and more serious perhaps than one would at first suppose. Witter Bynner profited, of course, from his own joke, carrying Spectric humor over into his subsequent work; and there were others who may have benefited as well. Witter Bynner had known Wallace Stevens at Harvard, and both he and his collaborator admired Stevens's work. When "Sunday Morning" first appeared in *Poetry*, Arthur Davison Ficke wrote to Harriet Monroe that it tantalized him "with the sense that perhaps it's the most beautiful poem ever written." In the original draft of the Anne Knish preface, now in the Yale Library, is a passage at the very end, referring to the Spectric method, which was dropped in the printed version. "Poe used it in 'Ulalume', and to a lesser degree, in 'Helen, thy beauty is to me'," it reads. "Among recent poets, apart from a small clan soon to be heard from, we have noted only one who can be regarded in any sure sense as a Spectrist. This one is Wallace Stevens. In his work appears a subtle but doubtless unconscious application of our method; and though a certain antiquation of touch prevents him from being fully classifiable as a Spectrist, it must be admitted that his work is by implication related to ours, a fact which we gladly acknowledge."

The passage was too serious for inclusion in the preface; but on Anne Knish's list of writers and critics who received complimentary copies of the volume appeared the name of Wallace Stevens. There is no record of Stevens's acknowledgment of the book, but as one of the few poets of the time possessing a real sense of humor, he must surely have enjoyed it. And it seems even possible that he found sense in the nonsense. For was he not engaged in carrying Cubism over seriously into poetry, just as

the Spectrists had done jokingly? In *Harmonium,* first published
in 1923, we find a mingling of nonsense and sense and a use of
"color" words reminiscent of Anne Knish: the colors of the
poet's spectrum appear to have come to proper focus in the work
of Wallace Stevens.

The situation in poetry today is not unlike that which prevailed in 1916 when *Spectra* made its appearance; it is a boom
time. There has been less talk of schools than there was then, but
only because the word "school" has gone out in favor of the
word "generation." A new "generation" comes into being every
month or so. The Beat Generation has replaced the Silent Generation overnight; and the center of poetic activity has moved
farther west. The San Francisco poets are in the news today just
as the Pittsburgh poets were some forty years ago (they have
been, as were the Spectrists, the darlings of the columnists) ; and
oddly enough they share many of the same traits. Speaking of
the youngest group of poets, Kenneth Rexroth says, "They are
all interested in Far Eastern art and religion; some even call
themselves Buddhists." Jack Kerouac speaks of the "New Poetry" as "a kind of new-old Zen lunacy poetry." The Orient
also attracted the Spectrists; and one is reminded of the response
of Louis V. Ledoux, a young poet and art collector, who wrote
to Emanuel Morgan, "Some of the poems, quite naturally, appeal to me more than others do, but in most of them is that
curious Oriental quality that interested me especially because
that particular Orientalism is unusual in our literature."

Although the Spectrists were more restrained in their references to their personal behavior, there was a certain aura of
free love and sin that surrounded them, and a certain aggres-
siveness and violence that characterized their self-expression.
Their antics, of course, seem mild in comparison with the
belches, sexual grunts, and general incoherent exhibitionism of
the "New Poetry" of today; but the wild rambling of recent
poetic manifestoes, stripped of the shock value of their reiterated

four-letter words, is perhaps only the Spectric theory of Anne Knish carried to its extreme, just as the excesses of the Abstract Expressionists might be said to be merely an attempt of the artist to respond to his own spectres, the "light of infinite existence falling on the spectrum," his own mystic vision. The language of the Spectric introduction seems mild in comparison also with that used by some art critics in speaking of certain of these paintings, one of which was recently described as "haunted, like the shining skin of an opulent eggplant by the clay-colored echo of a final and unbreakable promise."

The question of authenticity in art is a very complex one; and there is no doubt that in poetry, as in painting, fakes are often vociferously acclaimed. Ours is an age of criticism; but their fine-spun theories frequently fail our critics of modern poetry when they are confronted with the simple choice between good and bad. The element of common sense, which should shape all judgment, is today in eclipse. Witter Bynner has written that D. H. Lawrence, who was much amused by *Spectra*, used "to nod occasional assent to my belief that finally only common sense persists with purity and force." Now in poetry when so often dullness triumphs in the guise of novelty, when as Emanuel Morgan put it:

> Fun
> Is the mastodon
> Vanished complete . . .

Spectra is a tonic reminder that it is always both helpful and healthful to laugh.

[1961]

VI

THE POETRY
OF ROBERT
HERRICK

ONE

AFTER suffering complete neglect during the entire
eighteenth century, Robert Herrick regained his
place in the pantheon of English lyric poets. The
nineteenth-century estimate of him seems best summarized by
Swinburne, who said that "he is and will probably be always the
first in rank and station of English songwriters. . . . Elegy or
litany, epicede or epithalamium, his work is always a songwriter's; nothing more, but nothing less, than the work of the
greatest songwriter—as surely as Shakespeare is the greatest
dramatist—ever born of English race." Herrick knew what he
could do, said Swinburne, "a rare and invaluable gift," and having been born a blackbird or a thrush, he did not "take himself
(or try) to be a nightingale." John Masefield said also in 1906
that perhaps no English poet has shown "a more complete mastery of the art of delicate writing." But Masefield is careful to
define Herrick's limitations: "He is never quite 'a man of this
world'. He creates, or adopts, a fictitious world, which one has to
accept in accepting him. The things of that world are the dainty

and luxurious things, which are pleasant to catalogue in dainty verses. The people of that world are either Watteau shepherds or Fragonard nymphs; and in either case they are unreal, but adorable, playthings. . . . He was not a lover of human beings. He was a lover of parts, of points, of separate qualities or beauties." It is this very pleasantness and prettiness that has led in our time not only to a popular acceptance of Herrick but also to a different sort of neglect.

The qualities that make Herrick so delightful a lyricist also seem to make him one of the major English poets least fitted for careful study and critical evaluation. Modern scholars have devoted themselves to the background and sources of his poems, and only recently we have had the first complete critical edition of his work. But critics have paid him little attention for the simple reason that his poems present few difficulties. What is there to discuss or analyze in a poet who writes so simply, so delicately, and so directly? Undergraduates today like him and read him in the same uncritical way that they do a modern poet like E. E. Cummings; and their professors are apt to let them do so and to devote their major efforts of analysis and explication to the more difficult and meatier work of a poet like Donne. In his poem "False Nightmare," Allen Tate in the "sleep-awakened mind" assigns these words to Walt Whitman:

> "I give the yawp barbaric
> Of piety and pelf
> (Who now reads Herrick?) . . ."

The answer is, "Not many," if we mean something more than superficial reading.

"Herrick was a real gentleman, sir," said a Southern student to his professor, "a man like that could never use a dirty word." Herrick did use many, as the student would have discovered had he examined the complete poems. But a gentleman he was, and a gentle man. *Two Gentle Men*, Miss Marchette Chute entitles a recent study of the lives of George Herbert and Robert

Herrick. But since so little is known of Herrick's life, Miss Chute has had to limit herself to a detailed discussion of background and to a portrait of the poet as he emerges from his poetry. With her conclusion that for "all its oddities and its many failures, *Hesperides* is one of the most beautiful books ever written" one must agree, but the reasons for that particular beauty are difficult to define. Herrick's uniqueness appears somehow to escape us. What was it that he alone among English poets was able to do?

Of delicacy it is always difficult to speak, and because Herrick is so modest a poet and so clear about what he is doing, a weighty treatment will inevitably appear to labor the obvious. The last words of "The Country Life" are *cætera desunt*—"the rest is wanting"; and this is true of many of Herrick's poems. Because he is a master of understatement, he knows what to omit. What is only hinted at or suggested is often the most important part of the poem. Herrick chooses always a small frame in which to work. It best fits his "little note," and "little" is one of his favorite adjectives. Herrick is a perfect miniaturist; nothing is too small for him to notice or too great to reduce in size. Lafcadio Hearn found him of all English poets closest in spirit to the Japanese, not only because of his love of short and delicate verse forms, but for his perceptions as well. He is a supreme watercolorist, and with his quick brushstrokes he suggests the *haiku* and the *tanka* centuries before they were known in English. Herrick's world is a small world, depicted with a spring freshness and an early-morning shimmer.

The principal inhabitants of this world are girls and flowers, and together they act out over and over a strange series of little dramas, changing one into the other at will. What is the sense of all these playthings and this play? No poet has ever presented his readers with such a bevy of beauties. They appear separately and together, moving about the alcove like succubi, ever ready to serve their master. Primping and pouting, they always seem prepared at a moment's notice for whatever game their master would designate. Readers of Herrick have tried for years to discover which, if any of them, had a counterpart in real life. Anthea, Electra, Sapho, Myrha, Corinna, Perilla, all are mentioned at least seven times, and Julia more than fifty. All the mistresses are identified with flowers, but Julia is preeminently the rose. She is the Queen-Priest who is to burn incense to appease love "for our very-many Trespasses." It is she who is asked to throw his book into the fire if the poet dies before it is completed. But, for all the attention she receives, is she, as Edmund Gosse seems to think, any more real than the others?

If she is, it seems strange that the most graphically sensual of the poems, "The Vine," should concern not Julia, but Lucia. And what of Corinna, one of the mistresses least frequently mentioned, but who receives the tribute of one of the most elaborate poems? Herrick is precise in his detail and everything in his book seems to be there for a reason. We, therefore, naturally expect that the names he gives his mistresses have some significance. And yet while he is precise, he is purposely vague in wishing to give an all-pervading dreamlike quality to his work. His mistresses drift in and out of his pages as delicate as the silk that clothes them and as insubstantial as the air that surrounds them. If there is any reason for the names, it is usually the verbal setting. In the poem "Being once blind, his request to Biancha," the name, meaning white, is appropriate for the contrast with darkness imagined in the poem; and the *b*'s prepare the reader for the falls and stumblings of the blind man mentioned. No other name could possibly be substituted in the famous line:

Come, my *Corinna*, come, let's goe a Maying.

It does not matter that Corinna was the feigned lady love of Ovid (and of many other poets) ; she here becomes the only Corinna who has ever existed, and the only one associated with Maytime and the country.

Miss Helen Bevington has called our attention recently in

a most amusing way to the curious fact that Julia had a double chin.

> Black and rowling is her eye,
> Double chinn'd, and forehead high

writes Herrick. The detail is not so curious, however, if we think of Julia, as presented in the poems, as rather less than life-size. Herrick lays such stress on the daintiness and simplicity of his mistresses and on the smallness of their features that his reader begins to wonder if he is speaking of grown women at all. He is, of course, since there is nothing morbid in his portrayal, but the girls *are* girls rather than women, and like Ronsard's nymphets they have the plump and pleasing features of children. Following these nymphs and shepherdesses through the pages of the *Hesperides*, the reader cannot escape the feeling that he is witnessing the enactment of a series of scenes by Roman *amorini*. The games of these maidens and these "younglings" are children's games—and Herrick made use of all the children's games of his day, push-pin, chop-cherry, cherry-pit, stoolball—but they naturally play all the adult games as well since they are projections of adult feeling. Herrick loved real children, and many of his poems are addressed to them. But his dream children are his greater love. They never existed, and they never will exist, except in a pagan paradise where experience is innocence and where sex is as natural as the air one breathes. They exist side by side with the fairies of Herrick's England. They belong to the western isles that he imagined, the Eden on earth, that is inevitably linked with childhood.

All this is not to say, of course, that Herrick did not know women intimately. He insists, quoting Ovid, that although his muse was jocund, his life was chaste, but he protests too much and one cannot believe that he expects to be taken literally. He was thirty-two years old before he entered the church, and certainly during his years in London he had ample opportunity for a worldly life. But even when he is writing of women that we know existed, he often makes us see them, if only briefly, in miniature. This is not in any sense a diminution of their value nor is it merely a reflection of the Anacreontic spirit of his day; it is his own peculiar angle of vision that carries over even into his longest and most serious pieces. Herrick's merry nature loved infinite variety. He treated language as if it were an accordion: his stanzas open from the shortest to the longest lines and close back again. His eye ranges over the broadest landscape only to come to rest on the most minute detail, and from there to return to the whole. In this same fashion, he can move from the world of the imagination to the world of everyday reality without the slightest difficulty. He can put scenes of pagan rites side by side with the rural customs of the Devonshire of his day, and he can reconcile Christianity with an eroticism that is virtually Oriental.

In the true spirit of the Renaissance, Herrick wanted to encompass everything, the old and the new, the good and the bad. For him it was all part of the great wheel of life, and the circle is one of his favorite figures. In Julia's petticoat he sees all the splendors of the heavens, and in a fly in amber, Cleopatra in her tomb. If the reader of the *Hesperides* finds himself pelted with roses and sprinkled with perfumes and spices on every page, he also encounters other sights and odors that have not been to everyone's liking. Herrick's epigrams have always been a source of embarrassment to his editors. (Pollard in his 1897 edition printed them, along with the other objectionable poems, in a detachable appendix.) "It is one of the paradoxes of literature," writes Percy Simpson in his introduction to his Oxford reprint of Herrick, "that this exquisite artist, experimenting in minute satire, should have composed a monotonous and, on the whole, pointless series of poems on merely nauseous themes. A reprint of Herrick among the Oxford poets, side by side with the complete text already issued, gives a welcome opportunity of clearing away these weeds from the flower-garden of the *Hesperides*." Herrick's reaction to this would have been that every flower garden, however formal, must have its weeds. The flowers shine all the brighter by reason of the contrast just as jewels are best seen against the dark. Perfection must have its flaw; a "sweet disorder" in a lady's dress is not only desirable but necessary since it heightens and accentuates the lady's beauty:

> Love's of it self, too sweet; the best of all
> Is, when loves hony has a dash of gall.

Herrick's is a bittersweet world, and to remove the bitter completely is to do injustice to the sweet since the two are inseparable.

Weeds, by their very nature, must be rank and lush; flowers are nourished by compost. If Herrick's flowers are children, symbols of love, his weeds are the aged, emblems of hate. It is true, as Marchette Chute remarks, that the individuality of Herrick's epigrams lies in "their real, ruthless hatred of physical ugliness." "He cannot hide his fury," she writes, "at the existence of bleary eyes and sweaty feet, toothless gums and bad breath. His delight in the surface of things—silks, flowers, perfumes, crystals, the softness of a woman's flesh—made him feel a sense of betrayal when they disappeared; and he turned on the pitiless victims of poverty and old age with the slingshot pebbles of his epigrams." When Herrick writes of silks, flowers, jewels, he describes their surface brilliance in order to stress the greater loveliness that lies beneath them or the deeper beauty that they exemplify. In his epigrams, however, he remains on the surface —with the traits of physical decay—and does not relate their foul aspect to life and death. This is their defect; they have no dimension.

The epigrams stand in the foreground of Herrick's landscape; they are surface blotches that hold the eye, even if only momentarily, rather than let it wander in perspective to ever-deepening vistas. The best of them do have, as Edmund Gosse remarks, a broad Pantagruelist humor, but in them Herrick is usually too close to his subject; the results are blurred and muddied. The finest of Herrick's poems are little dramas, sparkling with action; his epigrams are static. They present gross, larger-than-life caricatures, drawn without relish.

In "Oberons Palace," after a long and highly intricate description of a miniature fairyland, the poem ends with these words: "This flax is spun," *i.e.*, the web is completed, the matter has been dealt with. We may indeed look upon many of Herrick's poems as woven together since the texture appears to be the most important element: they are made up of shining surfaces, and are technically brilliant in the flash and interplay of the facets of words one upon another. Often the play is the point, and the surface is the subject. But is there nothing beneath that surface? "The important thing about a poet," A.E. said, "is finally this: 'Out of how deep a life does he speak?' " How deep, then, is Herrick?

TWO

L ET US LOOK at two six-line poems, each concerned
with a surface that particularly interested Herrick,
i.e., silk. "The silken Snake" is the epitome of the
diminutive Herrick:

> For sport my *Julia* threw a Lace
> Of silke and silver at my face:
> Watchet the silke was; and did make
> A shew, as if't'ad been a snake:
> The suddenness did me affright;
> But though it scar'd, it did not bite.

From the point of view of sound, the subject is immediately and
perfectly conveyed. What other poet has used *s*'s more tellingly,
and turned that most defeating of consonants into such a small
triumph? The subtle alternation of *s* and *l* throughout presents
the slithering of the snake: at once the snaky quality of the silk
becomes the silken quality of the snake; and the alternating short
and long vowels suggest the snake's uncoiling and striking. The

247

long *a*'s, coming at the end of each of the first four lines, carry forward the feeling of the coldness of the silk, that reaches its climax in the word "snake" and its denouement in the word "scar'd." "Watchet" is, of course, a cold blue green, sky blue, a serpent's flashing blue, cold to the eye. The poet plays throughout with dental sounds, suggesting with them the play of the serpent's tongue: we have them in the very word for the silk's color "watchet," and then the final flickering in the fourth line "as if't'ad been a snake." The dentals, tripping up the tongue, draw attention away from the other consonants and from the uncoiling effect of the vowels, and rightly so because they are concerned with presenting the poem's most important element— the serpent's bite. The fact that the serpent has no bite is the poem's point, and its conclusion.

In Herrick's Eden the serpent is a child's toy, and its purpose is play. The snake, rather than destroying its victim, startles him and awakens him with its coldness. But the snake is the silk and the silver, and in the phrase "Watchet the silke was" there is in the sound of the *w*'s and the *a*'s an effect completely opposed to that of coldness. While the color gives coldness to the eye, the words themselves convey warmth to the ear. We realize that irony has been minutely at work, for the total effect on the reader is not one of chill, but of amusement and warmth.

Herrick's careful understatement builds by indirection, and the simile of the snake takes the reader away from the overall metaphor. This is a "silken" snake, but the most important word in the poem is "Lace." The simile of the snake is loose and ambiguous; it is a lace of silk and silver that Julia throws. The lace is, of course, Julia's girdle, made of an openwork fabric of silk and silver threads, inwrought probably with patterns. The lace becomes the snake, but being lace, it remains the surface, the cold skin, of the snake. Its loops, uncoiling, present the snake striking, but the lace is still a net. The poet, rather than being bitten by the serpent, is enmeshed in its scales: the surface literally triumphs.

248

In another, and far greater, lyric concerned with silk, "Upon Julia's Clothes," the sounds again constitute one of the triumphs of English poetry:

> When as in silks my *Julia* goes,
> Then, then (me thinks) how sweetly flowes
> That liquefaction of her clothes.
>
> Next, when I cast mine eyes and see
> That brave Vibration each way free;
> O how that glittering taketh me!

We have again in the first three lines the mellifluent quality of silk in the *s*'s and *l*'s, and again in the overall vowel pattern of the poem; and in the alternation of long and short vowel sounds, first, the flow of silk and then, its frou-frou and crinkle. Dr. Tillyard says:

A fresh and unaffected sensuality pervades the poem. Not only is the speaker's excitement expressed by 'then, then', but from the flow of the clothes and their vibration the hint of the body beneath is not absent. The full emphasis and the fall of the third line express how well the spectator's excitement is satisfied by the downward flow of the silk. We may even derive from 'liquefaction' a hint of the word 'satisfaction.' 'Liquefaction' is a sophisticated word, and as such is more important than as describing a quality of silk which (incidentally) had been already indicated in the word 'flows'. More important probably than any of the factors noted above is the contrast on which the poem is constructed. The spectator first sees the downward flow of Julia's silks and he experiences satisfaction. He then sees the silks vibrating, perhaps moving in little horizontal eddies, and he is captivated. . . .

Dr. Tillyard, in his concern with the oblique, has been a victim of Herrick's obliquity. There is, of course, far more than a "hint of the body" beneath the clothes. What Herrick is saying of Julia is quite simply: (a) I like her with her clothes on, and (b) I far prefer her with them off. But Dr. Tillyard is not alone in being misled in this case. Herrick's mastery of sound, as evidenced in the first three lines, has made many readers believe this to be, as it indeed is, one of the finest poems on silk ever written. But it is much more than that.

For a poem whose chief appeal is sensuous, the language is strangely abstract. The two most important words in these six lines are "liquefaction" and "vibration," both abstract—and sophisticated, as Dr. Tillyard observes—nouns of Latin derivation, "liquefaction" meaning the act or process of making or becoming liquid, or the state of being a liquid. And here, of course, it is both things: the silk becomes water and is water. "Vibration" means oscillation; and suggests immediately the moving to and fro of the silk and of the lady's body, that is, the liquid not only moves, flows, it also oscillates and glitters. There is a progression in the poem underlined by the words, "Then, then," and the word "Next," that opens the second stanza. The lines do not merely say that Julia's silks are like water, and that when she walks, they move glittering back and forth. The words "each way free" can only mean unconfined in every direction. The silk surely cannot be said to be entirely free; what is free must be Julia's body. The lady's clothes have been removed, or are being removed, before our eyes, and what Herrick is saying, as he does so often, is that he prefers the nude to the clothed figure, no matter how lovely the fabric that covers it, that he prefers nature to art. The central metaphor of the first tercet is that of a river flowing forward, confined within its banks; that of the second, the waves of an ocean moving freely to and fro, and all is contained within the abstract framework of "liquefaction" and "vibration." In the first tercet, it is the external qualities of the lady, her dress, that impress themselves on the internal in the observer, the mind, "me thinks." In the second, the situation is reversed; it is the internal, the lady's body that impresses itself on the external, the eyes, the vision of the beholder.

We have witnessed in the poem a peculiar alchemical process whereby a base material is transformed before our eyes into gold; and it is no mere accident that the entire work hinges on a word with alchemical overtones, for the alchemist, like the poet, while going through his complicated labors, may be said, in a sense, to have explored the depths of the human unconscious. Herrick, in his early years an apprenticed goldsmith, has wrought with the mind a metal of inestimable value. And it is not too farfetched to say that his work as a goldsmith in some ways prepared him for the greater and more difficult craft of poetry.

Many of Herrick's poems treat the same subject. In "Clothes do but cheat and cousen us," he writes, "mine Eye/ Is wone with flesh, not *Drapery*," just as his master Ben Jonson had said: "Such sweet neglect more taketh me/Than all the adulteries of art." "To his Mistresses" of Herrick also provides a parallel:

> Put on your silks; and piece by piece
> Give them the scent of Amber-Greece:
> And for your breaths too, let them smell
> Ambrosia-like, or *Nectarell*:
> While other Gums their sweets perspire,
> By your owne jewels set on fire.

So likewise, in this poem, it is the lady's "owne jewels" that fire the silk.

Now if this poem fails in any respect, the reason must lie in the fact that the surface is so skillfully presented that it attracts undue attention to itself at the expense of the basic content. Here is a work of art of which it may be said that the texture is the text: it is concerned with the texture of woman's clothing, but more than that, with the texture of her flesh. If it is often taken to be merely a description of the quality of silk, it must be because the mellifluence of silk is so powerfully expressed in the word "liquefaction" that the reader is almost forced to view the second stanza as a mere amplification and restatement of the first. But the reader is at fault then in not appreciating the full subtlety of the poem, and in missing the impact of Herrick's miniature drama.

Several critics have been aware of "the hint of the body" in this poem, but a good deal of nonsense has been written about Julia's extraordinary physical features accentuated by the glittering of overlaid silk. In *The Personal Heresy: A Controversy*, Dr. Tillyard and Mr. C. S. Lewis argue for pages on the subject. Mr. Lewis holds that what the poem tells him about is silk; the experience the poet is communicating is one the poet had regarding silk. Dr. Tillyard contends that Mr. Lewis is concerned only with things, and that it is the state of the poet's mind that is communicated, "the qualities of unaffected sensuality, keen observation, sophistication, and sense of decorum." While the critics keep bickering, not unlike two women over a bolt of silk at a counter, Julia in all her unadorned splendor has passed them by. And Herrick continues to smile from between the lines.

Both the poems we have been discussing might have been written by a painter; they are clearly the work of a poet for whom the visual imagination is paramount. In each case, it is the eyes that act and are acted upon. The exciting "glittering" of Julia's nudity "taketh" the whole poet, but it reaches him through his eyes; the excitement is visual. In the case of the silken snake, there is the same type of "glittering" connection between the poet and his mistress. In that poem, however, it is the mistress rather than the poet who casts the glance, and it is a captivating one. The girdle of blue silk and silver is also a metaphor for Julia's tempting and flirtatious gaze, her rolling eye. Both pieces present us with miniature dramas enacted in the boudoir. Both are concerned with surfaces, with the clothed and the unclothed figure; and both are indeed the works of an "unaffected sensuality." What is most important, as so frequently in Herrick, is, of course, what is left out. There is clearly a before and after, and therefore the poems expand in their small frames. We need not dwell at length on the sexual implications of "The silken Snake." A psychologist might devote pages to a study of the male and female symbolism in these six lines. This is a trifle, and Herrick is here playing with play; it is all "for sport." But even in this lesser lyric the vision of depth should not be lost because of the surface shimmer. A greater lyric such as "Upon Julia's Clothes" has retained our attention because it is at the same time so simple and direct and so endlessly complex.

In his sonnet "Pur Sang" on one of his favorite pictorial subjects, a racehorse, Edgar Degas speaks of the horse as:

Tout nerveusement nu dans sa robe de soie.

Herrick's Julia is likewise "nervously naked in her silken gown." And the diminutive ballerinas of Degas come to mind in connection with Herrick, for Degas also created a world of his own, based on the real world but apart from it, in which delicate and lovely figures move, animated by feeling. Herrick was a lover of beautiful things and not of human beings in the ordinary sense. If we want people presented as in Chaucer, we shall not find them here; Herrick's beings are projections, distillations, of human feeling; and for those readers for whom "feeling is first" he will have no inferior. It has been said that the ballet as an art form appears devoid of feeling perhaps because it is all feeling. Although Herrick may seem at first merely childlike, playful, and innocent, it is the maturity of his feeling that in the end must command our attention. And, in this sense, he is surely not without depth, for feeling may have a complexity of quite a different order from that of thought. Viewed from this angle, Herrick is as mature as Donne, although to modern, if not to

Elizabethan, eyes he may appear as far removed as it is possible to be.

In pointing out some of the rewards of reading Herrick, I have only touched the surface, but I have tried to show how intricate and deceptive that surface can be. "With an old serving-woman in a tumbledown country parsonage," Edmund Gosse said of Herrick, "his life passed merrily among such dreams as Oriental sultans wear themselves out to realize." And yet for all the brightness of his dreams, he has his darker side that cannot escape the careful reader. Grosart found that the "unlifted shadow of melancholy must have lain broad and black over Herrick." His merry nature had a "dark thread interwoven in it." Herrick may not appear to insist upon it, but then it is not his nature to insist. He prefers a music that "sighs" rather than "sounds." But for all his instinctive gaiety, he could write:

> Putrefaction is the end
> Of all that Nature doth entend.

And death is a theme recurring on every page. Professor Musgrove has pointed out that Herrick's series of poems on women's clothes is not complete without the silks as seen "with more serious eye, as the vesture of decay," as in "The Transfiguration":

> Immortall clothing I put on,
> So soone as *Julia* I am gon
> To mine eternall Mansion.
>
> Thou, thou art here, to humane sight
> Cloth'd all with incorrupted light;
> But yet how more admir'dly bright
>
> Wilt thou appear, when thou art set
> In thy refulgent Thronelet,
> That shin'st thus in thy counterfeit?

Herrick leaves much to his reader; the very nature of his art is to conceal itself. But a vision such as this, at once so contained and so transcendent, will always hold the attention of those for whom the imagination has value.

[1962]

VII

IN THE
CLASSIC
MANNER:
Notes on the
Tellers of Tales

TWO RETURNS
TO AFRICA
(*Isak Dinesen and Evelyn Waugh*)

T
HE NAME of Isak Dinesen is today so familiar to all of us that we may forget that just over twenty-five years ago it was completely new to the world. When *Seven Gothic Tales* first appeared in 1934, published in the United States for the first time anywhere, its readers knew only that it was the work of a Danish author writing in English. Soon afterwards they learned, of course, that Isak Dinesen was in reality Baroness Karen Blixen of Rungstedlund near Copenhagen. Dinesen was her maiden name; Isak she had chosen because it meant literally "laughter" in Hebrew. From her own account in *Out of Africa* her readers discovered, moreover, that Isak Dinesen was a woman quite as extraordinary as any tale she had told, that she had lived for seventeen years in Kenya, had run a coffee farm, hunted lions, walked with Masai warriors, and sat with Arab sheikhs. While waiting for the rainy season in Africa, she had begun to put down some of the tales and fantasies that she told to entertain a friend on his return

from his safaris, one who had, she said, "a trait of character which to me is very precious, he liked to hear a story told."

"Who are you?" the lady in black asks the Cardinal Salviati in one of the Baroness's tales; and the Cardinal replies, "Allow me, in order to save my modesty, to answer you in the classic manner, and to tell you a story." Isak Dinesen's answer is always in the classic manner; and her stories like the pleats of an accordion fold one into the next, or rest like Chinese boxes one within the other.

In her new book,[1] she returns to the Africa she knew and loved. She returns to it now in dreams just as she returned during her African stay to the dream world of Europe in her *Seven Gothic Tales*. In "Barua a Soldani" ("The King's Letter"), which is the central story of this collection and as fine as any she has produced, she describes killing a lion one New Year's morning long ago with her friend Denys Finch-Hatton. She thought that the lion, which was feeding on a giraffe, was the exact image of the *lion posant or* on the royal coat of arms of Denmark, and she decided therefore that it was only fitting that the skin should be sent to the king of Denmark. It was; and many months later, she received a letter from King Christian X, written in his own hand, thanking her for the gift. She had the letter in her pocket when she rode out on the farm to find a native whose leg had been smashed by a falling tree. Since she had no medicine to ease his pain, she held to his chest the king's letter and it proved to be what she said it would—*mzuri sana*, very excellent indeed. The letter, covered with blood and filth and passed about in a pouch, became a relic cherished for its miraculous powers.

"Barua a Soldani" ends thus:

The blood on my sheet of paper is not proud or edifying. It is the blood of a dumb nation. But then the handwriting on it is that of a king, *mokone yake*. No ode will be written

---

[1] Isak Dinesen, *Shadows on the Grass* (New York: Random House).

about my letter; still, today it is, I believe, history as much as the relic of Rosenborg. Within it, in paper and blood, a covenant has been signed between the Europeans and the Africans—no similiar document of this same relationship is likely to be drawn up again.

When I had the honor of introducing Isak Dinesen at the Poetry Center in New York, she told "Barua a Soldani" to a large, enthusiastic, and astonished audience. And "told" is the right word: she did not read and she did not recite. Her first words, uttered in a voice amazingly firm and commanding to rise from so frail a body, were that she came from a long line of storytellers. And so she began to tell this story, and many members of her audience returned to hear it a second and then a third time, no doubt realizing that they would never again hear another like it.

The wording of it was almost exactly as it is printed here with only the subtlest variations from one evening to the next, for each telling seemed to her a new experience; but the ending was, as I recall, different. Perhaps because she was aware of her physical presence, and of the audience's interest in her as a teller of tales, her last sentence, although I do not have her exact words and put them badly, was to the effect that if any words of hers could, like those of the king, in any way alleviate human suffering, she would not have written in vain. Isak Dinesen may have excised this final sentence because she did not wish there to be any suggestion of condescension or self-aggrandizement. But she has at the same time always been aware of the noble, and ennobling, role of the artist. In one of the *Last Tales*, "Converse at Night in Copenhagen," the poet, speaking of his role in life, says: "Crushing in its weight is my own covenant with the Lord, yet it is, at the same time, highly gay and glorious!"

It is this same crushing covenant that has produced the great stories of Isak Dinesen; and it is curious but significant that her recent work, produced at a time of great personal suffering and dictated often a few paragraphs at a time from her bed, has still the "gay and glorious" quality of some seventeenth-century classic.

"The introduction into my life of another race, essentially different from mine, in Africa became to me a mysterious expansion of my world," Isak Dinesen says here. Her world has been expanding ever since. Evelyn Waugh has also returned to Africa in his new book.[2] He returns physically, and so little does his world expand with his journey that some readers of *Tourist in Africa* may feel that he might better have stayed at home. Mr. Waugh declares that at fifty-five he is not at the age best suited to travel—"too old for the jungle, too young for the beaches"— and then it is difficult in a world laid waste by tourism and politics to find anywhere to go. India, where wine is prohibited, cannot be long endured; Africa "without preoccupations, with eyes reopened to the exotic" seems to be the ticket. And off he goes to escape the rigors of the English winter to Genoa, and then through the Suez Canal and down the East Coast of Africa, to Kenya. Then leaving his ship at Dar-es-Salaam in Tanganyika, he continues by land through Rhodesia and the Union of South Africa, where he rejoins his ship. He steps ashore at Southampton buoyantly, "very different from the old fellow who crept into the train south two months ago."

How different? Here is Mr. Waugh in Kenya: "The Club is unchanged since I was last here, a spacious, old-fashioned building designed to catch every breath of air. The monsoon was blowing. It was deliciously cool, but it is not easy to read *The Times* India-paper edition in deep shade and a brisk wind. Have the editors, I wonder, considered what a high proportion of their copies are perused under fans?"

The ruffling of the pages of *The Times* continues throughout these pages, and Mr. Waugh looks up from time to time to make his crotchety, pointed, and often very funny comments, but

[2] Evelyn Waugh, *Tourist in Africa* (Boston: Little, Brown).

one cannot help feeling that he is really more interested in his paper than in his surroundings or his companions. "As happier men watch birds, I watch men," he writes. "They are less attractive, but more various." The man-watching, however, does not add up to much here, and the places that seem to have been waiting for years for Mr. Waugh's sharp eye are passed over far too lightly.

It may be wrong to compare two such totally different books, and certainly any literary pantheon would include both writers. But in their present return to Africa Mr. Waugh goes further and sees less, while the Baroness, distant, old, and ill, is always infinitely closer to her subject.

[1961]

THE LEOPARD
(Giuseppe di Lampedusa)

W HEN *Il Gattopardo* was nominated for the Strega award, Italy's highest literary prize, Alberto Moravia is said to have remarked that anyone who voted for it was voting against the modern Italian novel. And at first glance, he seems to have been right; for this historical opus complete with romantic trappings looks as out of place among works of recent Italian fiction as a carefully executed representational painting would in a room filled with abstractions. The fact that the book was the sole work of a literary amateur, a recently deceased Sicilian prince, based on the life of his paternal great-grandfather, appeared to bear out Moravia. But the novel found backers all the same, chief among them Ignazio Silone, who can certainly not be considered a reactionary. It won the award, and was hailed in Italy, and later throughout Europe, as a novel not only of merit but of genius. Now magnificently translated by Archibald Colquhoun, it will surely enjoy a long life in English as well as in Italian.

The story behind the composition of *The Leopard*[1] is as

---

[1] Giuseppe di Lampedusa, *The Leopard* (New York: Pantheon).

romantic as the tale itself. Giuseppe di Lampedusa, whose widow is a Baltic noblewoman and a practicing psychoanalyst, had lived in London and Paris as well as his native Palermo and had read in the original all the best of European literature. Although he had contemplated writing his novel for twenty-five years, he did not get around to it until after he was sixty and completed it only a short while before his death at sixty-one in 1957. He submitted one copy of his manuscript to the novelist Elio Vittorini, a fellow Sicilian, who read it for one of Italy's most important publishing houses. Vittorini decided that it was more an essay than a novel, and rejected it as unpublishable. Five days after receiving this news, Lampedusa died; and it was not until months later that another unsigned copy of his manuscript found its way into the hands of Feltrinelli, the publisher of *Doctor Zhivago*, who published it with enthusiasm.

Vittorini and Moravia will probably find their rejection of *The Leopard* as hard to live down as Gide did his rejection of Proust. It is always difficult, as Proust himself remarked, to judge something completely new. We are shocked by things to which we are not accustomed; and a style long out of fashion may seem new by reason of the audacity of its reintroduction at the appropriate historical moment. Stylistically *The Leopard* is clearly of the old school: in its panoramic sweep, it recalls Tolstoy; in the precision of its writing, it reflects the influence of several nineteenth-century French novelists. The author's model is Stendhal (his hero's name is Fabrizio), but there are echoes also of Flaubert and Mérimée. It is not merely the mechanics of style, however, that evoke the French novelists. The author is so schooled in French literature that *The Leopard* gives the curious impression of having been written by one who thought in French but wrote in Italian.

Italian the novel certainly is in its baroque operatic sweep: the plot is simple, but somehow at the end the reader is left feeling that he has covered a vast amount of ground, emotional as well as historical. The action begins in Palermo in May 1860 when Garibaldi lands in Sicily on his way to overthrow the Bourbon monarchy in Naples and ends with the fiftieth anniversary of the landing in May 1910. The principal character is Don Fabrizio, prince of Salina, a benevolent nobleman and part-time astronomer who realizes that the arrival of Garibaldi means the end of his way of life and the rise of a new class. Skeptical and smiling, he broods like a giant over the changing scene, a timeless figure caught between past and present, his eyes fixed on the stars.

This is no ordinary historical novel to be followed for the sake of its fast-moving action; Lampedusa is more interested in the psychological interplay of his characters and in their symbolical extension. The *gattopardo* of the title is the spotted wild-cat rampant on the Salina coat of arms; it is the prince of Salina himself with his huge frame, fair skin, and light hair betraying his German background. Moreover, it represents with its tawny hide the true ruler of Sicily, the savage sun, which "kept all things in servile immobility, cradled in violence as arbitrary as dreams." It is also the product of that sun, the Sicilian landscape itself with its flaming hillsides "yellow with stubble, black with burned patches." *The Leopard* is, in essence, a study of Sicily. It is the power of Lampedusa's visual imagination that gives the book its strange and haunting vitality: he sees everything in panorama, complete down to the most minute detail. Each fragment of landscape is given its precise and poignant equivalent. Huge bougainvillaeas cascade over the gates of a villa "like swags of episcopal silk." The prince's telescopes are pictured as lying quietly, dazed by the sun "with black pads over the eye-pieces, like well-trained animals who knew their meal was given them only at night."

It was the design of an earlier Sicilian novelist, Giovanni Verga, with whom the modern Italian novel began, to compose a series of novels about Sicilian life at its various social levels. He completed only two of these, the first about a family of peasants, the second about a *petit bourgeois*. Lampedusa concerns himself with the view from the top of the ladder; but because he has set down, as Croce said in speaking of Manzoni, "all the tragedy and comedy of a subtle moral conscience," his vision of Sicily, and of existence, is no less moving.

[1960]

F. SCOTT FITZGERALD:
A Poet's View

"THE TALENT THAT matures early is usually the poetic type," Fitzgerald wrote late in his short life, "which mine was in large part." Poetry played an important role in his development from college on. He wrote to his daughter at Vassar, advising her to take courses in which she would read poetry; it was his contention that anyone who was not subnormal could read prose for himself. But with poetry, he said: [1]

> It isn't easy to get started on by yourself. You need, at the beginning, some enthusiast who also knows his way around. John Peale Bishop performed that office for me at Princeton. I had always dabbled in "verse" but he made me see, in the course of a couple of months, the difference between poetry and nonpoetry. After that one of my first discoveries was that some of the professors who were teaching

---

[1] All quotations, except as noted, are from *The Letters of F. Scott Fitzgerald*, edited by Andrew Turnbull (New York: Charles Scribner's Sons, 1963).

poetry really hated it and didn't know what it was about. I got in a series of endless scraps with them so that finally I dropped English altogether.

Poetry is either something that lives like fire inside you—like music to the musician or Marxism to the Communist—or else it is nothing, an empty, formalized bore around which pedants can endlessly drone their notes and explanations. "The Grecian Urn" is unbearably beautiful with every syllable as inevitable as the notes in Beethoven's *Ninth Symphony* or it's just something you don't understand. It is what it is because an extraordinary genius paused at that point in history and touched it. I suppose I've read it a hundred times. About the tenth time I began to know what it was about, and caught the chime in it and the exquisite inner mechanics. Likewise with "The Nightingale" which I can never read through without tears in my eyes; likewise the "Pot of Basil" with its great stanzas about the two brothers. "Why were they proud," etc.; and "The Eve of St. Agnes," which has the richest, most sensuous imagery in English, not excepting Shakespeare. And finally his three or four great sonnets, "Bright Star" and the others. . . . In themselves those eight poems are a scale of workmanship for anybody who wants to know truly about words, their most utter value for evocation, persuasion or charm. For awhile after you quit Keats all other poetry seems to be only whistling or humming.

It was when he had learned about poetry, he said at another point, that he first began to develop a style of his own. Much of his work seems in many ways so close to poetry that perhaps a brief examination of his poetic quality will throw some light on his unique sensibility and his style.

F. Scott Fitzgerald for most people calls now immediately to mind the period of the twenties with all their trappings, their gaiety and frivolity, their emptiness and superficiality perhaps more than their tragedy. When I myself open one of his books I think of wonderful long summer afternoons when I was eight or nine on an army post on the edge of the Mississippi and a mammoth —or at least it seems mammoth to me in restrospect—white roadster would draw up in front of our house. In it was a lovely teen-age girl surrounded by several of her current admirers. They would be singing some popular songs of the time such as "In a Little Spanish Town" or "Doodle-dee-doo." The fact that the girl was not only the very essence of sophistication but had just returned with her father, a major, from three years in China made her all the more glamorous. Here to my young eyes was life as it should be lived.

I spoke recently with a lady who declared that her mother, referring to Fitzgerald and the twenties, had said, Yes, that she *had* danced the Charleston, but that no one had ever poured *shampoo* from her shoe. Many critics still think that Fitzgerald's writing is more shampoo than champagne. But at its best, champagne it really is—and champagne of the finest vintage.

Scott Fitzgerald's daughter, Frances Fitzgerald Lanahan, has recently written in her introduction to her father's letters to her: [2]

> During the last five years of my father's life, he couldn't have bought a book of his in any bookstore: he probably couldn't even have asked for one without getting a blank stare from the saleslady. I am not sentimental by nature, but once a few years ago when I walked into the bookshop of a remote town and saw a whole shelf of F. Scott Fitzgerald sitting there as naturally as if it had been the works of Shakespeare, I burst into tears. A sick wife, poverty, bad luck—we all have to contend with some of these

[2] *Scott Fitzgerald Letters to His Daughter*, edited by Andrew Turnbull, with an introduction by Frances Fitzgerald Lanahan (New York: Charles Scribner's Sons, 1965), p. xi.

things, and Daddy had helped bring on a good bit of it himself. But the writing part wasn't fair; God had played one of those trump cards which can defeat even the most valiant of us.

One recent writer on Fitzgerald has said that it was not entirely true that he had been completely neglected because at the time of his death a number of his books were still in print. Books in print, however, are not always obtainable—especially if the author is not one that booksellers know and approve of. I am well aware of this fact from my own experience. A few years ago I went into a book store in Los Angeles and asked for one of my own books. A saleslady with a voice like an electric carving knife said, "Yes, we had that but it didn't sell so we sent it back."

Born in 1896 at St. Paul, Fitzgerald died in 1940 at Hollywood. Most of his writing, except for his last unfinished novel begun shortly before his death, was done in the twenties; his reputation suffered a serious decline in the thirties; he died at the opening of the forties. And, of course, it was not until the fifties that there was a real revival of interest in his work.

Much has been written about Scott Fitzgerald, and much of it has been irrelevant and nonsensical. Much of it also has been about the *man* rather than the *writer*, for Fitzgerald was an unusually interesting personality as well as a fine writer. This is far from true of most writers. But so many people who knew him have testified to his great charm—and we have his letters and his notebooks to back them up—that even so notable an authority as his supposed friend Ernest Hemingway was hard put to it to make us feel that it would not have been a delight to have known him.

It is extremely difficult, in fact, in Fitzgerald's case to separate the man from his writings—just as it is in the case of Keats, that is, the Keats of the letters from the Keats of the poems. Fitzgerald put so much of himself into everything that

271

he wrote—in this case, the style was certainly the man—that we have great difficulty in judging his work objectively. Perhaps one of the best ways to begin is with the most objective of his novels and clearly his masterpiece, *The Great Gatsby*.

The French novelist Huysmans, speaking of the poet Jules Laforgue, said, "Jules Laforgue—quelle joie!" And it would be equally exact, I think, to say, "F. Scott Fitzgerald—what joy!" For it is the happy aspect of his style—even when he is writing of tragedy—his surface brilliance, his delight in words, his inimitable wit—which is so difficult to pin down and to classify.

When *The Great Gatsby* was published in 1925, one of the most enthusiastic responses came from a poet, and this response has now become quite celebrated. T. S. Eliot, in a letter to the novelist, wrote:

> *The Great Gatsby* with your charming and over-powering inscription arrived the very morning that I was leaving in some haste for a sea voyage advised by my doctor. I therefore left it behind and only read it on my return a few days ago. I have, however, now read it three times. I am not in the least influenced by your remark about myself when I say that it has interested and excited me more than any new novel I have seen, either English or American, for a number of years. When I have the time I should like to write to you more fully and tell you exactly why it seems to me to be the first step that American fiction has taken since Henry James. . . .

It is not at all astonishing that Eliot should have been so enthusiastic for certainly the novel owes a great deal to him: it could probably never have been written had it not been for Eliot's poems, particularly "The Waste Land." Much of the imagery of the early Eliot has been absorbed, transformed, and presented dramatically in the novel.

I should like to quote a brief and excellent summary of the plot by Charles E. Shain: [3]

> The short novel tells the story of how James Gatz, a poor farm boy from North Dakota, imitates the example of Benjamin Franklin and other proven American moralists and rises at last to be a rich and powerful criminal named Jay Gatsby. Along the way when he is an anonymous young lieutenant in a Kentucky training camp, when American "society" is open to him for the first time, he meets and marries, in his mind, in an act of absolute commitment, a lovely Southern girl named Daisy Fay. But he has to leave Daisy behind when he goes to France and he loses her to a rich American from Chicago, Yale, and Wall Street. The only course conceivable to him when he returns is to pursue Daisy and in the American way to convince her of her error, to show he is worthy of her by the only symbols available to them both, a large house with a swimming pool, dozens of silk shirts, and elaborate parties. But Daisy believes in the symbols themselves, and not in the purer reality, which (for Jay Gatsby) they only faintly embody. She loses her nerve and sacrifices her lover to the world.

It has been said that poetry is all in nouns, nouns and verbs, and that furthermore adjectives in poetry are like leeches—they draw the blood away from the nouns. Scott Fitzgerald had this to say to his daughter:

> About adjectives: all fine prose is based on the verbs carrying the sentences. They make sentences move. Probably the finest technical poem in English is Keats's "The Eve of Saint Agnes." A line like: "The hare limped trembling through the frozen grass," is so alive that you

[3] *F. Scott Fitzgerald* (Minneapolis, Minn.: University of Minnesota Press, 1961).

race through it, scarcely noticing it, yet it has colored the whole poem with its movement—the limping, trembling, and freezing is going on before your own eyes.

The verbs in *The Great Gatsby* carry the prose forward so skillfully that the reader races ahead scarcely cognizant of the care with which the author has selected them. Notice the verbs in these sentences: "The lawn started at the beach and ran toward the front door for a quarter of a mile, *jumping* over sundials and brick walls and burning gardens—finally when it reached the house, drifting up the side in bright vines as though from the momentum of its run." "The lights grow brighter as the earth *lurches* away from the sun, and now the orchestra is playing yellow cocktail music . . ." "On Sunday morning while church bells rang in the villages along shore, the world and its mistress returned to Gatsby's house and *twinkled* hilariously on his lawn." "I'll tell you God's truth. His right hand suddenly *ordered* divine retribution to stand by."

Surely the most significant verb in the book is *lean:* the characters are always leaning toward one another—when standing, when seated, when moving in taxis or cars—leaning in anticipation one to the other just as Gatsby, the solitary figure, leans toward the starry night and toward his dream. They are all like sculptured figures on a frieze or on a Grecian urn—moving toward their destinies, but frozen in time. Time itself is suspended, literally suspended, leaning—as the clock at the time of the reunion of Gatsby and Daisy leans forward from the mantelpiece and falls into Gatsby's hands.

The very basis of poetry, of course, is metaphor and *The Great Gatsby* is filled with these, cast, as Maxwell Perkins put it, in "phrases that make a scene blaze with life." All these that I quote attain, of course, their maximum effectiveness only in their context. "We ought to plan something, yawned Miss

Baker, sitting down at the table as if she were going to bed." "And so with the sunshine and the great bursts of leaves growing on the trees, just as things grow in fast movies, I had that familiar conviction that life was beginning over again with this summer." "Twenty miles from the city a pair of enormous eggs, identical in contour and separated only by a courtesy bay, jut out into the most domesticated body of salt water in the Western hemisphere, the great wet barnyard of Long Island Sound." "We drove over to Fifth Avenue, so warm and soft, almost pastoral on the summer Sunday afternoon that I wouldn't have been surprised to see a great flock of white sheep turn the corner." "The very phrases were worn so threadbare that they evoked no image except that of a turbaned 'character' leaking sawdust at every pore as he pursued a tiger through the Bois de Boulogne." "She wouldn't let go of the letter. She took it into the tub with her and squeezed it up into a wet ball, and only let me leave it in the soap dish when she saw that it was coming to pieces like snow." " 'Perhaps you know the lady,' Gatsby indicated a gorgeous, scarcely human orchid of a woman who sat in state under a white plum tree. Tom and Daisy stared, with that peculiarly unreal feeling that accompanies the recognition of a hitherto ghostly celebrity of the movies."

Metaphors are repeated, echoed as in a poem, for the desired effect of resonance. The black wheel wrenched from the car is repeated in the black funeral wreath on the door of the house that Gatsby purchases, and in the black wreath that Mrs. Wilson wants to obtain for her mother's grave; all are echoed by the black earth wheeling through the heavens.

The horns of the motorcars are echoed by the horns of Gatsby's dance orchestra; and they both are heard in the metaphorical horns calling Actaeon (Gatsby) to Diana (Daisy) so that he may be devoured in the end by his own hounds. And in the horns themselves the reader hears the echo of the lines from T. S. Eliot's "The Waste Land":

> But at my back from time to time I hear
> The sound of horns and motors, which shall bring
> Sweeney to Mrs. Porter in the spring.
> O the moon shone bright on Mrs. Porter
> And on her daughter
> They wash their feet in soda water
> *Et O ces voix d'enfants, chantant dans la coupole!*

And he hears also the voices of the innocent children singing in the cupola as in the line from Verlaine:

> When Jordan Baker had finished telling all this we had left the Plaza for half an hour and were driving in a victoria through Central Park. The sun had gone down behind the tall apartments of the movie stars in the West Fifties, and the clear voices of little girls already gathered like crickets on the grass, rose through the hot twilight:

> > I'm the Sheik of Araby,
> > Your love belongs to me.
> > At night when you're asleep
> > Into your tent I'll creep—

A paragraph in the first chapter not only sets the airy tone of the novel but prepares us for the image we return to at the end:

> The only completely stationary object in the room was an enormous couch on which two young women were buoyed up as though upon an anchored balloon. They were both in white, and their dresses were rippling and fluttering as if they had just been blown back in after a short flight around the house. I must have stood for a few moments listening to the whip and snap of the curtains and the groan of a picture on the wall. Then there was a boom as Tom Buchanan shut the rear windows and the caught wind

died out about the room, and the curtains and the rugs and the two young women ballooned slowly to the floor.

At the conclusion of the novel on the pneumatic mattress in his swimming pool Gatsby's body is buoyed up while a thin red circle of blood revolves in the water around it, water whose surface is but "scarcely corrugated" by a small gust of wind. And the reader knows that the anchored balloon is again adrift but bearing now its true, final, and deadly burden.

The force of Fitzgerald's visual imagination is nowhere more clearly demonstrated than in *The Great Gatsby*. Brooding over the valley of ashes—the wasteland area adjoining the Long Island millionaire garden paradise presided over by Gatsby—are the huge eyes of Dr. Eckleburg. As described at the opening of the second chapter:

> The eyes of Doctor T. J. Eckleburg are blue and gigantic—their retinas are one yard high. They look out of no face, but, instead, from a pair of enormous yellow spectacles which pass over a nonexistent nose. Evidently some wild wag of an oculist set them there to fatten his practice in the borough of Queens, and then sank down himself into eternal blindness, or forgot them and moved away. But his eyes, dimmed a little by many paintless days under sun and rain, brood on over the solemn dumping ground.

Toward the end of the book Wilson, the garage man, looks up at these eyes and remarks, "God sees everything." Throughout the book the eyes of the characters are stressed: they are watching one another and in turn they are all being watched by Nick Carraway, the narrator. It has frequently been pointed out that we find it easy to believe in all the happenings of *The Great Gatsby* because we believe in Nick Carraway. His point of view is clear from the beginning. In the first chapter he says: "This isn't just an epigram—life is much more successfully looked at from a single window after all." He is himself involved in the action but never so involved that he cannot view it all objectively. The eyes watching over the garden paradise are his eyes. Dr. Eckleburg's glasses provide the frames through which he watches the horror of the action unfold. Gatsby also is staring out—staring at the green light on the Buchanans' dock across the way. But the vision is inner as well as outer. Describing his reaction to New York, Nick Carraway says: "I was within and without, simultaneously enchanted and repelled by the inexhaustible variety of life."

Scott Fitzgerald remarked that in criticizing a sonnet sequence, one did not use the same approach as with a larger work. And it is for this reason that the special qualities of *The Great Gatsby* are so difficult to assess. The author works within a small frame. That is not to say that he treats, in any way, a small subject. Quite the contrary, he deals with the largest possible subject: the nature of the American dream, the nature of America, the nature of man himself. But everything in the book is understated. All is held in perfect balance from the first sentence to the last. It is a balance not of intellect but of feeling. Nick Carraway *is* a man of feeling: with him and through him we experience not only the place, but we follow him step by step as he witnesses the whole revelation of horror. We see with him the ashes floating in the wake of Gatsby's dream.

Edith Wharton, who greatly admired the book, remarked that Gatsby could probably have been made to seem greater if Fitzgerald had depicted for us in detail his early life. But she was right to add that doing so would no doubt have been wrong because that would have been the *old* way. Fitzgerald's new way —and it appears less new to us now because so many other novelists have taken it since—is to understate, to suggest. What Fitzgerald omits—and this is the poet's approach—is as important as what he puts in.

From the very beginning a wind is blowing through *The Great Gatsby*. A summer storm is brewing—colors keep shifting

—light becoming dark—objects are glimpsed only fleetingly as on a windy day: the color of everything seems about to be washed away.

And then in the famous conclusion about the nature of the American dream Nick Carraway says that we are all boats struggling against the current, "borne back ceaselessly into the past." Only when we reach the final word do we realize that the boat has been the important and unifying metaphor throughout. We have been "borne back," and we have been approaching the island—Long Island—throughout, just as the Dutch saw it for the first time—a green light wavering upon the water. The boat is analogous to Queequeg's coffin in *Moby Dick* or the raft in *Huckleberry Finn:* it is the receptacle of the author's sensibility that has carried us along—a symbol of hope, of triumph, and of ultimate release and salvation from the horror of death itself. It is ultimately the symbol of the triumph of art over chaos. The boat is bobbing on the water like the girls in their innocent-appearing white dresses in the very first scene ballooning on the sofa, bobbing up and down like the pneumatic mattress on which rests the body of Gatsby in the swimming pool that he had not used all summer. The pool itself becomes in miniature the ocean that all of us as Americans have crossed—the gateway to the past held within a frame in one still moment.

The Great Gatsby is in so many respects a lyrical composition that one must think of it in musical terms. Description and conversation are constantly breaking off into song. The author interjects the words of popular songs: their ordinary—even silly —lyrics in a new context are like musical notations highlighting, urging the action on.

The novel is analogous to a musical composition—not a symphony, however, but a tone poem in which color predominates. Indeed, color takes on a real symbolic value. The work might be said to be—like *The Portrait of A Lady* of Henry James in a different fashion—a study in *chiaroscuro*, moving back and forth from light to dark, beginning with white, the absence of color, and ending with blackness, the combination of all colors.

The novel opens, as I have mentioned, with the vision of the two ladies—Daisy and Jordan, on the sofa—so fresh-appearing in their white frocks that they are to the narrator like angels that have come momentarily to rest after a flight around the room. Everything about Daisy—her house, her rooms, her clothes, the sails on her boat—are white, just as everything about Gatsby is black: he is a creature of the night, of dream, shrouded in mystery. Much is made of the pink suit that he wears—pink, the color of his own blood as it will mix with the water when he lies drifting in the pool. White also is Daisy's pearl necklace, Gatsby's gift to his golden girl whose voice is like money; white also are the human molar cuff links worn by Meyer Wolfsheim, Gatsby's companion in crime. A white dust drifts through as the action unfolds: as the terrible heat of the summer dissolves the powder on the women's faces—a white dust that settles finally on the valley of ashes, the dumping ground where the action is concluded, and the festive flowers are thrown away and left to rot beside the foul river.

There is only one child in the book—Daisy's daughter—and she appears but once, led in by her laundered nurse to say hello. She is dressed in white and notices that her Aunt Jordan also has on a white dress. Her mother says to her, "You dream, you. You absolute little dream." And a dream of innocence she is, little knowing the world of horror to which her parents will ultimately introduce her.

A different sort of child, the narrator realizes, is this child's father, Tom Buchanan, the athlete, who whips his mistress with a dog leash. "I shook hands with him; it seemed silly not to," Nick Carraway says in the last chapter, "for I felt suddenly as though I were talking to a child. Then he went into the jewelry store to buy a pearl necklace—or perhaps only a pair of cuff buttons—rid of my provincial squeamishness forever."

There are other children just offstage—those dressed up in

white on their way to church on Sunday when Gatsby's parties are just breaking up. (I think there is in this novel a significant echo of Scott Fitzgerald's lapsed Catholicism.) The innocent child is set against the murderous parents just as the innocent Middle Westerner is set against the evil Easterner—the new against the old world.

In the course of the action of what I have termed this tone poem we have a profusion of color—yellow, blue, lavender, green—"shirts with stripes and scrolls and plaids in coral and apple-green and lavender and faint orange with monograms of Indian blue," and Daisy throws herself upon them, weeping as if on his body for the wealth of the world that she wishes to possess.

In conclusion I should like to quote a poem of my own relating to Fitzgerald and the twenties. It is very short but may require a few words of explanation. Harry Crosby was a wealthy American expatriate living in Paris at the same time as Fitzgerald. He was a dilettante—his poems and journals are bizarre but not without interest. He lived a fast life, and he died a strange death. He literally worshipped what he termed the Black Sun; and this fact as well as the circumstances of his life and death seem surely to have been on Fitzgerald's mind when he wrote *The Great Gatsby*. Harry Crosby was found dead one morning in a hotel room beside his mistress. They had painted the bottoms of their feet black, and he had shot her and himself.

His widow, Caresse Crosby, tells in her autobiography about the time when they lived in a former mill on the outskirts of Paris that Harry used to play *Petits Chevaux* with his friends —those lead or wooden horses that you move along the floor, usually on shipboard; and he had devised what he called the Bedroom Stakes, and had given the horses names such as Fidelity, Frivolity, and Concubine.

When Zelda Fitzgerald suffered her mental breakdown, she became more and more preoccupied with dancing. It was her ambition to be a ballet dancer and someone said that at the time of her collapse her dancing became so compulsive that it resembled the dancing of those possessed during the Middle Ages. In 1947 a fire broke out in the sanitarium where she was confined, and had been off and on for many years before Fitzgerald's death. She was one of seven patients trapped on the top floor and she perished in the fire.

PETITS CHEVAUX: THE TWENTIES

I

Harry Crosby one day launched the
  Bedroom Stakes—
Frivolity out in front, Fidelity over-
  taken by Concubine.
The play was fast, the bets were high.
  Who lost? Who won?
Green baize drank the tilting shadows
  of the sun,
And Death left the players' goblets
  brimming with blood-red wine.

II

Scott Fitzgerald organized the Crack-
  up Stakes—
The horses galloped ahead; victrola
  records turned.
He downed his drink and wrote; wife
  Zelda whirled and swayed;
The goblets shattered, but the words
  survived Time's raid,
And Zelda danced on madly till the
  asylum burned.

F. Scott Fitzgerald: A Poet's View

At the time of the novelist's death, Glenway Westcott wrote: "The great thing about Fitzgerald was his candor; verbal courage; simplicity. One little man with eyes really witnessing; objective in all he uttered, even about himself in a subjective slump; arrogant in just one connection, for one purpose only, to make his meaning clear." His meaning is clear; and I could point out further examples of the sort that I have taken from *The Great Gatsby*. The poetic qualities that I have stressed are nowhere in greater evidence than in his final unfinished novel, *The Last Tycoon*. Fitzgerald did win in the end; "the words survived Time's raid," the words of a valiant spirit and a great artist.

[1966]

THE LANDSCAPE
OF MADNESS
(*J. M. G. Le Clézio*)

I N HIS FIRST NOVEL, *The Interrogation*, which won
the Prix Renaudot, J. M. G. Le Clézio admits in a preface to two secret ambitions. "One of them is to write
one day," he says, "a novel of such a kind that if the hero
dies in the last chapter—or, at a pinch, develops Parkinson's
disease—I shall be swamped beneath a flood of scurrilous anonymous letters." The second is to write a really effective novel
later on, "something in the spirit of Conan Doyle, appeal-
ing not to the readers' taste for realism—along the broad lines
of psychological analysis and illustration—but to their senti-
mentality." In *Terra Amata*,[1] which now appears in a fine
English translation by Barbara Bray, he may have realized both
ambitions, although perhaps not quite in the way he had anticipated. The hero of this new novel dies, causes unspecified, and is
buried in the last chapter; but I doubt that M. Le Clézio will be
swamped by anonymous letters of any sort. And while it may
not appear so on first reading, *Terra Amata* is, in a sense, very

1 J. M. G. Le Clézio, *Terra Amata* (New York: Atheneum).

284

much in the spirit of Conan Doyle: while presented in the guise of psychological analysis and illustration, its basic appeal is sentimental. It is really a little fold-out puzzle, or, as M. Le Clézio himself says of *The Interrogation*, a "kind of game or jigsaw puzzle in the form of a novel."

What we have now is simply a do-it-yourself piece, a happening in which the author does everything possible to make the reader feel not only that what is happening is happening to him but also that he is making it happen, that he is the writer as well as the reader. "Come up on stage," the author seems to say, "let's see what we can make of all this. Your guess is as good as mine." M. Le Clézio's interest is simply in spreading the scrambled jigsaw before us and letting us focus on the pieces. He has a predilection for prologues, and he indulges himself, and his reader, again here. This novel begins: "You've opened the book at this page. You've turned over two or three pages, glancing idly at the title, the name of the author . . ." and ends:

> What does it matter that there was one to write and another to read? In the last resort, in the very last resort, they are one and the same, and they've always known it. There is not just one word, one sun, one civilization. There are millions of things everywhere. Isn't the poem there, or there, or in your eye, the eye of the beholder? I didn't really write what you've just read. . . . But I've said enough. Now it's your turn.

And so, if it is not too old-fashioned a question to ask, what is it all about? It is about nothing less than the entire universe, about one person who is born on this insignificant earth, born by chance, that is, and whose name happens to be Chancelade (*de la* Chance, you see), who kills potato bugs, grows up, has a girl friend who by chance is called "Mina," makes love, peoples the earth ("Another thing you could do was have a son"), tries to communicate (and, of course, tell the whole truth along the way), dies, and is buried. Chancelade, the hero of this miniature saga, is a kind of Lucky Jim, who projects his anguish and frustration into timeless space. And there is—as in every French film—a girl beside him watching and admiring him while he does. Chancelade is Everyman everywhere and at every time. The book is all paradox from beginning to end—the structuralism of Claude Lévi-Strauss linked to the existentialism of Sartre and the absurdity so dear to the authors of the *nouveau roman*. It seems a terribly youthful work, that of a philosophy student in a cold room who has stayed up too late, read too much in too many dusty tomes, and is trying to put it all down—utterly without humor—before turning on the gas. But in the paradox, in the shifting of the jigsaw pieces, there is, all the same, a certain poetry.

M. Le Clézio is frequently very good at communicating sensations. In one section entitled "In a region that resembled Hell," he describes in detail the sights, sounds, and smells of driving along the Côte d'Azur in a traffic jam, and he does give his reader the definite sensation of being in hell. "He felt that he was gliding into the landscape of madness, in time with the electric music. Soon he would be one of them, an insect among insects; the crowd would close around him like a mouth and digest him greedily." The novel begins by detailing the landscape, "a stretch of earth and dry rubble, with a few mountains, a few hills, and, on the other side, the great plateau of the sea." And it ends with the landscape still the same under "the inescapable sun": "There is nothing figurative anywhere, because everything is self-sufficient. There is no imagination. Nothing is isolated, and nothing communicates."

For a novel concerned with nothingness, in which there is no communication, a great many pages are devoted to attempts at it. There are Chinese characters sprinkled throughout. One section is composed of invented, incomprehensible words; the hero and heroine communicate for pages at another point in sign language. I was going to try to decipher that, but I looked first at another section in which Chancelade addresses his mistress by blinking a flashlight in Morse code. The message, printed in code (and, of course, translated from French to English in code), begins: "Dear Mina are you there I want to say what I've never been able to say before. . . ."

When I got that far, I gave up. It may well be that, as Lévi-Strauss maintains, society's myths and beliefs are as fundamental to its form as language. But still one wishes that M. Le Clézio would give greater vent to his poetic self, and realize that language, like life, may be a prison, but it may also be a privilege and a promise.

I read *Terra Amata* in Paris at Christmas while the astronauts were circling the moon. The novel seemed representative of Paris at the moment, with all its buildings washed clean and already beginning to get dirty again, Paris obsessed by its manmade beauty and its logical heritage, trying to break free in so many ways into the greater modern world, but still held back, in its attempt, by its sentimental self-concern. I went at the same time to see Jean-Louis Barrault's wonderful spectacle, a recreation of Rabelais, which is held on the planks of a former wrestling arena. Rabelais, with his grotesque, but always human, characters, his long lists of invented, earthy words, seemed infinitely more modern, yet more in touch with all that is primitive and eternal on this blue, beloved earth than this at times brilliant, but fundamentally pretentious, little puzzle.

[1969]

VIII

THE SKIES
OF VENICE:
A Variety
of Views

THE SKIES OF VENICE
(Adja Yunkers)

HOWEVER one looks at Venice, it is a mirror—water mirroring air, air mirroring water, baroque buildings reflected in water and air—the whole a mirror so that the skies of Venice are Venice itself. Venice is a mirror, not one in which man finds himself reflected full and bodily, but one in which he sees himself reduced to spirit, to complete airiness. If the buildings of Venice did not exist, they would have to be invented: on Torcello, the true, original Venice, the buildings have gone (only the Duomo, grass-enclosed, remains), but the buildings are there more than ever—in the clouds that touch the water, in the forming and reforming of color broken by a single oarblade invoking in one sweep the majesty of a brushstroke across the heavens. From a single Cyclopean Etruscan wall one can reconstruct a whole Etruscan city, opening on a mountain height with all earth's buried secrets, as in Etruscan tombs all the brightness of sea and sky may be found recommitted to the earth. From a single stone wall, from the grass bank of a canal on Torcello, one can, looking up, around, and about, reconstruct Venice as it was and relive it as it is. Here the city is reduced to essence, to total abstraction. Mathematics and poetry meet; form lives in space, and space is everywhere. The sky is everything.

Arthur Symons has spoken of the architecture of Venice as one "which seems to have grown up out of the water in order that it may be a flower on the surface of the water." And as a surface flower, it is for me the coral atoll in reverse. In the lagoons of many Pacific islands, where, as in Venice, sea and sky meet with unimpeded and shimmering clarity, the white ledges branch down into the water, folding one into the other until an entire dream world rests below a blue green surface. In Venice the coral palaces branch up above that surface; they are the surface, water's gift to the air.

It is impossible to "paint" Venice; the painter must, in a real sense, remain powerless when confronted with dream in its pure essence, and yet the great painter will always strive for the impossible. Adja Yunkers is a believer in Jean Cocteau's dictum that an artist must find out what he can do and then do something else. No medium is alien to him because he must prove that he can test its limits. Not content to be the foremost print-maker in America, Yunkers has shown that his technical accomplishment is such that he could give undreamt-of dimension to pastel and that he could return to oil with the assurance gained from his graphic explorations. Now, in these lithographs, he attacks the medium of stone, and, for this attack in typical fashion, has chosen the most impossible subject—the furthest thing from stone, the air itself, the skies of Venice. The result is that he has taken the mirror that is Venice and rubbed it bare. The back of the mirror here becomes the mirror itself, and what we have is reflection reflected. All color is suggested by the absence of color, by the subtle shimmering grays; the quality of light is conveyed by the light inherent in the black.

The "Skies" are for Yunkers a logical continuation of the series of large pastels that he recently completed. In these the colors glow like coals in a brazier, contained but expanding, re-vivifying one another. *Bewitchers' Sabbath*, 1958 is a brilliant example, a cauldron of color, the hot reds held in suspension as if the molten liquid had congealed as it flowed over the lip, the contrasting blacks evoking a group of wild dancers frozen in their frenzy. With the intensity of contrast and gradation of color, Yunkers carried this medium further than one would have thought possible. He set fire to chalk and the filmy pinks and blues characteristic of eighteenth-century pastels that had made of the pastel such a scorned medium were burned away. In striving to intensify his medium, Yunkers piled layer on layer of chalk and gave it the density, the look and feel of oil; the total effect was one of power with lightness; he gave weight to transparency. Now, reversing the process, he has made weight all lightness and air; he has given transparency to stone.

It is astonishing how much of the baroque nature of Venice is here put down in black and white—the great moving mosaic above the veined marble of the water, the clusters of gondolas at the horizon's edge, black lines rising and falling, the lights of lanterns bobbing above the canals against the lacework of moldering palaces. Here, in spirit, is a record of the "Sposalizio del Mare," and the echoing words of the Doge: "Desponsamus te, Mare"—"We espouse thee, Sea, in sign of true and lasting dominion." Here, abstracted, are the fury of Tintoretto and the sweep of Tiepolo. In Tintoretto's *Marriage of Ariadne and Bacchus*, Venus slowly turning in the air as she arrives with her crown of stars is a distillation of the skies of Venice; and it is that distillation that Yunkers has carried forward. The high point of the group is No. VIII, the oval, an opal in X-ray, containing in miniature the reflected outline of all force, human and divine.

Adja Yunkers has quoted Melville on the sea: "It is not a vista but a background. People living on it experience it on the foreground." Venice *is* the sea, and by giving us, in these powerfully original graphic statements, its very essence, he has

293

reminded us that it is not only possible for an artist to transcend his medium but that by setting down with accuracy and fullness the shadow of a thing he may bring us close to the thing itself.

[1961]

ON BEING MERRY

SOME WORDS like coins worn smooth by constant exchange become so dulled with use that in time they risk being withdrawn from circulation; one that has lost much of its brightness is the word "merry." Ours is far from being a merry world like that of Shakespeare's merry England, and we approach festivity with hesitation and restraint; for with so much unpleasantness everywhere how can any occasion be a pleasant one, and with so much darkness around us, how can we really make light of anything? And yet merriment and the need to make merry are deeply human: we come wailing into this world, but soon learn that we can obtain what we want easily with a smile. Behind our laughter may always be tears; but if we lose the ability to laugh we are in danger of losing our human qualities.

Originally, merry meant pleasant or agreeable, and hence, secondarily, productive of pleasure—amusing, comical. Perhaps as we approach the word today, we should think first of the secondary meaning; for if we want an enjoyable world, we must produce it—we must be gay, we must be able to laugh. Everything tends, however, in the opposite direction to make us sober if not solemn. And solemnity sets our facial expressions and fixes our minds: we can see only what lies straight ahead of us, and but one thing at a time. It demands absolute answers, a rigid outline of black and white. Gaiety forces us, on the other hand, to see two things at once, black and white, not together as gray, and yet mingled and mixed—the two interwoven, interplaying, as in the checkered fabric of Harlequin. Laughter animates the business of life, the dead furniture of daily living; it makes things happen; it creates a varied, fabulous, multicolored existence. Laughter destroys our fixed ideas, upsets our stereotypes of thought and feeling, and surprises us at every turn. By eliminating perspective and making us see what is remote as suddenly close and what is close as suddenly remote, it gives us a world not rigid and heavy but shifting, ever changing and light.

The face of the clown, the comedian, is a moon mask seemingly incapable of change; but while doing one thing—counting money, playing cards, shaving, or making love—the comic artist is always thinking of something else; his mask is constantly about to break into pieces with the slightest twitch or pull, like the moon in one of its phases. Laughter provides no answers, it deals with the concrete, the here-and-now; its abstract nature forever eludes us. And if we realize that much of life cannot be catalogued or defined, that some questions can only be answered by further questions, then we are in all seriousness coming close to an evaluation of the mercurial quality of merriment and a true appreciation of pleasure.

[1958]

CREATIVE WRITING

IN HER INTRODUCTION to *Aromas and Flavors of Past and Present*, Mrs. Poppy Cannon, gourmet cooking editor of *House Beautiful*, tells of using the term "creative cooking" in addressing Miss Alice B. Toklas, who provides the recipes in this remarkable cookbook. Miss Toklas's voice and eyebrows rose. "What would that be?" she asked. "For me it has always been the highest accolade," Mrs. Cannon interpolates, "to achieve imaginative originality." And she adds rather wistfully that she will not soon forget Miss Toklas's "snort and scorn" on hearing the phrase. For Miss Toklas, schooled in the traditions of French cuisine, cooking is an art, and like any art it involves certain classical disciplines; to call it "creative" is as nonsensical as it is redundant. The Sunday pages of our newspapers are filled with examples of such "creative cooking," many of them as weird as Edward Lear's Crumboblious Cutlets. Frankfurters with sliced pineapple and parsley may be strikingly creative, they may save time, look heavenly, and satisfy thousands of palates; they are not art.

What then of "creative writing?" The term brings not the slightest flicker of an eyebrow today, and yet to me it is just as meaningless. The expression came in with progressive education along with "creative play" and "creative mathematics"; we now also have the "language arts," which I take to be English and public relations somehow mysteriously combined. If "creative writing" is writing by means of which something is created, then its opposite, "noncreative writing," must be writing by means of which nothing whatever is created; copying or typewriting, since they involve only mechanical skills, would therefore, I should think, be "noncreative writing." Writing, to whatever end it is applied, whether technical, scientific, historical, or artistic, is in fact a craft, one which in the hands of a master becomes an art, in the hands of a genius, great art.

[1960]

THE BLUESTOCKINGS
OF NEW ENGLAND

MARTHA BACON begins her *Puritan Promenade* [1] in eighteenth-century Boston, and ends it in New Haven at the turn of the twentieth century; in the course of it, she takes her reader down the rich Connecticut River valley, the heart of commercial and intellectual New England; her discerning eye is focussed on more than scenery, although that also does not escape her attention. Her subject is New England women, and they seem to be all over the place— in houses, churches, libraries, universities, lecturing from platforms, strolling by the river, even perched in the trees. All of them are nonconformists, who, rebelling against the arbitrary limitations of society, science, and religion, had an impact on their time. *Puritan Promenade* presents in miniature and in a delightful, witty fashion an important segment of American social and literary history.

By 1820 the common reader had come into his own. The popular writers who emerged to fill the expanding leisure time

[1] Martha Bacon, *Puritan Promenade* (Boston: Houghton Mifflin).

299

in England and America were, Miss Bacon points out, frequently women:

> They wrote fluently and prolifically. They wrote tracts, dramas, stories, essays and poetry. They were industrious and ambitious and with the exception of a few they regarded themselves as poets.

One of the precursors of these prolific wrtiers was Phillis Wheatley, the second woman poet to be published in America and one of the earliest of either sex. She was a Negro slave, a modest, pretty, and pathetic creature whose heroic efforts in heroic couplets were "valued in her time for all the wrong reasons by many of the wrong people and some of the right ones."

The next of Miss Bacon's ladies was anything but modest. Lydia Sigourney, the Sweet Singer of Hartford, the "American Hemans," author of some sixty volumes, had reason to consider herself a literary light. "Glossily ringletted and monumentally breast-pinned," as Henry James described her, she claimed thousands of readers. "We are, as you doubtless know, emphatically a *reading people*," Mrs. Sigourney wrote to Lady Blessington. And she knew exactly what those readers wanted. No writer of her day "caused so many luxurious tears to flow or addressed so many public monuments." She even addressed stone walls. "Rise, lofty column," she told the Bunker Hill Monument, and it apparently did—for thousands of Americans brought up on *Poor Richard* and eager for patriotic and respectable subjects. Mrs. Sigourney was a one-woman Woman's Page, bad in the truly grand manner. Most of her poems begin with "Ho!" or "Hail!" There is one canto of her *Traits of the Aborigines of America*, which opens:

> Say! who again will listen to the call
> Of the returning Muse?

Catharine Beecher, a minister's daughter, was another fervent lady. She published in 1836 her *Letters on the Difficulties*

of Religion in which she sought to refute Jonathan Edwards'
theory of hellfire; and she made people listen. When asked late
in her life to join in the hymn beginning, "I am nothing, Lord,
nothing," she refused. "I am *not* nothing," said Catharine
Beecher.

The career of Delia Bacon, the central figure on this frieze,
may be summed up simply:

> Delia Bacon
> Was very partial to Sir Francis
> Bacon;
> She maintained that he was Shake-
> speare, the Bard of Avon.
> They locked her up and let her rave
> on.

And rave on she did in *The Philosophy of the Plays of Shakespeare Unfolded,* a "marvelously contrived gargoyle, a monument to misapplied scholarship." All these ladies were, in one
way or another, poets, bad, but bad in no ordinary way.

Good women poets have often had a difficult time with the
men in their lives (Emily Dickinson and Christina Rossetti come
immediately to mind); bad women poets, on the basis of these
examples, seem to flee them like the plague, or, at least, to take
momentary refuge from them, along with their largely female
audience, in a torrent of words. Phillis Wheatley, admired by
Voltaire (who never bothered to read her) and by George Washington (who did), got on famously with men as long as she
stayed away from them, but not long after she married John
Peters, a drunken no-good free Negro who dressed like the
gentlemen with whom she had associated, she ended her career
in abject poverty, dying along with the third of her children, a
copy of *Paradise Lost* at her elbow. Phillis almost never referred
directly to herself in her poems; the eighteenth-century style
had a way naturally of eliminating the personal, and Phillis,

being a slave and having become a slave to Boston, was the soul
of reticence. Lydia Sigourney, in Miss Bacon's words, idealized
her husband, "the thin-lipped little Yankee merchant who resembled a featherless owl," into a nobleman "who had con-
ferred inestimable honor on a humble but adoring bride." But
Miss Bacon points out that she frequently revealed in her writings that she felt otherwise; in *The Intemperate*, for example,
which concerns the downfall of a drunkard, she declared that
there is "no tyranny so perfect as that of a capricious and alienated husband." One senses that she may well have been referring
to her own. When Catharine Beecher's fiancé was lost at sea,
she took up her pen; and undismayed by a total absence of any
verbal gift, sought to make clear that if *she* could not have him,
then only God could.

"Literary," wrote Julia Moore, the Sweet Singer of Michigan, "is a work very difficult to do"; and these ladies would have
agreed. They worked hard and long to give the public what it
wanted—consolation in the face of disaster; and disaster was
apparently omnipresent. Gordon Haight, Mrs. Sigourney's
biographer, describes her work as dealing with "deaths of in-
fants, dying boys' last bequests, the death of consumptive girls,
of missionaries in Burma and Liberia, of poets, lunatics, artists
and sailors."

In the preface to *Water-Drops*, her temperance poems,
Lydia Sigourney wrote: "Women, by the courtesy of modern
times, have been styled the educating sex." As educators they
set—or met—the standards of taste. And it is with taste that
Puritan Promenade is ultimately concerned. Mrs. Sigourney,
Miss Bacon says,

> . . . molders in the literary attic, smelling of mice and moth-
> balls, among the stuffed birds . . . the odd bits of chipped
> porcelain, the quaint clothing and the bundle of letters
> almost too faded to read. They are impermanent things but
> they shape the past for us in small ways. Through them we

know how our obscure ancestors lived their daily lives. The Gettysburg Address, *Leaves of Grass*, the lyric poems of Ralph Waldo Emerson may tell us something of the genius of the age, but we can learn nothing from them of how people whiled away a rainy summer Sunday in the middle of the nineteenth century. If we wish to know how this was done we turn to Lydia Sigourney.

Martha Bacon, herself a member of the family that figures prominently in her pages, demonstrates in her writing, the Puritanical virtue of restraint together with the un-Puritanical one of ebullient wit. Her book deserves a permanent place beside Dame Edith Sitwell's *English Eccentrics*. The small detail lights up the whole; the ladies in her frieze shine like fine silver in a Connecticut house.

[1965]

MARY McCARTHY
AND THE MEDICI

N O ONE needs to be reminded at this late date that Mary McCarthy is a daring, original, and forceful writer; and never has she been bolder in her attack on any subject than in the present volume [1] in which she gives us what she considers the essential Florence. She sets out to clear away the picturesque clutter that came in with the Victorians, all that has gone to build up the "tooled-leather idea of Florence as a dear bit of the old world," a city that belonged only to its foreign residents, to the "old maids of both sexes," retired librarians, governesses, gentlemen painters, dabblers of all kinds, who wanted somehow to keep it preciously to themselves. In so doing, she writes with none of the ecstatic sighs and awed whispers that we associate with the late nineteenth-century travelers. She speaks calmly and coldly as if she were attacking the stones of Florence themselves: her sentences have a nervous chiseled quality; and occasionally, when she seems to feel that her reader's

[1] Mary McCarthy, *The Stones of Florence*, with photographs by Evelyn Hofer and others (New York: Harcourt Brace Jovanovich, Inc.).

304

attention is about to wander, she comes down hard and intro-
duces an image calculated to shock him into recognition. The
cruel tower of the Palazzo Vecchio pierces the sky, she writes,
"like a stone hypodermic needle." This is certainly not the city
of the guidebooks nor of the conventional art history.

Florence today, Miss McCarthy begins, is for the summer
traveler something to be endured more than appreciated. It is
full of banks (indeed this city of bankers, although she fails to
mention the fact, has given the world its standard bank architecture), loan agencies, insurance companies, shops selling place-
mats, doilies and tooled-leather desk sets. With its dreary main
piazza, its forbidding fortresslike buildings, its lackluster cafés,
it strikes the traveler at once as dull and provincial. The noise,
confined within narrow stone canyons, is deafening; the traffic,
intolerable ("one old American lady, the mother-in-law of an
author, walking on Via Guicciardini, had the distinction of being
hit by two bicycles, from the front and rear simultaneously").
One is cheated, robbed, poorly housed, miserably fed, devoured
by mosquitoes; and in constant danger of being killed by motor
scooters and bits of falling masonry. The Florentines appear to
be just what Dante said they were, "stingy, envious, and proud";
and extremely reluctant to give one proper directions. The mu-
seums are the worst-hung and worst-organized in Italy; there is
no night life. "How can you stand it?" the traveler asks and
usually gets out. Miss McCarthy stayed; and her answer to the
question, in the remainder of her book, as she weaves in and out
among Florentine artifacts as if through traffic, is that one en-
dures it all because it is there to be endured, a "terrible city, in
many ways, uncomfortable and dangerous to live in, a city of
drama, argument, and struggle."

With her clinical eye Miss McCarthy views Florence as
constantly at war with itself, split into rival factions, Black and
White, Guelph and Ghibelline, throughout its long history. But
it was not just the masses that veered back and forth; the individual Florentine was "liable to shifts of passion or lapses into

barbarism, as though he constituted a mob in himself." The tension within the individual was sexual as well as political; homosexuality was rampant in this new Athens. Only in the pursuits of the intellect was the energy of Florence properly channeled; only in art did it achieve a powerful and tragic unity. It is no wonder that its colors were the colors of stone and metal, and that its music was that of the hammer and chisel. The drama of Florentine life resulted, in the case of Brunelleschi, in the art of perfect balance. This plain bald little man who raised the dome of the cathedral at its center epitomizes for Miss McCarthy the greatness of the city; and it is against him that she measures all other artists. Not all of them achieved his balance by any means. Uccello, to whom she devotes some of her most interesting pages, is for her the first modern artist who was really "cracked."

"In daring," Miss McCarthy remarks, "the Florentines excelled; that is why their architecture and their sculpture and much of their painting have such a virile character." Florence, unlike Venice or Siena, is a masculine city, descended from a pioneer version of Rome established in the wild mountains; many of its streets still run straight out toward the mountain of Fiesole "like streets in the raw towns of the American Far West." The Florentines were innovators, and felt a compulsion to be first in everything: they wrote the first important work in the Vulgar tongue, indeed, they gave Italy its literary language; they raised the first massive dome and created the finest statuary since antiquity, composed the first opera, and the first literary and art criticism in a modern sense; they were the first political scientists; they discovered perspective; they tried literally to move mountains and to fly through the air. The list is unending simply because Florence invented the Renaissance, which is the same as saying that it created the modern world. Not, of course, Miss McCarthy adds, "an unmixed good."

There is nothing new in this cataloguing of Florentine achievement; but the peculiar merit of Miss McCarthy's book is that it makes us look at all these things close-up and in our own terms, as if they had happened yesterday, not isolated but related one to the other, reported upon and examined by an intelligence that is nervously concerned with them. She sees her job as that of a restorer, like one of those modern Florentines in whom the old skills survive, at work on a crumbling fresco, removing the layers of overpainting and getting down to the original.

But the danger of the restorer is that in removing paint and dirt he may make the original appear too bright and new; in bringing everything close-up, the writer may tend to magnify the insignificant. Miss McCarthy's predilection for gossip whether five years or five hundred years old makes some of her paragraphs seem patchworks of trivia. Speaking of the Florentine Mannerists, who were, she says, the first modern painters in the sense that their work could not be understood and appreciated by a great proportion of their contemporaries, she rightly remarks that the "faculty of eliciting inappropriate comparisons is always a mark of strain in art." She herself is not without it. The description of the "Deposition" of Pontormo looking "as though Cecil Beaton had done the costumes for a requiem ballet on Golgotha" may be suggestive but it is certainly strained; and, her characterization of Michelangelo's figures of Night and Day, Twilight and Dawn as "somewhat rubbery" is sure to rub many readers the wrong way. But no matter; better her brightness than the tedium of the "tooled leather" commentators; and one who can see the Pitti Palace "with wings extended in a glaring gravel courtyard, like a great brown flying lizard, basking in the terrible sun," has an eye that is far from ordinary.

The 128 black-and-white photographs, principally by Evelyn Hofer, and the 12 color plates, which accompany the text, are, on the whole, magnificent. I agree with Miss McCarthy that Miss Hofer's work has "an astonishing, even uncanny fidelity" to the "essential Florence." But it is a Florence one never sees; and how Miss Hofer managed some of the shots "amid the hazards of Florentine traffic" without being suspended at times by rope from the palazzi is a mystery. The freakish angles and the

odd choice of detail give many of the photographs a chichi quality that is not wholly absent from the text. They all seem to
have been taken at high noon or at midnight and in midsummer;
there is a minimum of shadow, and nowhere a hint of the fog
and haze so typical of Florence in autumn and winter. An unreal
and incongruous silence hangs over the scenes; the streets have
been vacuumed of litter and of people. Expert though she is,
Miss Hofer like Miss McCarthy has cleaned things up a trifle too
much; and as if to bear out the fact that the two ladies have been
overly concerned with their dusting, we are given at the very
end of the book a glorious and totally pointless close-up of Florentine garbage-collecting equipment, made to look like modern
or pre-Columbian sculpture, a bicycle-propelled platform complete with two cans and a twig broom.

Florence itself is sure to be torn apart by the book; those
Florentine professors who bother to read it will be all for it because even if they disagree with most of her judgments they will
feel that she is championing them against the omnipresent tasteless tourist; the members of the Anglo-American colony will be
violently against it because they will find themselves neglected,
indeed eliminated. It will be the old story of Florence divided
against itself; for Florence today is not just Tuscan Florence nor
has it been for some time. The city did not entirely stop developing with the fall of the republic and the final arrival of the
Medici, as Miss McCarthy with her neat democratic bias would
like us to believe. (Her antipathy to the Medici in general is such
that she seems at times almost literally to sicken at the sight of
the pills on their coat of arms, a reaction as extreme in its way
as that of writers like G. H. Young, who felt on the contrary
that the great old dynasty could really have done no wrong.)
Florence is a small provincial city, but in a sense it does
belong to the world. Miss McCarthy overlooks the essential fact
that on her death in 1743 Anna Maria Ludovica, the last Medici, gave to the state of Tuscany forever all the art treasures

collected by the family throughout the centuries on condition that they should never be removed from Florence, and should be for the benefit of the public of all nations. Were it not for that legacy, Florence would still be a city like Lucca, its ancient enemy that in many ways it resembles; and without it Miss McCarthy would not have written this book. No matter how violently one may object to some of its pronouncements nor how unsettling one may find its vague and frequently incorrect use of Italian, it is brilliantly conceived, bold, and refreshing.

[1959]

IX

FROM OTHER SHORES

IN PRAISE
OF CHILDHOOD
(St.-John Perse)

IN A REMOTE ISLAND in the New Hebrides I once met
a French planter who spoke of the years spent on his
plantation with the hesitation of one who had grown
accustomed to silence. He said that the visit of a planter from a
neighboring island was indeed a splendid thing, that a face, even
a familiar one, became an event of importance. People who have
lived such solitary lives learn to use their eyes: they see the
common things that surround them freshly each day with the
clear vision of children. They can look on the world as if they
were really seeing it for the first time. It is this vision that gives
Eloges, the product of a similar isolation in fabulous surroundings, its immediate and universal appeal.

Published in Paris in 1911, it was the first volume of poems
by one of France's greatest living poets, Alexis St. Léger Leger,
or, as he has become known to us, St.-John Perse. Much has been
written of M. Leger's career as one of France's foremost prewar
diplomats, first in the Orient, then as secretary to Briand, and of
his subsequent exile in Washington. It is true that his diplomatic

travels and experiences in various parts of the world have influenced his work in subtle ways. But it is interesting that most of the poems in this volume were written while he was a student in his twenties before he had given up his medical studies. Although some of the poems were added later, the volume presents mainly the poet's earliest work, which grew out of his youth on the small island of Saint-Léger-les-Feuilles near Guadaloupe. The subject of *Eloges* is childhood itself, and the poems, as the title indicates, are poems of praise. *Eloges,* parts of which have been translated into Spanish, Italian, and German, was first published in an English translation by Louise Varèse in 1944. The Bollingen Series has now reissued Mrs. Varèse's translation in revised form.[1]

Berlioz once wrote, describing a vivid scene of his adolescence: "Life was evidently outside me, far away, very far." It is this outside, far-off world that St.-John Perse gives us in these poems. While the subject is shadowy, almost legendary, the approach to it is luminous and direct: St.-John Perse writes of what he knew and of what he knows. "Childhood, my love," the poet exclaims; and the poems are an apostrophe to his own specific childhood in the Antilles. He writes of the town where the candy vendor "battles the wasps whose flight is like the bites of sunlight on the back of the sea," and where the walls, to the child returning from his missionary school, "smell of hot bread," and of the plantation where the mute faces of the servants" paused like burnt-out stars behind our chairs," of the country around it where the old people in the courtyards drink "punches the color of pus." Childhood is addressed with reverence; the recurring words throughout are "joy," "esteem," "praise," and "celebration."

One of the characteristics of the poetry of St.-John Perse has been its sustained psalmlike fervor; and we find him here at

---

[1] St.-John Perse, *Eloges and Other Poems*, Bollingen Series, bilingual edition, translated by Louise Varèse (New York: Pantheon).

the beginning of his work writing in a veritable intoxication of reverence that no modern poet, not even Dylan Thomas in his Welsh rhapsodies, has ever equaled.

He recreates from memory the living world of childhood through a reiteration of sensuous images: bright everyday household things are evoked alongside old and indistinct ones like the disparate objects heaped up by a hurricane, grown over with old roots and green vines. The long, winding *versets* themselves —and in this the form is superbly fitted to the subject—suggest the gnarled and twisted lianas reaching out to claim everything in their path. Images recording the long, slow, hazy sweep of time and memory gather slowly: the dresses of the servant girls sweep across the floor, voices are heard from the different levels of the garden, the

> . . . dreamer with dirty cheeks
>   comes slowly out of
> an old dream streaked with
>   violences, wiles, and splendor,
> and jeweled in sweat, toward the
>   odor of meat
>   he descends
> like a woman trailing: her linen, all
>   her clothes, and her hanging hair.

Again,

> Rhythms of pride flow down the
>   red mornes.
> Turtles roll in the narrows like
>   brown stars. . . .
> Trees were rotting at the far end of
>   creeks of black wine.

The wind, rising between the islands, sweeps above the houses and over an old man's chest; the smell of coffee drifts up the stairs. The child speaks:

315

> "When you stop combing my hair, I'll
> stop hating you."
> The child wants his hair combed on the
> doorstep.
> "Don't pull like that. It's bad enough
> being touched.
> When you've finished my hair, I'll have hated you."
> Meanwhile the wisdom of day takes
> the shape of a fine tree
> and the swaying tree,
> loosing a pinch of birds,
> scales off in the lagoons of the sky a
> green so beautiful,
> there is nothing that is greener except the waterbug.
> "Don't pull on my hair so far . . ."

Everything is drawn out threadlike, worn away. The heart itself, under its burden of love and memory, drags as if along the decks of a ship, more exhausted than an old swab.

The effect of all this is to suggest a primitive painting in which everything is seen on the same plane, where light and shadow are one, where perspective does not exist—or rather, where everything is seen in unending perspective, and events occur in an eternal now.

Those who have followed the poems of St.-John Perse carefully are struck by his constant use of the image of the doorway, the entrance to the house, through which life comes and goes, and of the great gates through which civilization has passed. Indeed, this book begins with a poem, "Ecrit sur la Porte," which should be read alongside T. S. Eliot's "Marina." The door, the gate, means both welcome and farewell. It becomes, in a specific sensual sense, that gateway of the body toward which all desire is directed. Psychologically, it marks the division between the inner and outer world: to the child, on the threshold of experience, there is no such division, but to the adult, and to the artist, there is the constant passage between, the balance kept between light and dark, present and past. In the later poetry of St.-John Perse the exile becomes a common figure—man uprooted from his homeland, civilizations lost and buried by time and conquest; and yet the exile always returns. He returns in the triumph of language, in the magnificence of his artifacts, in the depth of his dream. St.-John Perse speaks for that rich human exchange that is the glory of man.

[1957]

LAND OF POETS
(*Haitian Poetry*)

HAITI IS A LAND of color—orange, lemon, magenta, and green blending together in incredible and unpredictable patterns of light and shadow, against a sky of so intense a blue that it seems to burn slowly on the horizon, consuming tree, mountain peak, and ocean wave. The Haitian landscape is constantly shifting, the patterns change, the geometric designs like giant crystals form and reform; and against this mobile landscape the people move: they arrange themselves in patterns within the everchanging patterns of nature, they move as the light moves, and the slightest gesture, a lifted hand, a nodding head, becomes a note in a symphony. The air is alive with sound, and in the sound there is color. Singing and dancing to the Haitian peasant are as natural as breathing, and as complex and beautiful. The native Creole speech is itself a reflection of the contour of the country; there is nothing smooth about it; it is like the mountains, rugged and unyielding; it has the warp and woof, the twist and tangle, of a wild uneven land. One can hear in it at times a sound such as that produced by large pieces of tin slapped together; at others, the single melancholy note of the *vaccine*, a long bamboo horn, and always in the background the slow pulsing beat of drums.

It is important to mention speech, for, like dancing, talking is an art in Haiti: words roll and ripple from every tongue, and even silence can be strangely eloquent. Haitians have always been tellers of tales, and a whole story may be summed up in a simple Creole proverb. The tradition of the African *samba*, who was musician, storyteller, and poet combined, is kept alive today. So, too, is the African rhythm: the hypnotic, staccato beat that gives power to the dance, animates the speech, and through the speech the tales, songs, and poems. Haiti is a land of poets, of lyric poetry, poetry of feeling rather than intellect. With the Haitian peasant poetry is a living, day-to-day thing, as it has always been. With the intellectual of the upper classes this instinct has been strengthened by a French classical education, which has stressed the fact that the writing and appreciation of verse is to be expected of any normal, intelligent, cultivated person. The result is that there are surely more poets per square mile in Haiti than anywhere else in the world, and these poets range from the simple peasant singer to the exponent of the most complicated modern school. A recent anthology of modern Haitian poetry contains a map showing the birthplaces of the poets, and the map is so dense with dots that it looks like a black swarm of bees. A U.S. poet entering such a hive cannot possibly be aware of all that is going on; the best he can hope to do in a brief space is to give some general impression of this fresh and lively spectacle.

The number of poets is all the more astonishing in view of the fact that most of them are *published* poets. Publication in Haiti means paying a private printer or the state to bring out one's book. The audience is small, since the majority of the people, even if they could read French, could not afford anything so expensive as a book of poems. The poet usually dis-

319

tributes the entire edition to his friends; recognition consists of remarks from them or mention in a few newspaper reviews, and sometimes, but not often, a notice abroad. Yet poetry goes on, and much of it possesses an extraordinary vitality.

The basic conflict in poetry, as in other fields of Haitian endeavor, has constantly been between native tradition and French influence. Haiti has deep cultural ties with France, and French influence upon Haitian literature naturally continues even today, when Haiti is considerably less oriented to Europe politically than it once was. This influence is often important and valuable. In the early part of the century, however, Haitian poetry followed the French Parnassian and Symbolist schools so closely that it seemed at times a poor copy of an already fading original. Some poets of this period, whose names now sound like poems in themselves, Coriolan Ardouin, Ignace Nau, Pierre Faubert, Oswald Durand, Christian Werleigh, Justinien Ricot, Madame Ida Faubert, produced much that was original, but much that seemed borrowed and secondhand. As René Bélance, one of the most sensitive poets of the younger generation today, has expressed it, Haitian poetry "was elegantly bored: little lyrics for young ladies, insignificant descriptions of sunsets. In this incandescent island, it was dying of cold. . . . There was no fundamental fidelity to the air we breathed. People wrote not of being, but of objects. . . . And when poets began to rewrite the fables of Lafontaine two centuries too late, the asphyxia was complete."

Around 1925 a group of young writers, some of them recently back from France, sought to break with the older traditions. No account of the development of modern Haitian poetry would be complete without some mention of this "Generation of the Occupation," as they were called. *La Revue Indigène* became their focal point; and although the magazine itself was short-lived, its influence was far-reaching. The fundamental belief of these writers was expressed in the name of the magazine: poetry, they held, should be *indigenous*; they strove to

320

"Haitianize" the Muse. In this they succeeded, and in the process were responsible for producing some of the finest works in Haitian literature. Among the leaders of the movement were Normil Sylvain, Jacques Roumain, Antonio Vieux, Philippe Thoby-Marcelin, and Emile Roumer. Carl Brouard, one of the talented poets among them, captured the spirit of the moment when he spoke in his forthright poem *"Nous" ("We")* of "the madmen, . . . the poets" with "hearts powerful as motors." There was the force of affirmation in this revolt; and as M. Bélance has pointed out, few of the reputations of the older poets survived it. Only Oswald Durand, the author of the Creole poem *"Choucoune,"* one of the lyric masterpieces of Haitian literature, seemed in touch with the modern spirit. This movement was not merely a protest against the style of older writers, but a passionate declaration of faith in the Haitian people, and in things Haitian. In reacting against the U.S. occupation, Haitian writers saw as never before that their real strength lay not in emulating Europeans but in being themselves, and in giving the world at large the true picture of the ordinary Haitian in all the beauty and dignity of his difficult position. That is precisely what the late Jacques Roumain, novelist, poet, and ethnologist, did in his *Gouverneurs de la Rosée* (published in English as *Masters of the Dew*), an extraordinary novel that needs no introduction. Jacques Roumain is certainly the leading prose writer of the modern period; the leading poet is Emile Roumer.

Like Jean Brierre, one of the important young poets to follow him, M. Roumer was born in Jérémie, southern capital of the Haitian poetic scene. He studied in Port-au-Prince, and afterwards in Paris and England; and in 1925, when he was twenty-two years old, he published his *Poèmes d'Haïti et de France*. Soon after the appearance of this book, M. Roumer retired to Jérémie, where he lives today. He has written occasional prose pieces for Haitian newspapers since then, but has produced no other book of poetry. It is said that he is no longer writing, but as recently as 1947 a special Christmas issue of *Haïti-Journal* devoted to his work contained many previously unpublished pieces, some of them among his finest. Although his famous *"Marabout de mon Coeur"* ("The Peasant Declares His Love"), worthy to stand beside Durand's *"Choucoune,"* has been printed in anthologies in this country in a fine English translation by John Peale Bishop, his work is scarcely known to American readers. It is to be hoped that it will soon be collected and made available to the wide audience it deserves.

The title of M. Roumer's book is exact; his poems are both Haitian and French—French in that they show an unusual genius for handling varied verse forms, deeply Haitian in vocabulary, outlook, and essence. They are the robust lyrical expression of a man who can with reason call Villon his ancestor. He can combine the earthiness of the Haitian peasant with the elegance of the Parisian dandy: he is at home anywhere, for he is proud to be what he is, a man of feeling and intelligence. In his poems he writes of a great many different things—childhood reminiscences of Port-au-Prince, the English landscape, foreign women, Haitian history, and Indian legend. "I am black," he says, *"Niger Sum,"* and says it with humor and without self-pity. He can be savage, too, in his attack on those of his countrymen who would forget their African antecedents:

> *Bête comme ses pieds, rouge comme un kaki*
> *je présente au lecteur le mulâtre Bouqui. . . .*
> As dumb as his feet, and as pink as khaki,
> I give my reader the mulatto Bouqui. . . .

M. Roumer's poetry is a poetry of the senses, but there is nothing soft or sentimental about it. It has a rare toughness; he can laugh with the body as well as with the mind:

> *Midi sonne en mon ventre aussi sûr qu'à l'horloge.*
> It is noon by my stomach as it is by the clock.

M. Roumer delights in evoking the Haitian landscape through the use of Creole words that have what he calls "the hot perfume of mangoes" *("le chaud parfum des mangues")*. His work has both gusto and charm, vigor and delicacy; and his love poetry is among the finest this century has produced anywhere.

Another leader of the modern movement in poetry and one of the most prominent figures in Haitian letters is Philippe Thoby-Marcelin. Although he first devoted himself almost completely to poetry, publishing three collections of poems between 1924 and 1941, he won international recognition as a prose writer when his novel *Canapé Vert*, written in collaboration with his younger brother, Pierre Marcelin, received the prize for the best novel in the second Latin American contest sponsored by Farrar and Rinehart in 1943. The publication of this book, which treats of peasant life in a small district near Port-au-Prince, was an important event in modern Haitian literature, for it showed the world how authentic Haitian material could be handled within the traditional framework of the novel. Since its appearance, the Marcelin brothers have written *La Bête de Musseau* and *Le Crayon de Dieu*, which appeared in English as *The Beast of the Haitian Hills* and *The Pencil of God*. In the meantime, however, Philippe Thoby-Marcelin has not forgotten poetry; he published in Paris this year his most distinguished collection of poems, *A Fonds Perdu (Invested for Life)*.

What is remarkable in the Marcelin novels is that the exploration of the Haitian peasant mentality is accomplished with the most complete objectivity: the characters are human beings first and Haitians second. The Marcelins seem to say that the situation of the Haitian peasant is bad, but it is nonetheless a human situation. There is a basic tension created between the primitive material and the sophistication with which it is presented. One is reminded in reading their books of the Sicilian novelist Verga, whose masterly prose became a sensitive instrument for recording at close range the tragedy and comedy of the Sicilian peasant. The ears of the Marcelins likewise are faithful to the rhythm of Haitian speech; they can record because they have been trained to listen. The result is something unique in literature today.

Philippe Thoby-Marcelin, while keenly involved in Haiti's problems, is one of the poets in whom one senses the effect of a careful reading of much of modern French poetry: there are echoes here of St.-John Perse and Valery Larbaud, stylistic reminders of Jules Romains and Jean Cocteau. In *"Poème Liminaire"* ("Introductory Poem"), he strikes the note of traditional Haitian lyricism in a fresh and modern way:

> *Le bleu inaltérable de nos saisons*
> *Était mon élément, et le vert.*
> *Je vous parle d'une alliance indéfectible*
> *Avec la mer et les campagnes,*
> *—Toute la joie des Isles*
> *Et leur aisance profonde!*

> The unalterable blue of our seasons
> Was my element, and the green.
> I speak to you of an unfailing alliance
> With the sea and the countryside,
> —All the joy of the Islands
> And their profound ease.

The poem continues in the manner of Whitman, but of a Whitman with a certain Gallic grace:

> *J'étais le maître incontesté des altitudes,*
> *Je connaissais l'odeur exacte de chaque source,*
> *J'évaluais le silence des oiseaux,*
> *Je percevais le chant multiplié des plantes,*
> *Le bavardage globuleux des poissons.*
> *Et tous les hommes ignorant mes richesses!*

> I was the uncontested master of altitudes,
> I knew the exact odor of every stream,

I valued the silence of birds,
I perceived the multiplied song of plants,
The globular prattling of fishes.
And all men are unaware of my wealth.

The verbs "know," "value," and "perceive" are important; M. Thoby-Marcelin does not deal merely with pleasant surfaces; he goes to the heart of the matter. In *"Le Marron Pathétique"* ("The Pathetic Runaway"), he evokes in the simplest words the moment of terror of the escaped slave, a moment that becomes eternal by reason of the contrast of the slave's state of mind with the lush jungle in which he has taken refuge:

Était-ce de jour ou de nuit
De joie ou de douleur
Était-ce d'hier ou de toujours
Il s'était allongé
Dans les herbes lyriques de l'année
. . .
Et l'oreille au ras de la folie
(Dieu ayant mis sa main
Sur la bouche du vent)
Il écoutait battre
Au rythme élancé
De blessures pleines de cris
Les pas de sang d'une dansante émeute.

Was it by day or night
In joy or sorrow
Was it yesterday or forever
That he had reclined
On the lyrical grasses of the year
. . .
And his ear bent to madness
(God having put his hand

On the wind's mouth)
He listened
Through the pulsing rhythm
Of his howling wounds
To the bloody footsteps of a dancing revolt.

A gifted and original poet who exemplifies the modern revolt in a different area is Magloire St. Aude. Although his total poetic output consists of only two pamphlets, *Dialogue de Mes Lampes* and *Tabou*, which come to little more than thirty pages, he is one of the most widely discussed poets in Haiti today. One reason for this is undoubtedly the fact that, more perhaps than any of his contemporaries, he has made Haiti aware of a new poetic idiom. Although educated Haitians were acquainted with the technique of French surrealist poets through books reaching them in Port-au-Prince, Magloire St. Aude has localized it and made it a Haitian reality; and for this he deserves the highest praise.

M. St. Aude writes in the most sophisticated French; his truncated style is wholly modern and yet owes much to classical French tradition. To understand how he has arrived at a style that is entirely personal and yet linked to the best modern French poets anywhere, a style capable of expressing his own personal problems as well as those of his milieu and race, one must know something of the man himself. Magloire St. Aude is a native of Port-au-Prince; he received the traditional French education of the son of a well-to-do family; he has rarely left the city except for occasional trips to Cap-Haïtien and Jacmel. He has read the classics, and mentions among his favorite writers Montaigne and Emerson; he knows also Rimbaud, Mallarmé, Lautréamont, and Apollinaire; but because of the difficulty of obtaining books in Haiti, his reading in more recent French poetry has been by no means thorough. It is important to stress this fact, for M. St. Aude is not the follower of any particular modern French poet: his development has been individual.

While writing in a cultivated way, Magloire St. Aude has broken with the world that made this cultivation possible; he has turned his back on society. He now lives on the edge of Port-au-Prince in a typical peasant's hut, the walls of which display, together with an odd array of pinup girls, a picture of a Negro's head by Picasso and a photograph of President Roosevelt. He may be found at odd hours wandering on the back streets of the city or seated in a rum shop reciting lines from his poems to an audience that does not know quite what to make of this "feverish and sullen poet."

At first sight, M. St. Aude's poetry seems to consist of a host of disparate images drawn from the poet's subconscious, and in this sense is like any other surrealist work. But to call him a surrealist one must think of the peculiar meaning of surrealism in Haiti. The Haitian is never far removed from the world of the supernatural. For the masses, religion, even in its more remarkable mythical aspects, is an everyday reality; the gods of the Voodoo pantheon are familiar to every peasant, and as the Marcelin brothers have shown in their novels, are powerful forces constantly at work. Whether the Haitian believes in them or not, he is reminded of their presence—in the names of his towns and his buildings and even his public conveyances, in his Creole speech with its patchwork of proverbs. Moreover, there is everywhere a juxtaposition of the old and the new: the jukebox resounds in a crowded nightspot while the ancient African drums beat in the distance; a sleek modern station wagon may be seen drawn up beside a Voodoo temple or *houmfor*. The ordinary Haitian, too, seems to have a horror of the symmetrical: everything is somehow strangely askew, the roofs of the houses slant at odd angles, the lettering in signs is a mass of ornate scrolls and curlicues. The shortest distance between two points is never a straight line. In this asymmetrical world where mysterious forces are a part of the air one breathes, a roundabout way of speaking comes quite naturally; Magloire St. Aude has made a special literary use of something that is quite instinctive to the Haitian peasant.

The symbol of the veiled lamp in his *Dialogue* provides the key to the poetry. The lamp may be said to represent the vision of the poet, sealed, cut off from the world, but still lit by the intensity of feeling:

> *De mon émoi aux phrases,*
> *Mon mouchoir pour mes lampes.*
> From my feeling to my phrases,
> My handkerchief for my lamps.

The handkerchief, as in the poetry of Mallarmé, symbolizes the poet's departure from the everyday world, and at the same time his arrival in a world of greater reality. This exploration of the inner world reminds one that while the Haitian expresses emotion readily and is involved in the world around him, he is at the same time deeply concerned with the life of the spirit. The poetry of Magloire St. Aude is strangely negative, as his frequent use of such words as "silence," "emptiness," "nothing," poison," indicates; it is bitter and ironic:

> *Le poète, chat lugubre, au rire de chat.*
> The poet, lugubrious cat, with a cat's laugh.

The words of the poems appear to emerge from what the poet calls a "curtain of curling voices" *("rideau des voix bouclées");* as Philippe Thoby-Marcelin has expressed it, they seem "whispered as if between sleep and waking on a feverish night." André Breton has spoken of the poet's "irony which subdues the tumult." It is as if Magloire St. Aude, by denying everything, sought clearly to affirm the validity of human passion and suffering:

> *A mon mur de suie*
> *Le sable des années.*
> On my wall of soot
> The sands of the years.

In exploring his own unconscious, the poet goes to the depths of the Haitian unconscious, and gives symbolic intensity to the psychological strains and stresses that are at work everywhere. One senses in this dynamic, truncated style the staccato rhythms of his people. The brief poem *"Phrases"* shows something of his special quality:

> *Sept fois mon col,*
> *Dix-sept fois le collier,*
> *Le vent bossu du fiel.*
> *Informe, froid,*
> *Les yeux sans eau comme la fatalité.*
> Seven times my neck,
> Seventeen times my necklace.
> The wind with its hump of gall.
> Ugly, cold,
> Dry-eyed like fate.

With the map of modern Haitian poetry open before me, I have touched only a few of the many spots of interest. There are others: the fine free-verse poems of Roussan Camille and F. Morisseau-Leroy, for example. The latter writer has given new impetus to poetry in Creole with his recently published collection *Diacoute*. In his introduction to this book, Morisseau-Leroy speaks of the Creole tongue as the "ideal vehicle for a kind of revolutionary wisdom." Something of this same wisdom is in the fascinating Creole poems of Milo Rigaud. The map is large, and not limited merely to the physical contours of the country; for the more one reads the Haitians, the more one is convinced that the diversity and vitality of their talent is important to the world.

[1953]

POET OF THE CITY
(C. P. Cavafy)

ALTHOUGH KNOWN to English and French readers through scattered translations over the years, the most famous modern Greek poet, C. P. Cavafy, did not acquire an audience in this country until a translation of his poems by John Mavrogordato appeared in 1952, nine years after his death in Alexandria at the age of seventy. Even then the poems received less attention than one would have expected; now with Miss Rae Dalven's new translation of the complete poems he seems destined to attain a somewhat larger degree of the regard that he merits. Ironically, the way was prepared for Miss Dalven's translation not so much through the work of Mavrogordato and others or through the critical appraisals of E. M. Forster or C. M. Bowra as through the novels of Lawrence Durrell. Mr. Durrell's Alexandria quartet teems with characters but there is none more important than the one who broods in the wings over the entire work, although he never comes on stage in person to take part in the action. He is referred to simply as the "old poet" or the "poet of the city," and without him it is safe to say that Lawrence Durrell would not have composed his quartet.

Alexandria, with its blend of sensuality and skepticism, was the focal point of C. P. Cavafy's life and work; he almost never left it literally, and it spiritually never left him. Constantine P. Cavafy, as he is generally known to the English-speaking world, was the son of a wealthy cotton broker. In 1881, at the time of an uprising in Alexandria against the foreign communities, his mother took him and his brothers to Constantinople, where he applied himself to the study of Byzantine and Hellenic history, for which he developed a passionate interest. It was here also that he began the study of demotic Greek, and wrote his first poems. When he returned to Alexandria three years later, he continued his study and writing. Then, the commercial life of the Greek community having been virtually destroyed, he found it necessary to earn his own living, and went to work as a temporary clerk in the Ministry of Irrigation. He remained at this temporary post for thirty years until his retirement in 1922.

E. M. Forster described Cavafy to English readers the following year in an essay in *Pharos and Pharillon* as a Greek gentleman in a straw hat whom one might chance to meet on the streets of Alexandria, "standing absolutely motionless at a slight angle to the universe." He is on his way, Forster says, either from his flat to his office, or from his office to his flat. If it is the former, he will vanish at once "with a slight gesture of despair." If it is the latter, he may be prevailed upon to begin a sentence dealing with "the tricky behavior of the Emperor Alexius Comnenus in 1096, or with olives, their possibilities and price, or with the fortunes of friends, or George Eliot, or the dialects of the interior of Asia Minor." The sentence, delivered with ease in Greek, English, or French, stands also, Forster feels, "at a slight angle to the universe," for, he concludes, it is "the sentence of a poet." Out of such sentences, and from this odd angle, Cavafy wrote his poetry.

Cavafy spent his life in the old Greek quarter of Alexandria, at 10 rue Lepsius, where he lived in a lamp-lit and candle-lit house amid old-fashioned Arabian furniture and untidy bookshelves. According to one biographer, he "would honor an especially beautiful guest by lighting another candle, taking care to remain in the shadow himself." The gesture is significant, for as Robert Liddell has put it, Cavafy was as reticent in conversation as he was outspoken in poetry: "some things he said needed art to make them beautiful." Out of the shabby and sordid, the dim, confused, and neglected aspects of life he wrote poetry; and it is the sharpness of his eye that made it possible for him to do so. He focuses on a small historical detail or a minor figure of history, and then to these fragments he holds the candle of his attention close-up as to a face. The fragment remains a fragment but every portion of it is so clearly delineated and intensified by the light of his vision that it suggests and illuminates an entire frieze, which the reader is left to complete for himself.

Cavafy's poetry is a poetry of moments, carefully chosen from his own life and from the historical past. His poems are brightly lit small dramas, pieces of polished mosaic, each complete in itself and each evoking the entire pattern of a life and a civilization. He is in the tradition of the Greek epigrammatists, Callimachus, Appollonius of Rhodes, and the Alexandrine poets of the Greek anthology. Cavafy, remembering perhaps the words of Callimachus, librarian at Alexandria, that a "big book is a big evil," wrote short poems; there is in them no excess verbiage and no unnecessary description. They are dry and understated, not without compassion but rarely marred by self-pity. He is said to have written about seventy poems a year, of which he saved only four or five. Cavafy called himself a "poet-historian." "I, I could never write a novel or a play," he once remarked, "but I feel in me a hundred and twenty-five voices that tell me that I could write history."

It is no accident that the characters in Mr. Durrell's quartet refer to the "*old* poet." Cavafy began as a middle-aged writer: his first book, containing only fourteen poems, was published when he was forty-one. Throughout his later poems, which he circulated privately among his friends, he speaks always as an old man, looking back over his life as if it were part of history, relying on his memory to record accurately and dispassionately the events and characters of earlier years. His love poems frequently have titles such as "Days of 1896," "Days of 1901," "Days of 1908," as though based on the notes in an old agenda. Two words that recur frequently throughout are "memory" and "vision." Cavafy seems at times to be looking down a long, dusty, and ever-narrowing corridor on to which, from side rooms, brightly lit but ghostly figures enter and depart and then blend again with the dark. He has been compared to Proust, whose work he scarcely knew; and the poems do at times suggest a Proust in miniature. But rather than exemplifying Bergsonian "duration," they grow out of the "space-time" relation that Lawrence Durrell explores in his "word continuum."

Cavafy said he was neither Hellene nor Hellenist but Hellenic. He took his themes not from the classical Greek world of Homer and Pericles, but from the periphery of Greek civilization, from Asia Minor, from cities like Antioch and Alexandria, with their blending of races, languages, and creeds. As C. M. Bowra has said, "What Yeats found for a time in old Irish legends, what Eliot found for *The Waste Land* in figures and events from anthropology, Cavafy found much less laboriously in the Hellenistic past." Supreme among Cavafy's heroes was Antony, symbol of Alexandria and the defeat of the East. Cavafy's poems have been said to fall into three categories: erotic, philosophic, and historical. Although the greatest number are historical, the erotic poems, because they are so candidly homosexual, are perhaps the best known. One European critic deplores the introduction into the later work of a "*louche* and boring company of workmen or shop assistants in pink or mauve shirts," and would make an understanding of Cavafy hinge completely on his sexual abnormality. Certainly homosexual love in its unenduring nature and its attendant guilt has not been so coldly

333

and carefully presented anywhere in modern poetry. But to say that Cavafy's erotic bent is the sole controlling factor of his entire work is surely to simplify what is simple only on the surface.

If in reading Cavafy one is at times reminded of Whitman, it is usually when he is being, as he is only in passing, general:

> The years of my young manhood, my sensual life—
> how plainly I see their meaning now.

One can imagine where Whitman would have gone from there —to a vague and mystical picture of young manhood all over America; how different is Cavafy's conclusion:

> Deep in the dissolute life of my young manhood
> the designs of my poetry took shape,
> the scope of my art was being plotted.

> This is why even my repentances were never stable.
> And my resolutions to restrain myself, to change,
> lasted for two weeks at the very most.

The scope of Whitman's art was also being plotted in his young manhood, and there are in his poems moments of remorse for his dissolute life, but he would have been entirely incapable of so direct and self-revealing a statement. From his sensual life Whitman developed a vision of the resurgence of a young nation, an optimistic outlook; from his, Cavafy summoned up a vision of an old decayed civilization, a pessimistic view that spares itself nothing in its cold analysis. For all his cataloguing of particulars, Whitman is never anything but general; Cavafy is nothing if not particular. Cavafy's art is clearly art for art's sake; Whitman's is art in spite of art. And yet for all the sharp outlines of his poetry, Cavafy is not without his mystical moments; he delights in the Byzantine traditions of the Greek church. And perhaps, through touching the East in such different ways, if only by combining something of life's religious and sensual aspects, they are closer than they technically and temperamentally might at first seem.

In his introduction to Miss Dalven's translations,[1] W. H. Auden speaks of his debt to Cavafy, whom he first read in translation thirty years ago. Since poetry is, of course, untranslatable, Mr. Auden is perplexed by the fact that Cavafy should have come through so clearly to him in English and French translations; it is his conclusion that the poet survives translation because of his distinctive tone of voice, his personal speech. A poem of Cavafy, even translated by different hands, is unmistakable; no one else would have written it. Mr. Auden is right; and Cavafy's tone of voice is so clear that it reaches us in this volume even through Miss Dalven's awkwardnesses, inaccuracies of English idiom, and plain grammatical errors. (Why these errors should have been necessary when the lines are frequently given correctly in Mr. Mavrogordato's translation is not clear.) Miss Dalven's labor is not without its bright moments, however, and her book is especially valuable for the versions of the early and previously uncollected poems that she has taken great pains to assemble. The reader, coming to Cavafy for the first time, will want to read the Dalven and Mavrogordato translations together; and to "transplant" from the two, as Lawrence Durrell does in the notes to *Justine*, his own version.

Balthazar in *Justine* says of the "old poet" that to "the Cartesian proposition: 'I think therefore I am,' he opposed his own, which must have gone something like this: 'I imagine, therefore I belong and am free.' " With him one "had the feeling that he was catching every minute as it flew and turning it upside down to expose its happy side." In Cavafy's poem "Tomb of Iases" the epitaph is addressed to the traveler who, if an Alexandrian, will know "the rushing torrent of our life; what

[1] *The Complete Poems of Cavafy*, translated by Rae Dalven with an introduction by W. H. Auden (New York: Harcourt Brace Jovanovich, Inc.).

ardor it has; what supreme pleasure." It is of this torrent that Cavafy wrote, and because he could envisage its continuity he could bring it to rest in the clear pools that constitute his poems.

[1961]

THE LEGACY
OF LAFORGUE

W HEN JULES LAFORGUE, early one November
morning in 1881, left Paris by the Gare de l'Est
to join the German Court in Coblentz and take
up his position as French reader to the seventy-year-old Em-
press Augusta, he was an intelligent, inexperienced, and un-
formed young man of twenty-one; he was traveling, as he
expressed it, "into a great dream." A dream it was, the fantastic,
artificial life he led at the Prinzessinnen-Palais in Berlin and
the watering-places of Germany, reading daily from French
books and newspapers of the time to that descendant of Catherine
the Great of Russia who was such a Francophile that she refused
to tolerate a word of German in her presence. Throughout the
dream, however, the dreamer's eyes were open and attentive,
capable of creating what Laforgue called those "lightning flashes
of identity between subject and object—the attribute of genius."
The man who returned to Paris five years later possessed an extraordinary maturity of mind, and had produced imaginative
works whose importance would grow with time. The poet died

of tuberculosis the following year at the age of twenty-seven, but he would be remembered by generations of writers in Europe and America: many would look on him as the most gifted of the Symbolists.

Warren Ramsey's book,[1] which won the Modern Language Association–Oxford University Press Award, is the first complete study of Laforgue to appear in English; and is of value not only for the light it throws on many aspects of the poet's life and work, but also for an extended attempt to define his position with reference to modern poetry. "Laforgue's life is as interesting as that of most pure poets is dull," writes Mr. Ramsey in his opening chapter; and to that interesting life he devotes considerable space, presenting much that was hitherto unknown or buried away in the columns of forgotten newspapers and magazines. From the unpublished manuscripts to which he has had access, he quotes with care and translates with gusto. This earnest and judicious work will provide the general reader with an excellent introduction to a writer whom Ezra Pound has called "an exquisite poet, a deliverer of the nations."

It would be difficult to quarrel with the critical appraisal of Laforgue's accomplishment as given here. Mr. Ramsey sees him as the finest of French Romantic ironists, reaching the fullness of his powers with his final poems in *vers libre*, and in the volume of prose tales, *Moralités légendaires*. In his *Hamlet*, as well as in the *Derniers vers*, he experimented with a stream-of-consciousness technique that was to be continued by Edouard Dujardin and James Joyce. It was Laforgue who, influenced to some degree by Walt Whitman, composed the greater part of the genuine free verse written in France in the nineteenth century, verse that was, of course, to leave a mark on the early poems of T. S. Eliot. His first efforts in *Le Sanglot de la terre* were, Mr. Ramsey states, a real attempt to broaden the subject matter of poetry, and impress one today as fine poetry of ideas. Although his lit-

---

[1] Warren Ramsey, *Jules Laforgue and the Ironic Inheritance* (New Haven, Conn.: Yale University Press).

erary criticism was fragmentary, consisting largely of notes for essays he did not have time to finish, Mr. Ramsey is indeed correct in saying that no poet until Valéry wrote so well about Baudelaire. Laforgue possessed a strong plastic sense; and his art criticism, although hurried and incomplete, is none the less of interest. To all this one is tempted to add the freshness and charm of his letters, unequaled except by Keats, and the brilliance of his book on Berlin and the German Court, which, for all its roughness, remains one of the most spirited volumes of travel impressions of the time. But about a poet like Laforgue no one would wish to be dogmatic. His only real dictum in art was that it be new and that it not be boring; and that he always observed.

Jules Laforgue and the Ironic Inheritance is concerned, for the most part, with the ideological background out of which the poet wrote, the concepts which he carried over into his poetry, and the way in which the imaginative formulation of these concepts was to influence the poets of a later generation. No single book was as important to Laforgue as Eduard von Hartmann's *Philosophy of the Unconscious*, and he was familiar with it even before he went to Germany. Hartmann's book, says Mr. Ramsey, tells us what Laforgue meant by the Unconscious, "a world principle working for diverse means, 'loves, religions, languages, sciences, arts, social apostolates, mysticism,' to regain an original unity that philosophers and artists had glimpsed within the Absolute." To Laforgue, artistically and philosophically, the Unconscious was like the Imagination in our time to Wallace Stevens: it was the one real good, the "necessary angel."

All this is very well, and in writing of it and of other material with which Laforgue was inevitably familiar, the ideas being, as they were, in the air at the time, Mr. Ramsey gives us a good general basis for understanding Laforgue's work. But when he interprets individual poems completely in the light of these things, in an attempt to give an argument to his own book, he gives arguments to Laforgue's poetry that will not bear close inspection. He finds the phrase "music of ideas" that Matthies-

sen used to describe Eliot's poetry as even more justly applicable
to the work of Eliot's first master. "Music of ideas" does not for
me illuminate Eliot's poetry in the first place, much less Laforgue's. There are times when we must distinguish if possible
between thought and feeling, and Laforgue is certainly more
a poet of feeling than of thought; although his method is
oblique and he presents a hard rhetorical surface, he is nonetheless a Romantic, and is, in a sense, quite as close to Keats as he is
to Eliot. It was Laforgue's mastery of feeling that Alain-
Fournier appreciated, and that his friend Jacques Rivière did
not. It is nonsense to say that "not even in *L'Imitation de Notre-
Dame la Lune* are there more essentially Laforguian poems than
those four in *Prufrock* which Eliot placed 'under the sign of
Laforgue,' whose implications, more than any other poet, he
grasped and worked out." Laforgue, in other words, was most
himself when he was Eliot. I think I may not be the first to declare that while Eliot understood the implications of the poems,
his treatment of them, for all its virtues, gave a host of English
readers a false impression of the French poet.

Ezra Pound, who understood Laforgue better than has anyone else, spoke of him as a verbalist, one skilled in *logopoeia,*
who "writes not the popular language of any country, but an
international tongue common to the excessively cultivated." It
was natural perhaps that many of the American writers of the
twenties, whom Laforgue provided with what Malcolm Cowley
termed "a sort of crooked sentiment, a self-protective smirk,"
should not always have been in full possession of that tongue.
Mr. Ramsey gives us several examples, and consequently a number of false leads in tracing the real inheritance from Laforgue.
Except for Eliot, he leaves out the British Isles entirely; and although this may well have been a necessary limitation, it pro-
duces rather strange results. Among translators of individual
poems, for example, he mentions Walter Conrad Arensberg, but
omits Aldous Huxley, the author of interesting and subtle variations. He devotes only a sentence or two to James Joyce, who is

known to have been influenced by the *Moralités légendaires*, but gives over a whole chapter to Frances Newman from Atlanta, an enthusiastic critic of Laforgue whose translation of the *Moralités* is all but worthless.

A lack of proportion in the concluding chapters, however, should not dull one's eyes to this study's real merits : it is devoid of any academic sludge or triviality, and Warren Ramsey's perception and erudition should win him many readers. The book is well produced and illustrated with the Franz Skarbina portrait of Laforgue, some of the poet's sketches, and with reproductions of several unpublished manuscripts.

[1954]

A NOTE ON RAYMOND RADIGUET

IN THE POEMS of that young genius, Raymond Radi-guet, one finds the same qualities of disarming can-dor, quiet, penetrating vision, and cool self-possession that have made his novels famous. He seems to have had from the very beginning a strong sense of the deepest classical tradition in French literature : his model in prose was Mme. de Lafayette, author of the most classical of French novels, *La Princesse de Clèves;* his models in poetry were Ronsard, Malherbe, La Fontaine. Radiguet could lay claim also to the sure, unfettered brilliance of youth. He died in 1923 at the age of twenty; all his poems were written between 1917 and 1921, between the ages of fourteen and eighteen.

"The Language of Flowers or Stars," one of his earliest works, sets down so modestly the awakening of the senses that the poem almost passes us by. The words evoke such a still, breathless atmosphere that they seem to communicate without being spoken. There is in these lines something shimmering, fresh, and resonant. It is as if a child had made some astonishing pronouncement without quite realizing the depths to which he had reached. "To a Nude Walking," which resembles one of the songs of Ronsard, has all the directness, the classical control the writer admired: "Racine, at first, seems less audacious than Rimbaud. The daring of Racine is simply more refined than that of Rimbaud, for it pushes modesty to the point of going completely unnoticed."

It is perhaps significant that Radiguet, in "The Language of Flowers or Stars," should, in a sense, have domesticated the months of the year. To the very young the domestic scene possesses mythical dimensions that it loses as one grows older: beasts sleep in the child's bed, knights breakfast at his table, the fabulous is everywhere around him. And so it is that classical myths come to life again and again in terms of the ordinary and everyday. Radiguet sought out banality in order to come to terms with it, to raise it to the power of dream. "The striving for banality," he wrote, "will ward off strangeness, which is always detestable. That queerness that spoils much of Rimbaud one never finds in Ronsard." "The Flower Girl" is the tale of Leda and the Swan in reverse: the Swan is abducted, the heavenly creature made at home. The world of the Swan is the limitless realm of adventure; its reality is supplied by the child's vision, it is fed as the Swan is fed. If the celluloid toy lives and breathes, it does so through the child's sense of play, a faculty which in the adult becomes the freedom of the imagination. With Radiguet, on the edge of adulthood, play and imagination are interlocked in a very remarkable fashion. This rare combination lies behind the peculiar understatement and wit of this early sketch; it gives it the same luminous quality one remarks in the author's more important work.

Raymond Radiguet was aware that more than the record of a youthful heartbeat is demanded of writing for it to live. On the subject of the young writer, he said:

It is a commonplace, and consequently an inescapable truth that to write one must have lived. But what I would like to

343

know is at what age one has the right to say: "I have lived." Does not this simple past logically imply death? For my part, I believe that at any age, and at the very earliest age, one has both lived and begun to live. However that may be, it does not seem to me impertinent to lay claim to the right of utilizing one's memories of one's first years before one's last memories have arrived. Not that we condemn the powerful charm there is in speaking of dawn on the evening of a fine day, but different as it is, the interest is no less in speaking of it without waiting for night.

Radiguet did not wait for night. He spoke of the dawn, but he had what great writers, young or old, possess: the vision of the whole day, which is life.

[1954]

RAYMOND RADIGUET:
TWO POEMS AND A TALE
(Translation)

THE LANGUAGE OF FLOWERS OR STARS

I lived for some time in a house where there were twelve young girls who resembled the months of the year. I could dance with them, but that was my only privilege; I was even forbidden to speak. One rainy day, to avenge myself, I offered each one flowers I had brought back from my walk. Some of them comprehended. After their death, I disguised myself as a bandit to frighten the others. They purposely took no notice. In summer we all went out walking, and each of us counted the stars. When I found one too many, I said nothing.

Can it be that the rainy days have passed, and the sky is closed again? Your ear is not quick enough to catch the sound.

TO A NUDE WALKING

Model yourself upon the hill
That is pregnant with the grape.
She might also be content
To wear nothing but vine leaves.

And yet with grassy shawl
And fur piece of the thicket,
With headdress and muff of thyme
Where hidden rabbits frolic,

She costumes her beauty.
—And you, extravagant coquette,
Clothed only in your flesh,
April, you think it's summer!

THE FLOWER GIRL

Everyone still remembers under what mysterious circumstances a swan was once stolen from the zoo. Cabaret singers at the time insinuated that the theft was the result of the price of poultry, and a Socialist deputy took advantage of the occasion to attack the government. But the public refused to admit that there was not some extraordinary motive behind so unusual a theft.

The zookeepers all knew little Aline, the flower girl, who, when her generous clients rid her of her burden of violets and mimosa, would run to one of those multicolored stalls, those childhood paradises.

Aline did not carelessly distribute the rolls she bought to fill her apron. She would willingly have taken her dainty meal with her favorite swan, but he was too proud to invite her. As soon as the flower girl's apron was empty, her peculiar favorite would bid the innocent young thing farewell.

Such manners on the part of so majestic a bird might seem surprising to anyone who has not read romances of chivalry, in which it is by no means uncommon for a lovely lady to provide for her knight.

Aline lived on the fifth floor of a rather disreputable hotel. Her exemplary conduct was a subject of continual amazement to the other women who lived there.

"At the age of fourteen," they said, "we had other things to do than sell flowers."

On the wall of Aline's room hung a color print showing Leda seduced by Jupiter. Unacquainted with the classical story and seeing in Leda only a rival for her swan's affections, she would look at it indignantly, saying: "What an ungrateful wretch!"

One evening in a fit of anger she tore up the print. The next day she felt she noticed a reproach in the eyes of her swan.

"Why are you jealous?" he seemed to be asking. "My affair with Leda is ancient history."

The fashion of wearing flowers in one's buttonhole returned; Aline got rich very, very quickly, and rented a comfortable apartment in a nice section of town.

Aline was now earning enough to support two. So she wrote to the director of the zoo and proposed to buy the swan. But postmen being what they are, the letter went astray, and she got no answer.

She had always been honest. You can imagine with what trepidation she kidnapped her loved one one day at closing time. Since he was quite intelligent, he refrained from singing: he knew that Aline did not want him to die . . .

They both arrived safely at the door of her dwelling, where the swan was installed in the bathtub. And the little girl no longer envied other children the swans in their baths. The only difference was that hers was not made of celluloid—it was real.

[1954]

POEMS OF A MULTIMILLIONAIRE
(Valery Larbaud)

T HE OPENING YEARS of this century offered seemingly endless vistas of peace and calm: the world lay before the upper classes of England and America like a broad green lawn where the only sound to break in upon the afternoon was the gentle tap of a croquet ball. Newly discovered electric light dispelled all shadow; bright yachts rode at anchor in distant harbors; illuminated trains sped through the night, carrying to seaside resorts and mountain villages passengers whose supreme desire was to reach the places where society expected them to be. One of the most unburdened and adventurous of all Edwardian travelers, a gentleman whose feeling was equal to his fortune, was the South American multimillionaire, Archibaldo Olson Barnabooth; and he first quietly but decisively made his existence known to the public in a most curious fashion.

It is rare for a traveler of intelligence and sensibility to choose the medium of verse to set down his impressions; Barnabooth was an exception. In Paris in 1908 appeared a slim vol-

349

ume of poems entitled *Poèmes par un riche amateur* in an edition of one hundred copies. More than half of these were review copies, bound in pink with a green border—to look as much like the labels on American canned goods as possible. Something went wrong: the colors were softer than they should have been to achieve the desired effect. The other copies offered for sale were bound in yellow, and bore the title *Le Livre de M. Barnabooth, prose et vers.* The book was prefaced by a brief biography of the multimillionaire by a certain X. M. Tournier de Zamble. Barnabooth was depicted as a charming young man of twenty-four, "short, always simply dressed, rather thin, with reddish hair, blue eyes, very pale complexion, clean-shaven." He was born 23 August 1883 at Campamento, Peru, of a wealthy Swedish pioneer father and an Australian dancer mother, in the province of Arequipa, which, as it happened, was at that moment being disputed by Chile, Peru, and Bolivia. Barnabooth, being technically a man without a country, had become a naturalized American, a citizen of New York and of the world. When he was nine years of age, his father killed himself accidentally while handling a revolver; the following year his mother inadvertently pricked her finger on a poisoned knife at the bottom of a drawer. Thus Barnabooth, after certain amorous adventures and schooling at Europe's great universities, is, when we meet up with him, left to journey about on his yacht, an uprooted, sorrowful, and highly sensitive young man. This volume, like that of many another *riche amateur,* might have passed gently into oblivion, had it not been what Charles-Louis Philippe called "one of the most astonishing and original books to appear in France in years," and had it not been the work of a writer of the first rank whose name was, in reality, Valery Larbaud.

Writing to Larbaud at the time, Charles-Louis Philippe said he did not bear the multimillionaire any ill will, but would simply like to join him from time to time in order to experience a form of happiness with which he was unfamiliar. "You have created Barnabooth because you contained him." André Gide wrote of the work later in the newly founded *Nouvelle Revue française:* "This book is calculated to irritate some people, and to amuse others all the more; let us quickly put ourselves among the latter. . . . Barnabooth has roamed every country. I love his haste, his cynicism, his gluttony. These poems, dated from here, there, and everywhere, are as thirst-making as a wine list. . . . In this peculiar book, each picture of sensation, no matter how correct or dubious it may be, is made valid by the speed with which it is superseded."

When the poems were reissued in 1913, together with the *Journal* of Barnabooth, fifteen of them were eliminated and a number considerably shortened. The *Journal,* a fitting prose accompaniment to the poems, relates the struggle of Barnabooth, in his travels throughout Europe, to come to terms with life. The book cannot be called a novel : there is little plot, and yet it is filled with action; it is the record of a conflict between the inner and outer self. Gide suggested that it be called the journal of a "free man"—and one can see how he drew upon it in his own writing. The mind of Barnabooth acts as a mirror held up to people and places; what results is a series of acute observations on manners and, in its way, a judgment on life itself. In addition to the poems and the journal, the book contained *"Le pauvre chemisier,"* a parody of eighteenth-century tales, a morality whose moral is itself double-edged. The biography, which Gide had found contrived and out of place in *Poèmes par un riche amateur,* was dropped; and Valery Larbaud appeared simply as the literary executor. This edition, containing the complete works of A. O. Barnabooth in their final form, has been re-issued many times since. Witty and wise, paradoxical and profound, it has influenced many writers in France, and still attracts discerning readers today as one of the truly original books of the century.

Valery Larbaud is known to the English-speaking world chiefly as an authority on English literature. Well-grounded in Latin and Greek, he took his *licence* in English at the Sorbonne,

351

and his first literary effort was a translation of *The Rime of the Ancient Mariner*. He contributed articles to English magazines, some of them written in flawless English, and translated works of Walter Savage Landor and Samuel Butler into French. A friend and associate of James Joyce, he has the distinction of being the first person anywhere to speak out publicly on the merit of *Ulysses*. Larbaud, as a critic and scholar, or, more precisely, what the French call a *lettré*, read widely in the literatures of Spain, Italy, and Portugal, together with those of England and America; and the list of his pioneering essays on important writers in all these countries is too long to give in detail. To the English reader he is almost unknown except as a critic; although a Parisian jury a few years ago selected his *Fermina Márquez* (1911) as one of the ten best French novels of the twentieth century, it has never been translated. He began his long career as a poet, and it is his poetry that concerns us here.

Valery Larbaud was born in 1881 in Vichy, where one of the mineral springs had been discovered and exploited by his father. Brought up to know both the country and the city, he was taken at the age of seventeen to Russia. He made other brief visits to England, Spain, Italy, Montenegro, and North Africa; and it is these early journeys that form the background of the poems. Larbaud had not actually traveled nearly as widely as the poems seem to indicate, nor has he ever been as wealthy as his hero, although a private income has permitted him to live modestly and devote himself to writing. He has never left Europe: the America of Barnabooth is completely the product of his imagination.

It was around 1905 that Valery Larbaud decided to give up writing poems of direct inspiration, and to speak through the medium of Barnabooth. The discovery of Whitman had a profound effect on him: the freedom, the lyrical, "quotidian and prophetic" spirit of Whitman's verse, and his championing of the commonplace opened new horizons to writers such as Larbaud who felt the need to leave Paris behind them and to con-

sider it "only one of their capitals." Larbaud's interest in Whitman led him, as a frequent visitor to Brentano's in Paris, to read
all the American books he could lay his hands on. It was thus
that he found George Washington Cable and read with fascina-
tion *Old Creole Days*. He said later that he was thinking of a
poet along the same lines, "sensitive to the diversity of races,
peoples, and countries; who could find the exotic everywhere
(which, I suppose, amounts to the same thing) ; witty and 'international,' one, in a word, capable of writing like Whitman but
in a light vein, and of supplying that note of comic, joyous
irresponsibility which is lacking in Whitman."

What Larbaud was seeking was the successor to Rimbaud,
Laforgue, and Walt Whitman combined. Something of the
spirit of such a rare combination he discovered, to his surprise,
in the poems of Henry Levet. Levet was a French consular official who, after years in far-flung Oriental posts, returned to die
in France in 1906 at the age of thirty-two, leaving behind him
a few inscribed photographs of Indian rajahs and a handful of
poems. These poems, later collected by Valery Larbaud and
Léon-Paul Fargue, are, in some instances, poems of the sort one
might have imagined Rimbaud to write after his departure from
the Continent. One of the most powerful describes the Japanese
captain of the port of Nagasaki passing in a sampan alongside
the great ships lying at anchor in his harbor. He has just lost his
daughter in an attack of cholera, and he imagines suddenly, in a
moment of despair and delirium, that the sirens of the huge
vessels begin wailing, lamenting her death like a chorus of
Walkyries. Another of these *Cartes Postales*, describing the passengers on a ship tied up at Port Saïd, unable to disembark because of quarantine, ends thus:

> *Poète, on eût aimé, pendant la courte escale*
> *Fouler une heure ou deux le sol des Pharaons,*
> *Au lieu d'écouter miss Florence Marshall*
> *Chanter "The Belle of New York," au salon.*

We recognize here something of the broad yet contained humor and gaudy surprise we find in the early poems of Wallace Stevens. Levet was indeed one who found the exotic everywhere; but while he left us only a few of these beautiful, cryptic postcards, Larbaud presented us with an entire album. In Barnabooth he created a character who had not only seen, but who also possessed, the entire world.

Barnabooth, in his *poésie des départs*, is the spiritual descendant of des Esseintes, the hero of Huysmans' novel, *A Rebours*, who perfumed his room with tar so that he might imagine he was at sea, and papered its walls with advertisements of voyages, timetables of the Royal Mail Steam Packet Company and other shipping lines. To des Esseintes the pleasures of travel are imaginary: one enjoys the anticipation and the recollection of a journey rather than the actual experience itself. In spirit, also, Barnabooth is a follower of that earlier traveler, Xavier de Maistre, who, when confined to his barracks for forty-two days in 1790, produced his celebrated *Voyage autour de ma chambre*. (It is interesting that de Maistre, like Larbaud, actually traveled in Russia; and, in his stories, wrote of distant villages with precision and color.) While de Maistre carries the world into his room, Larbaud-Barnabooth carries his room into the world:

> Regardant de la passerelle de mon yacht
> S'ouvrir la baie verte et rose de Gravosa.

It amounts to the same thing, a triumph of the individual over time and space. And it is the carefully circumscribed point of observation—the bridge of the yacht—that makes the vista imposing. Each place to which Barnabooth journeys opens for him a new life; and yet in memory each place is reduced to a name so that the name itself, like *Gravosa* above, becomes a symbol, a sign, leading the mind on. Countries open before one, infinite and infinitely varied, and yet borne always in miniature projection, like the contour of a map reproduced on a postage stamp.

People are places and places are people; Barnabooth, above all, directs our attention to a humanized landscape.

In creating Barnabooth, Larbaud had in mind a very definite character with a precise background and distinct tastes. The poems as presented were intended to be those that only a man in his social, economic, and cultural position could write. While Larbaud was surely right to exclude the biography eventually, he made no mistake in putting it down in the first place; in doing so, he delineated, more for himself than for his reader perhaps, clearly the man he had in mind. It is significant, first of all, that Barnabooth is a South American, one who sings of Europe, "her railroads and theaters," and yet brings to his poems the "spoils of a new world." He can love Europe, all of it, more intensely than the European because he does not belong to it. He writes always as if he were at the edge of Europe, approaching it on an ocean liner, dallying in one of its outlying provinces, and yet in spirit at its very heart. It is one of Valery Larbaud's favorite ideas that history and art must be approached not always directly, but often obliquely. One will know the main road all the better for having wandered off from time to time along lanes and bypaths. In what is discarded or cast off one may find something to give meaning and dimension to the whole. The work of a little-known or neglected writer may illuminate an entire era, as Rome is defined by its periphery. The creation of Barnabooth was for Valery Larbaud a way out, a means of approach to the centers of London and New York. For us he is a way back: if the poet began with Walt Whitman, he ended with Henry James, and his hymn to a civilized Europe is more rewarding today than ever.

It is worthy of note that Barnabooth is from a Spanish-speaking country. Spain, next to England, has occupied a high place among Larbaud's interests. His early voyages to that country made a lasting impression on him. The characters in *Fermina Márquez*, students at a boarding school near Paris at the turn of the century, are the sons and daughters of wealthy South

Americans. Larbaud is careful to put in the mouth of Barnabooth expressions appropriate to a Peruvian-born gentleman. It
is impossible in English to convey the full undertone of comedy
in all this; the author, in any case, gets away with more than he
would under ordinary circumstances.

Perhaps the real force of *Poems of a Multimillionaire*, as I
have chosen to call them in English, lies in the fact that Barnabooth, for all his gaiety, knows that the price demanded for the
possession of the world can never be paid in full; it is the price of
human suffering:

> *Mais que du moins j'entende,*
> *Monter toujours*
> *Le cri de la douleur du Monde.*
> *Que mon coeur s'en remplisse ineffablement;*
> *Que je l'entende encore de mon tombeau,*
> *Et que la grimace de mon visage mort*
> *Dise ma joie de l'entendre!*

He sees the full horror of the room brightly lit by the raw electric bulb. That lighted room has grown larger with time, the
shadow outside ever more menacing. Larbaud often looks at
things through the innocent eyes of a child, through the wrong
end of a field glass, as it were, which he does again in the charming stories of *Enfantines* (1918); but if innocence exists, it is
always because of experience. Barnabooth is youthful and ebullient, but old beyond his years.

Often in these poems, bearing as they do the unmistakable
imprint of American poetry and speech, I have the feeling that
something has shifted—perhaps not out of, but into, focus. The
author catches remarkably well, it seems to me, that note of
nostalgia inherent in the American character, the heart quicken-
ing at night to the sound of a train whistle, the vision responding
to the beam of headlights cutting across broad plains. But the
emphatic gestures of Whitman he has subtly tempered with wit;

and he has added something the American has always sorely needed: the ability not to take himself, even in seriousness, too seriously.

[1955]

VALERY LARBAUD:
SEVEN POEMS [1]
(Translation)

PROLOGUE

Borborygms! Borborygms! . . .
Rumblings of the stomach and the bowels,
Lamentations of the constantly changing flesh,
Voices, irrepressible whisperings of the organs,
Voices, the only human voice that does not lie,
And persists even for a while after physiological death . . .

Beloved, how often we have paused in our love-making
To listen to this song of ourselves;
How much it had to say
While we tried to keep from laughing!
It rose from the depths of our being,
Compelling and ridiculous,
Louder than all our vows of love,
More unexpected, more irremissible, more serious—
Oh, the inevitable song of the œsophagus! . . .

[1] From *Poems of a Multimillionaire*, translated by William Jay Smith (New York: Bonacio & Saul with Grove Press).

A stifled cluck, the noise of a carafe being emptied,
A sentence slowly, endlessly modulated;
And yet there it is—the incomprehensible thing
I can no longer deny;
And yet there it is—the last word I shall speak
When still warm, I am a poor corpse "being emptied"!
Borborygms! Borborygms! . . .
Do they also exist in the organs of thought,
Rumblings one cannot hear, through the thickness of the
       cranium?

Here, are, in any case, some poems in their image . . .

ODE

Lend me thy great noise, thy powerful, gentle gait,
Thy delicate nocturnal glide across illuminated Europe,
O luxurious train! And the agonizing music
Running the length of thy gilt, embossed corridors,
While behind the brass knobs of lacquered doors,
Millionaires slumber.
Humming I pace thy corridors
And follow thy course toward Vienna and Budapest,
Mingling my voice with thy hundred thousand voices,
O Harmonika-Zug!

I experienced for the first time all the joy of living
In a compartment of the Nord-Express, between Wir-
  ballen and Pskov.
We were gliding over fields where shepherds,
Under clumps of huge trees like hills,
Were clad in filthy, raw sheepskins . . .
(Eight o'clock one autumn morning, and the beautiful
  blue-eyed
Singer was singing in the neighboring compartment.)
Wide windows beyond which I have seen Siberia and the
  Mountains of Samnium,
Bleak, blossomless Castile, and the Sea of Marmara under
  a warm rain!

Lend me, O Orient Express, Sud-Brenner-Bahn, lend me
Your miraculous deep tones and
Your vibrant string voices;
Lend me the light, easy respiration
Of your high, thin locomotives with their graceful
Movement, the express engines
Drawing effortlessly four yellow gold-lettered carriages
Through the mountain solitudes of Serbia,
And farther on, through rose-heaped Bulgaria . . .

Ah, these sounds and this movement
Must enter into my poems and express
For me my inexpressible life,
The life of a child whose only desire
Is to hope eternally for airy, distant things.

POET'S WISH

When I have been dead for several years
And cabs in the fog still collide
As they do today (things not having changed)
May I be a cool hand upon some forehead!
On the forehead of someone humming in a carriage
Along Brompton Road, Marylebone, or Holborn,
Who, thinking of literature,
Looks out through the yellow fog at the great black
    monuments.
Yes, may I be the dark, gentle thought
One bears secretly in the noise of cities,
A moment's repose in the wind that drives us on,
Lost children in a fair of vanities;
And may my humble beginning in eternity be honored
On All Saints' Day with a simple ornament, a little moss.

THALASSA

Seated on a couch at the rear of my cabin
And rocked like a doll in the arms of some mad girl
By the pitch and roll of the ship in rough weather,
I bear upon my soul this luminous circle—this porthole
Which might be a shopwindow where one offered up
       the sea;
And, in my somnolent state, dream
Of constructing, in a form as yet untried, a poem
To the glory of the sea.

O Homer! O Virgil!
O Corpus Poeticum Boreale! It is in your pages
That one must look for the eternal verities
Of the sea, for those myths expressing an aspect of time,
The fairylands of the ocean, the history of the waves,
Marine spring, and marine autumn,
And the lull preparing a flat, green path
For Neptune and his procession of Nereids.

I bear upon my soul this luminous circle as it travels
Up and down, now filled with the white-speckled, blue-
      gray
Mediterranean landscape, and a corner of pale
Sky, and now
The sky descends into the circle, and now
I sink into a glaucous, cold,
Whirling light, and now of a sudden
The porthole, blinded by foam, wheels dazzled into the
      clear sky.

On the constantly shifting line of the horizon,
No bigger than a child's toy, a white Roumanian
      steamer

Passes,
Meeting the waves as if they were deep ruts in a road,
       the screw
Emerging from the water and whipping up the foam;
And signals to us, dipping its ensign,
Blue—yellow—red.

Ship's noises: voices in passageways,
The creaking of the wood, the grating of the lamps,
The throbbing of the engines with their stale smell,
Cries swallowed by the wind, drowning the music
Of a mandolin which strums: *Sobre las olas del mar* . . .
The usual sound, the usual silence.

Oh, to think of the raging wind up there on deck, the
      pirate-wind
Which, as it whistles through the rigging, makes
Those stars and stripes of three colors
Crack like a whip! . . .

THE GIFT OF ONESELF

I offer myself to everyone as his reward;
I bestow the reward on you even before you have earned it.

There is something in me,
Deep within me, at the core of myself,
Something infinitely arid
Like the summit of the highest mountain;
Something comparable to the dead spot of the retina,
Which gives back no echo
But sees and hears;
A being with a life of its own, but one which
Lives all my life, and listens calmly
To all the gossip of my conscience.

A being made of nothingness, if such is possible,
Insensitive to my physical sufferings,
Which does not weep when I weep,
Which does not laugh when I laugh,
Which does not blush when I commit a shameful action,
Which does not complain when my heart is wounded;
Which stands motionless and gives no advice,
But seems forever to say :
"I am here, indifferent to everything."

It is void perhaps as is the void
And yet so vast that Good and Evil together
Cannot fill it.
Hatred dies in it of asphyxia,
And the greatest love never enters it.

Take all of me then : the sense of these poems,
Not what you read, but what comes through them in spite of me :
Take, take, and you have nothing.
And wherever I go, in the entire universe,

I shall always meet,
Outside myself and within myself,
This unfillable Void,
This unconquerable Nothing.

IMAGES

I

One day in a popular quarter of Kharkov,
(O that southern Russia where all the women
With white-shawled heads look so like Madonnas!)
I saw a young woman returning from the fountain,
Bearing, Russian-style, as Roman women did in the time of Ovid,
Two pails suspended from the ends of a wooden
Yoke balanced on neck and shoulders.
And I saw a child in rags approach and speak to her.
Then, bending her body lovingly to the right,
She moved so the pail of pure water touched the cobblestone
Level with the lips of the child who had kneeled to drink.

II

One morning, in Rotterdam, on Boompjes quai
(It was September 18, 1900, around eight o'clock),
I observed two young ladies on their way to work;
Opposite one of the great iron bridges, they said farewell,
Their paths diverging.
Tenderly they embraced; their trembling hands
Wanted, but did not want, to part; their mouths
Withdrew sadly and came together soon again
While they gazed fixedly into each other's eyes . . .
They stood thus for a long moment side by side,
Straight and still amid the busy throng,
While the tugboats rumbled by on the river,
And the whistling trains maneuvered on the iron bridges.

III

Between Cordova and Seville
Is a little station where the South Express,
For no apparent reason, always stops.
In vain the traveler looks for a village

Beyond the station asleep under the eucalyptus:
He sees but the Andalusian countryside: green and golden.
But across the way, on the other side of the track,
Is a hut made of black boughs and clay,
From which, at the sound of the train, ragged children swarm
        forth.
The eldest sister, leading them, comes forward on the platform
And, smiling, without uttering a word,
Dances for pennies.
Her feet in the heavy dust look black;
Her dark, filthy face is devoid of beauty;
She dances, and through the large holes of her ash-gray skirt,
One can see the agitation of her thin, naked thighs,
And the roll of her little yellow belly;
At the sight of which a few gentlemen,
Amid an aroma of cigars, chuckle obscenely in the dining car.

    Postscriptum

O Lord, will it never be possible for me
To know that sweet woman, there in Southern Russia,
And those two friends in Rotterdam,
And the young Andalusian beggar
And join with them
In an indissoluble friendship?
(Alas, they will not read these poems,
They will know neither my name, nor the feeling in my heart;
And yet they exist; they live now.)
Will it never be possible for me to experience the great joy
Of knowing them?
For some strange reason, Lord, I feel that with those four
I could conquer a whole world!

THE DEATH OF ATAHUALPA

Pues el Atabalipa llorava y dezia
que no le matasen . . .
                    Oviedo.

O how often I have thought of those tears,
Those tears of the supreme Inca whose empire remained so long
Unknown, on the high plateaus, at the far edge
Of the Pacific—the tears, poor tears,
In those great red eyes beseeching Pizarro and Almagro.
I thought of them while still a child when,
In a dark gallery in Lima, I would stop
To gaze at this historic, official, terrifying picture.
At first one sees—a fine study in expression and in the nude—
The wives of the American emperor, wild
With sorrow, asking that they be killed, and here,
Surrounded by crosses and lighted candles and priests
In their surplices, not far from Friar Vicente de Valverde,
Lies Atahaulpa, on the horrible, inexplicable
Apparatus of the garrote, with his brown nude
Torso, and his thin face seen in profile,
While at his side the Conquistadors,
Fervent and fierce, kneel in prayer.
This belongs to the strange crimes of History.
Encompassed by the majesty of the Law and the splendor of the
          Church,
So extraordinary in their agonizing horror,
That one cannot believe they do not live on
Somewhere, beyond the visible world, eternally;
And in this very picture perhaps there will always
Dwell the same sorrow, the same prayers, the same tears,
Like the mysterious workings of the Lord.
And I readily imagine at this moment
As I sit here writing, abandoned by gods and men,

In my furnished suite at the Sonora Palace Hotel
(In the Californian Quarter of Cannes)
Yes, I imagine that somewhere in this hotel,
In a room dazzlingly bright with electricity,
This same terrible scene,
A scene out of Peruvian history
That is dinned into us as children there in our schools,
Is enacted precisely
As it was four hundred years ago in Caxamarca.

—Ah, let's hope that no one opens the wrong door!

[1955]

X

EPITAPHS

MASTER OF SILENCES
(Walter de la Mare)

WHEN a poet of stature dies, a silence settles upon language. One becomes suddenly aware that words will never again be handled as they have been by this particular man. All that can be said or heard resides in his poems: the rest is silence. Walter de la Mare was a master of silences; his poems seem always to have been written on this or that side of sleep:

> We wake and whisper awhile,
>   But, the day gone by,
> Silence and sleep like fields
>   Of amaranth lie.

Each one like a stone dropped in a pool sends out ripples in the reader's consciousness that, surging backward, close in upon themselves until a calm surface is restored. In a sense, he stood always on the edge of time, composing again and again his own epitaph.

Walter de la Mare remained during his later years a towering, but dim, figure. England, which paid him tribute, did so often for the wrong reasons; America, which with references to his delicate "magic" had relegated him to the purgatory of schoolroom anthologies, had forgotten almost that he existed. For many he was a poet writing out of a past, and with a poetic diction, which had little, if anything, to say to the modern world. For all the truly complex nature of his work, he seemed to present no problems. And because he seldom raised his voice in his poems, and indeed spoke at times in a whisper, his qualities had to be listened for; few people had the patience. In de la Mare's lines on Vaughan, he might have been writing of himself:

> So true and sweet his music rings,
> So radiant is his mind with light
> The very intent and meaning of what he sings
> May stay half-hidden from sight.
>
> His flowers, waters, children, birds
> Lovely as their own archetypes are shown;
> Nothing is here uncommon, things or words,
> Yet every one's his own.

Nothing is uncommon in the special universe of Walter de la Mare, but his intent and meaning may not be immediately grasped.

Certainly the setting of many of his poems is not unfamiliar—the rambling Victorian house where in a cobwebbed chair a little girl, the picture of health and innocence, has just fallen asleep. Moonlight streams in through the window; a face appears and disappears; a horseman gallops away, swallowed up in mist. The characters who move in and out of the rooms and in and out of the poems are ghosts; only the child is alive, but she, too, is close to death in sleep. Outside in the garden worms and snails creep from under mossy stones; far off, the sea breaks on the gray sand.

It may be that it is too familiar; everything about it is a
bit too English, the haunted atmosphere too cozy; one would
rather that the ghosts did not all stay to tea. But to object at this
point is to lose sight of de la Mare's special qualities. The house
—and how often the word itself occurs in his work—is for him
the very habitation of the mind. Old, decaying, abandoned, it is
like the mind haunted by memory; it is the voice of an eternal
silence, choosing its speech in our almost involuntary utterances:

> Very old are we men;
> Our dreams are tales
> Told in dim Eden
> By Eve's nightingales. . . .

Walter de la Mare lived more and more in his dreams, he said,
as he grew older; and the area which he explores is that between
sleep and waking, past and present, life and death. The darkness
within the house is balanced against the dark without: when the
face at the window has vanished, all that remains is the gray
night that shines on in its "chaos of vacancy."

The passage between inner and outer worlds is achieved
technically in de la Mare's poetry through the frequent use of
subtly modulated dialogue:

> "Dark is the hour!" "Ay, and cold."
> "Lone is my house." "Ah, but mine?"
> "Sight, touch, lips, eyes yearned in vain."
> "Long dead these to thine. . . ."

The voices, rising from the edge of night, become at times the
sound of earth itself:

> "Come!" said Old Shellover.
> "What?" says Creep.

They break off, striving to reach too far:

> "Waiting to . . ."
> "Who is?"

375

> "We are . . .
> Was that the night-owl's cry?"

Throughout, the pattern continues, a shuttle moving back and forth, weaving together the threads of pervading mystery.

Walter de la Mare gazed within, as the title of that superb collection of lyrics, *Inward Companion*, published in his seventy-sixth year, indicates:

> Why, inward companion, are you so dark with anguish?
> A trickle of rancid water that oozes and veers,
> Picking its sluggish course through slag and refuse,
> Down at length to the all-oblivious ocean—
> What else were apt comparison for your tears?

And while his gaze became ever more probing and his understanding of the complexity of the psyche ever keener, he concerned himself with a dream-enriched, dream-haunted world, not with a world of explicit nightmare. Everything he wrote has in it somewhere, as Horace Gregory points out, the chill of ice, but, I think, of ice that is ready to melt away before a warmth that is conveyed at times only in the tone of voice. Rarer than anything in life, one poem states, are good nature and good sense; and he possessed too much of both to be able to gaze directly—for very long, at least—at blood-curdling horror. His style—the record of the workings of that inner eye, which he said sees clearly but never fixedly—is "lucent, dewy, rain-sweet" (his adjectives for the prose of Isaak Walton); and as a writer for children he is closer certainly to Madame d'Aulnoy than to the Brothers Grimm. His children's stories have the delicacy, wit, and luminous mystery of certain French or Japanese, as opposed to German, fairy tales.

Nor is he completely at home in the field of nonsense; he lacks the zany spirit of Edward Lear. In his stories, for all their fantasy and implied unearthly terror, he never truly abandons the real world; nor in his children's poems does he ever allow good sense to become nonsense. In his *Stuff and Nonsense* he tries; and although many of its stanzas are rollicking and ingenious, the words do not somehow tumble from his tongue; it is the least successful of his children's books. Always, however, he moves majestically in the intermediate area between nonsense and sense:

> Who said, "All Time's delight
> Hath she for narrow bed;
> Life's troubled bubble broken"?—
> That's what I said.

The words seem to rise from time itself as from the depths of those prehistoric vats that he describes in one of his stories. The *b*'s in the second last line, together with the short *u* sounds, suggest a mumbling attempt to say what cannot be said, to ask more than life can answer; they evoke also, with the question itself, the sound of the bubbling water carrying off the dead Ophelia. The voice of the speaker, the Mad Prince, becomes at once the voice of the child asking the impossible and of the adult reaching further back than one can reach, the voice of a universal unconscious.

Far-off experience de la Mare brings into focus; his best children's poems shimmer with the unreasoning clarity of early morning:

> Why does that bluebottle buzz?
> Why does the sun so silent shine?—

We hear not only the bluebottle, but, more miraculously, the very sound of sunlight itself. *Peacock Pie*, which is, in its own way, as perfect as *Inward Companion*, is similarly concerned with the ultimate questions of existence. In it problems are simply stated, as they would be by a child, but they are life's problems none the less:

> Do diddle di do,
> Poor Jim Jay

377

> Got stuck fast
> In Yesterday.

Because de la Mare can look back so clearly at life's first moments, he can hear in language those rhythms basic to all times and epochs. No poet of the century has used such a variety of stanzas and meters or has made more subtle use of off-beat folk rhythm and of the nursery lilt to which at passionate moments every lover, even the savage Swift, returns.

The ripples move slowly outward on the pool as we read over the poems of Walter de la Mare and the world begins to glow as if it had only just emerged from dream, shining forth with all its miniature perfections. And if we listen carefully, we can hear his voice, resonant and forever-questioning, speaking to us from the edge of that mysterious darkness, of which he wrote so well, and into which he now has gone.

[1957]

DEATH OF A REBEL
(Albert Camus)

IT IS A TRAGIC IRONY that Albert Camus, who wrote so eloquently of the continuing triumph of pointless cruelty in human existence, should die in a pointless automobile accident. One of the main themes of his work is that of execution; and it seems to have stemmed from an early personal shock. As a child, he is said to have heard his mother describe an execution that his father had witnessed; and the memory of it remained throughout his adult life, taking the form of recurrent dreams in which the dreamer walked alone toward the scaffold. The dreamer became himself, and to the end of his life, Camus was a spokesman for justice.

For his literary production, "which with clear-sighted earnestness illuminates the problems of the human conscience in our time," the Nobel Committee chose to honor him in 1957. In the passionate force of his intellect, Camus was a writer of a kind the French so often produce; but he was not, as he himself knew, a philosopher. And while his novels have a seemingly logical structure, the events they describe have the quality of a nightmare. It is this quality that reminds us that Camus was a native of Africa, part of that Algeria he loved, where, he liked to remind us, a mixture of races had often, as in America, produced happy results. The son of an Alsatian father, who was killed in the battle of the Marne when Camus was only one year old, and a mother of Spanish origin, he grew up to embody the spirit of the Mediterranean, where, he wrote, an intelligence "intimately related to the blinding light of the sun" has always collided with tyranny. Haunted by death (he nearly died of tuberculosis at the age of seventeen), he had in him something of the fervor of the Spanish mystics; but the terrible light of his vision was thrown upon this life rather than upon the mysteries that lie beyond. He was a rebel, but for him rebellion could not exist "without a strange form of love."

The forces of pointless cruelty are still triumphant: the last words of the Emperor in Camus' play "Caligula" are "I am still alive." And yet one cannot believe that Albert Camus, who wrote that the "real generosity toward the future lies in giving all to the present," has given that all so briefly and so brilliantly in vain.

[1960]

LIFE, LITERATURE, AND DYLAN
(Dylan Thomas)

D YLAN THOMAS told me once that he found it difficult to converse with actors because they had only one subject of conversation—themselves. The Welsh writer was, of course, himself an actor, inspired reader, superb mimic, irresistible comedian, soulful clown; words rolled and danced on his tongue; but more than an actor, he was a poet, and of himself he rarely spoke. When he did, it was in asides, quick, bubbly, embarrassed, as if he wanted to get on with something more important—the story to be told, the joke to be brought to the proper roaring conclusion. How much indeed there was to get on with, and how lively and real it was to those of us who listened!

Oddly enough we met at All Souls in Oxford. A. L. Rowse had invited us to lunch, and I shall never forget the first sight of Dylan and Caitlin in those august surroundings, Dylan in a bright checked suit and rakish pancake cap, Caitlin all gold and red, completely the dancer, seeming to whirl in her bright skirts even when still. They were "country," as one of Eudora Welty's

Mississippi characters might put it, and they didn't mind letting the world know that there was something more important than literature, and that was life. Let geese honk below the windows, and beer spill over the tables; life was to be lived. It was life that counted.

There was not much of the "literary" about Dylan Thomas, but he knew his craft as only the finest craftsman can; and he was brilliant, when he chose to be, in literary asides. If he spoke of poetry, it was usually to praise the poems of a friend, or to quote some lines from Hardy. He could be devastating, too, with quick thrusts at certain contemporaries, at the bumbling, the pretentious, and the boring.

This perhaps is worth putting down. I remember that once in the midst of a dinner party, when the conversation had turned to literary topics, he broke in. "There's nothing so beautiful," he said, and his hand shot up, "as a lark rising from a field. That's what we . . . we . . ." He left the sentence for us to complete.

I did not see him again after that year at Oxford but I never cease hearing of the effect he had in this country, of the sense of vitality—and nobility—he communicated wherever he went. His poetry, written from the roots of language, goes to the roots of life; and it touches us all.

In a house opposite the hospital in Greenwich Village where Dylan Thomas died a short time ago, I write these lines. I look up, beyond the neon lettering outside, toward those windows where he breathed his last; and as I do, the traffic noises subside, a familiar voice again fills the air. And the lark rises.

[1954]

ODD BIRD
(E. E. Cummings)

T
HE ENDURING VALUE of the poetry of Edward
Estlin Cummings has frequently been obscured by
his eccentric typography, which Harriet Monroe,
reviewing his first book, *Tulips and Chimneys*, in 1923, said
had nothing to do with the poem and obtruded itself irritatingly
"like scratched or blurred spectacles" between it and the reader.
With the experimentation that has taken place in all art forms
since then, those spectacles now appear less foggy; but they may
still hold off those readers who find obscurity of any sort an
excuse for not liking poetry. The fact is that Cummings could
write more simply and directly than any poet of this century,
and he had the courage and ability to do so. An anthology could
be made of his purely formal pieces, in which a wrenched syntax does nothing to detract from a deep regard for tradition.
"The poet is a penguin," he once wrote, "his wings are to swim
with." And the remark is typical of the "lower-case" Cummings, who prided himself on being an odd bird, a kind of
Cubist of the unconscious. No poet was more uneven, and none

did more to squander his great gifts. He became increasingly repetitious, abstract, and even mystical. At his worst, he was little more than a New England crank, whose political views reeked of the cracker barrel. Still, his art was always alive, and in the greatest tradition. Odd bird that he was, the world is not likely to see another such for some time.

[1963]

MASTER POET
(Robert Frost)

A FEW YEARS AGO one of America's leading poets remarked to me that if he were crossing the desert of Saudi Arabia and someone were to call out in a tone of reverence and concern, "Robert!" he would know at once which Robert was meant. Robert Frost was known the world over, and everyone who read him felt that he knew him as a friend. The voice was familiar, and the voice came through in his poetry.

He called his poems "talk-songs," and said that he was "on one of the scales between two things—intoning and talking. I bear a little more toward talking." Anyone who heard him read his poems remembers that he would often break off in the middle of one to add a comment on this or that phrase; it was impossible to know where the poem left off and the talk began.

The very individuality of his speech, however, may have worked against his international reputation. If there is any explanation for his not having received the Nobel Prize, it may be that his lyric gift did not—like good wine, or in this case, cider

—travel: it lost much of its flavor in translation. I have spoken with French and Italian writers who considered him too dry, matter-of-fact, and quaintly regional to be a great poet. It is true that Frost may have seemed to deny the poet something of his traditional bardic role; he was certainly averse to poeticizing. But to those who know English and can appreciate all its fine nuances, its real fiber and strength, there has never been anything small about Robert Frost. He is indeed one of the titans of our literature.

Robert Graves has said of Frost that he was the first American poet to be "honestly reckoned a master-poet by world standards." The others, by comparison, appear inevitably provincial. Certainly with his death an entire era in English poetry has come to a close, for he was the last living link with the great English poets of the nineteenth century. He began as a Georgian, one of that school of British poets who in the early years of this century attempted to bring over the simple diction of Wordsworth and the poets of the Romantic period. But the simplicity of most of the Georgians was unfortunately stale, dull, and literary. Because there was nothing false or feigned in the naturalness of Frost, he survived them all.

Robert Frost belongs to the world, but Vermont had a special claim on him. He said, of course, many times that he was neither an extrovert nor an introvert—"just a plain Vert from Vermont." It was typical of Frost that of all the honors he had received in the world none moved him more than being named poet laureate of Vermont. The neighborhood that he had made known to the entire English-speaking world did not disapprove of what he had written, not entirely, anyway, although it had waited nearly fifty years to say so officially.

It was at South Shaftsbury in June 1922 that he composed in one night the long blank verse poem, "New Hampshire." As dawn arrived, he went out for a walk and when he returned to the house he wrote "in one stroke of the pen" one of the greatest of his lyrics, "Stopping by Woods on a Snowy Evening." "Permanence in poetry as in love is perceived instantly," said Frost.

386

"It hasn't to await the test of time." "Stopping by Woods" did not have to wait; nor did Robert Frost's other great lyrics. One of them, "Away!" from his last book gives us his final testament, energetic, unadorned, and to the point, just as he wanted it.

AWAY!

Now I out walking
The world desert,
And my shoe and my stocking
Do me no hurt.

I leave behind
Good friends in town.
Let them get well-wined
And go lie down.

Don't think I leave
For the outer dark
Like Adam and Eve
Put out of the Park.

Forget the myth.
There is no one I
Am put out with
Or put out by.

Unless I'm wrong
I but obey
The urge of a song:
I'm—bound—away!

And I may return
If dissatisfied
With what I learn
From having died.

[1963]

XI

A FRAME
FOR POETRY

THE MAKING
OF POEMS

WHEN I think about the writing of poetry, about the making of poems, my own poems, three pictures come to mind. In the first, as a small child, I see myself waking in a room in a quiet house early in the morning. There is absolutely no sound except for the breathing of my brother, still asleep beside me. The room is dark, and I look toward the window. The shades are drawn —old, faded, dark shades—the green of which is like that of a stagnant pool. They have been on the windows for years in all the rooms I can remember. Through the green come small pricks and points of light scattered unevenly up and down and across, making, together with the rips in the green canvas fabric, a series of odd designs. As I lie awake, I try to shape these designs, these points and lines of light, into animals and plants, fabulous creatures, familiar and far-off places. It is like looking up at the sky, but this sky belongs only to me. The whole world—my parents, my brother, the house—is still asleep, still shrouded in night. Outside the world is waking; the crowing of roosters flutters the dark shades. I know that before long, out-side and in, all the familiar activities of that world will resume as they do day after day, but here it is still night, still the begin-ning of the world. On this side of darkness, out of the few specks of light, I can make my own world. The shades provide me a kind of code, which, if I can read correctly, brings me a vision I can carry in my head through this day and every other. Al-though the framework is virtually the same (except for new specks, new cracks, new tears that slowly appear), the possibili-ties are endless: the patterns exist within the room and within myself. I must have been thinking unconsciously of this years later when I wrote one morning at Arnhem in Holland:

> From the cassowary's beak come streaks of light,
> Morning, and possibility.
> In the countries of the north
> Ice breaks, and breaking, blossoms forth
> With possibility; and day abounds
> In light and color, color, sounds.

A second picture comes to mind; I am at the desk in my cabin on shipboard during the war and all night I have been decoding messages brought to me by the radioman. There is no sound except the muted and regular rumble of the engines and the slap of the waves with the pitch and roll of the ship. Finally I put the code book aside—all the groups of meaningless letters that I know must have their meaning—and gaze at the pages of blank paper on my desk. In my drowsy state, I see on them an-other kind of code: here, if I can only decipher it, is the key to the poems I have not yet written but which I still carry in my head. And then I go out on deck: dawn is breaking over an empty gray ocean, and a poem begins to take shape in the back of my mind as the stars slowly fade.

A third picture: I am in a room somewhere in a motel or hotel. On one wall is a vast mirror that reflects in its cold expanse a huge bad painting showing a classical ruin with unidentifiable flowers climbing an unidentifiable column in an unidentifiable country while two forlorn figures stand on the edge of mossy rocks and a ship sails for an unidentifiable destination. There is no sound except the ice machine down the corridor or the hum of traffic in the distance. I am thoroughly relaxed: only one other person in the world knows where I am, and I seem to have all infinity before me, although in reality it may be only a few hours, a day or a night. In one corner is an unopened briefcase packed with unanswered letters that are going to remain unanswered for a while longer. On the wide bed—or beds—are spread out, on bits of frayed paper, blurred notebook pages, backs of dog-eared envelopes, formless sentences or closely knit stanzas that I know have no meaning to anyone else but to me are the makings of the still unwritten poem on which I have been working for months or years. It will not be easy, I know, to fit all the bits and pieces together. Many, if not all, of my notes may prove useless, and I may still have to start from scratch. There are two or three other poems that I have carried in my head for months from room to room, house to house, city to city, that now seem infinitely more interesting than the one I have spread out before me. And it takes all my will power not to sweep all the notes off the bed and back into my bag and to crawl under the covers, shut out the world, and sleep. As the young Jules Laforgue, having "only the friendship of hotel rooms," put it:

> And so before long I began to write,
> But the Devil of Truth who hovered near
> Would lean and whistle in my ear:
> "Enough, poor fool, put out the light."

Somehow the poet subdues or at least comes to terms with the antipoet, and composition begins.

Poets have always been haunted by the blank page—to use a phrase of Louise Bogan's that I shall come to later—by that "stark unprinted silence." Of the white page the French poet Mallarmé developed a whole esthetic. Many of his poems are concerned with whiteness, with the danger of departing on a terrible voyage on which, as he put it in one of his most famous poems, "A throw of the dice will never abolish chance." W. H. Auden has summed up Mallarmé's obsession in the form of a clerihew:

> Mallarmé
> Had too much to say;
> He could never quite
> Leave the paper white.

There is something terrifying about the blank page, untouched, innocent, and pure. A poem often seems so complete in one's head and so inadequate when one begins to set it down. Richard Wilbur has said that he carries around the idea of a poem in his mind as if it were a precious possession; he wants to keep it to himself until the time comes to write down the entire poem. Then he wants to communicate it, to show it to someone as soon as it is finished.

Every poet is haunted by the blank page, by its cold, white, terrifying mystery. The Greek Nobel Prize winner, George Seferis, has a curious story to tell in this connection. At one time he was having a book of his poems printed in Greece, and, going over the final page proofs, he realized that there would be several blank pages if the book were to have its proper form. He saw at once that these were the pages on which the poem "The King of Asine" was to appear. What was simpler then than to insert the poem where it properly belonged? All very well, but the truth dawned on him: the poem, while it existed in his head, had not yet been written. And then a second horrible realization: he had sent off, with a friend, his manuscripts, among them all the notes for this particular poem that he had taken in the course of two years. The single reference to the King of Asine in *The Iliad* had haunted him for some time. Nothing whatever is known of this king. Homer refers to him only once as one of the kings who sent off ships to Troy; but this was enough for the poet: he had to give voice to the mystery, to make known the unknown, to fill in the blank. And so he sat down, without his notes, aided only by his concentration and his memory; he sat down, confronting the mystery, and wrote off the poem as it now appears. It is one of the great poems of the twentieth century, and, in its fine English translation by Edmund Keeley and Philip Sherrard, has much to say, I think, about the mysterious making of poetry:

THE KING OF ASINE

’Ασίνην τε . . .—ILIAD

We looked all morning round the citadel
starting from the shaded side, there where the sea
green and without luster—breast of a slain peacock—
received us like time without an opening in it.
Veins of rock dropped down from high above,
twisted vines, naked, many-branched, coming alive
at the water's touch, while the eye following them
struggled to escape the tiresome rocking,
losing strength continually.

On the sunny side a long open beach
and the light striking diamonds on the huge walls.
No living thing, the wild doves gone
and the king of Asine, whom we've been trying to find
    for two years now,
unknown, forgotten by all, even by Homer,
only one word in the *Iliad* and that uncertain,
thrown here like the gold burial mask.
You touched it, remember its sound? Hollow in the light
like a dry jar in dug earth:
the same sound that our oars make in the sea.
The king of Asine a void under the mask
everywhere with us everywhere with us, under a name:
" ’Ασίνην τε . . . ’Ασίνην τε . . ."

395

and his children statues
and his desires the fluttering of birds, and the wind
in the gaps between his thoughts, and his ships
anchored in a vanished port:
under the mask a void.

Behind the large eyes the curved lips the curls
carved in relief on the gold cover of our existence
a dark spot that you see traveling like a fish
in the dawn calm of the sea:
a void everywhere with us.
And the bird that flew away last winter
with a broken wing
the shelter of life,
and the young woman who left to play
with the dogteeth of summer
and the soul that sought the lower world squeaking
and the country like a large plane-leaf swept along by
        the torrent of the sun
with the ancient monuments and the contemporary sorrow.

And the poet lingers, looking at the stones, and asks himself
does there really exist
among these ruined lines, edges, points, hollows, and curves
does there really exist
here where one meets the path of rain, wind, and ruin
does there exist the movement of the face, shape of the
        tenderness
of those who've shrunk so strangely in our lives,
those who remained the shadow of waves and thoughts
        with the sea's boundlessness
or perhaps no, nothing is left but the weight
the nostalgia for the weight of a living existence
there where we now remain unsubstantial, bending
like the branches of a terrible willow tree heaped in
        permanent despair

396

while the yellow current slowly carries down rushes up-
    rooted in the mud
image of a form that the sentence to everlasting bitterness
    has turned to marble:
the poet a void.

Shieldbearer, the sun climbed warring,
and from the depths of the cave a startled bat
hit the light as an arrow hits a shield:
" 'Ασίνην τε . . . 'Ασίνην τε . . ." Could that be the king
    of Asine
we've been searching for so carefully on this acropolis
sometimes touching with our fingers his touch upon the
    stones.

The poem, as it moves from the mind to the page, seems
guided like the bat in the cave by some strange and inexplicable
radar. Louise Bogan's "Song for the Last Act" is so classically
and simply structured that one would never suppose that it had
not come quickly and completely from the mind of the poet:

SONG FOR THE LAST ACT

Now that I have your face by heart, I look
Less at its features than its darkening frame
Where quince and melon, yellow as young flame,
Lie with quilled dahlias and the shepherd's crook.
Beyond, a garden. There, in insolent ease
The lead and marble figures watch the show
Of yet another summer loath to go
Although the scythes hang in the apple trees.

Now that I have your face by heart, I look.

Now that I have your voice by heart, I read
In the black chords upon a dulling page
Music that is not meant for music's cage,

Whose emblems mix with words that shake and bleed.
The staves are shuttled over with a stark
Unprinted silence. In a double dream
I must spell out the storm, the running stream.
The beat's too swift. The notes shift in the dark.

Now that I have your voice by heart, I read.

Now that I have your heart by heart, I see
The wharves with their great ships and architraves;
The rigging and the cargo and the slaves
On a strange beach under a broken sky.
O not departure, but a voyage done!
The bales stand on the stone; the anchor weeps
Its red rust downward, and the long vine creeps
Beside the salt herb, in the lengthening sun.

Now that I have your heart by heart, I see.

What is most remarkable about this poem is its precision in movement and line. Every word from the opening *Now* to the final *see* is part of the whole; and the whole unfolds like the sides of a screen on which everything is depicted with the utmost clarity. The poem is, in form, a triptych in which the reader may *look* and *read* and *see*; indeed, those three verbs are the hinges on which the whole rests and unfolds. But it was not always so. Miss Bogan has told me of the composition of this poem: what she began with—what was given—was the sense of the stanza itself and the refrain. In her words, she had hit upon the form right off. What she did not know was how that form was going to change in the course of composition. She had originally set down four stanzas, inspired by the etchings of Claude Lorrain, the seventeenth-century French classical painter, whose landscapes are usually painted against the light and yet are always fully luminous, bathed with mysterious and subtle indirection. The poem had lain for a good many years in a folder just as she had originally set it down. When she took it up again, she went over it all carefully, getting the words just right, but still she was not sure of the final version. Although the poem was complete, something was wrong. She did what many poets in similar circumstances have done: she showed it to a friend and fellow poet, Rolfe Humphries. Mr. Humphries pointed out to her that to him the final fourth stanza was not only unnecessary but disconcerting. The poem, he said, was a triptych and should stand as such. She agreed, and the poem exists now in its seemingly inevitable magnificence. It is interesting that, although Miss Bogan calls her poem a song, it is not the *sound* that predominates. It is the *vision* that is all important, for even in the second stanza where she is speaking of music and the sound of music, it is music as depicted, as scored, on the page—music that must be *spelled out* and *read*. The simple, external vision of the garden at the beginning, the thing that is *looked* at, as one looks at the face of a loved one, becomes in the end the inner vision of the thing *seen*, seen truly, finally, and inevitably: "O not departure, but a voyage done!" What has been looked at has been read and seen, and the poet's journey has been completed.

There is no more fascinating, tantalizing, and, of course, questionable account of the making of poems than that in Coleridge's famous Prefatory Note to *Kubla Khan:*

> In the summer of the year 1797, the Author, then in ill health, had retired to a lonely farmhouse between Porlock and Linton, on the Exmoor confines of Somerset and Devonshire. In consequence of a slight indisposition, an anodyne had been prescribed, from the effects of which he fell asleep in his chair at the moment that he was reading the following sentence, or words of the same substance, in "Purchas's Pilgrimage:" "Here the Khan Kubla commanded a palace to be built, and a stately garden there-

399

unto: and thus ten miles of fertile ground were inclosed with a wall." The Author continued for about three hours in a profound sleep, at least of the external senses, during which time he has the most vivid confidence, that he could not have composed less than from two to three hundred lines; if that indeed can be called composition in which all the images rose up before him as *things*, with a parallel production of the correspondent expressions, without any sensation or consciousness of effort. On awaking he appeared to himself to have a distinct recollection of the whole, and taking his pen, ink, and paper, instantly and eagerly wrote down the lines that are here preserved. At this moment he was unfortunately called out by a person on business from Porlock, and detained by him above an hour, and on his return to his room, found, to his no small surprise and mortification, that though he still retained some vague and dim recollection of the general purport of the vision, yet, with the exception of some eight or ten scattered lines and images, all the rest had passed away like the images on the surface of a stream into which a stone has been cast, but alas! without the after restoration of the latter.

A. D. Hope has written a brilliant, pertinent, and amusing commentary on this passage:

PERSONS FROM PORLOCK

It was unfortunate: Poor S.T.C.!
Once in his life, once only among men,
Once in the process of Eternity,
It happened, and it will not happen again:
His dream unbidden took shape as poetry,
And waking, he recalled it, and his pen
Set down the magic lines—then came the dread
Summons from Porlock and the vision fled.

400

Fortunate Coleridge! He at least began.
Porlock was tardy, almost missed its cue;
Something at least was saved of *Kubla Khan*,
And Porlock's agent, give the man his due,
Paid him that single visit in the span
Of a long life of three score years and two.
The Ancient Mariner, it is fair to mention,
Escaped the Person's sinister attention.

The Swan of Porlock is a kind of duck;
It quacks and has a large, absurd behind—
Yes, on the whole, the poet was in luck.
Think of his fate had Porlock been less kind;
The paps of Porlock might have given him suck;
Teachers from Porlock organized his mind,
And Porlock's Muse inspired the vapid strain
Of: "Porlock, Loveliest Village of the Plain!"

And had his baffled genius stood the test,
With that one vision which is death to hide
Burning for utterance in the poet's breast,
Porlock might still be trusted to provide
Neighbors from Porlock, culled from Porlock's best,
The sweetest girl in Porlock for his bride,
In due course to surround him with some young
Persons from Porlock, always giving tongue.

Eight hours a day of honest Porlock toil,
And Porlock parties—useless to refuse—
The ritual gardening of Porlock soil,
Would leave him time still for a spare-time Muse—
And when with conscience murdered, wits aboil,
He shook the dust of Porlock from his shoes,
Some would be apt to blame him, some to scoff,
But others kindly come to see him off.

Porlock was gone: the marvelous dream was there.

"In Xanadu . . ."—He knew the words by rote,
Had but to set them down.
To his despair
He found a man from Porlock wore his coat,
And thought his thoughts; and, stolid in his chair,
A person fresh from Porlock sat and wrote:
"Amid this tumult Kubla heard from far
Voices of Porlock babbling round the bar."

There are everywhere those persons from Porlock who have succeeded in turning the poet into one of them. They are always
those who hold out the moneybags, those moneybags that Baudelaire showed his eyes riveted on in one of his drawings; they are
the givers of grants and fellowships, the offerers of advances, the
gravy without which the poet's usual crumbs seem meager and
dry indeed. They are often those closest to the poet—who is
always somewhere midway between Porlock and Linton—and
they offer him love and understanding. I remember my mother,
who encouraged me immeasurably in every undertaking, coming into the room when I had a glazed and far-off look in my eye
and remarking, "Are you doped up on that poetry again?" Like
all mothers, even non-Jewish ones, she wanted the best for her
son, and if he wanted poetry, she wanted him to have it, but
could she be sure, poor darling, that it was really *good* for him?

There is perhaps no better defense against the persons from
Porlock than that of turning their own nonsense back on them so
that they may see it shining and clear before they overtake us,
and no one was better able to do so than Edward Lear. Note this
entry of 9 April 1868 in his *Journal of a Landscape Painter in
Corsica:*

The night voyage, though far from pleasant, has not
been as bad as might have been anticipated. He is fortunate,
who, after ten hours of sea passage can reckon up no worse
memories than those of a passive condition of suffering—of

that dislocation of mind and body, or inability to think straightforward, so to speak, when the outer man is twisted, and rolled, and jerked, and the movements of thought seem more or less to correspond with those of the body. Wearily go by

> The slow sad hours that bring us all
> things ill,

and vain is the effort to enliven them as every fresh lurch of the vessel tangles practical or pictorial suggestions with untimely scraps of poetry, indistinct regrets and predictions, couplets for a new "Book of Nonsense," and all kinds of inconsequent imbecilities—after this sort—

Would it not have been better to have remained at Cannes, where I had not yet visited Theoule, the Saut de Loup, and other places?

Had I not said, scores of times, such and such a voyage was the last I would make?

Tomorrow, when "morn broadens on the borders of the dark," shall I see Corsica's "snowy mountain-tops fringing the (eastern) sky"?

Did the sentinels of lordly Volaterra see, as Lord Macaulay says they did, "Sardinia's snowy mountain-tops," and not rather these same Corsican tops, "fringing the southern sky"?

Did they see any tops at all, or if any, which tops?

Will the daybreak ever happen?

Will two o'clock ever arrive?

Will the two poodles above stairs ever cease to run about the deck?

Is it not disagreeable to look forward to two or three months of traveling quite alone?

Would it not be delightful to travel, as J. A. S. is about to do, in company with a wife and child?

Does it not, as years advance, become clearer that it is very odious to be alone?

Have not many very distinguished persons, Œnone among others, arrived at this conclusion?

Did she not say, with evident displeasure—

"And from that time to this I am alone
And I shall be alone until I die"?—

Will those poodles ever cease from trotting up and down the deck?

Is it not unpleasant, at fifty-six years of age, to feel that it is increasingly probable that a man can never hope to be otherwise than alone, never, no, never more?

Did not Edgar Poe's raven distinctly say, "Nevermore"?

Will those poodles be quiet? "Quoth the raven, nevermore."

Will there be anything worth seeing in Corsica?

Is there any romance left in that island? is there any sublimity or beauty in its scenery?

Have I taken too much baggage?

Have I not rather taken too little?

Am I not an idiot for coming at all?—

Thus, and in such a groove, did the machinery of thought go on, gradually refusing to move otherwise than by jerky spasms, after the fashion of mechanical Ollendorff exercises, or verb-catechisms of familiar phrases—

Are there not Banditti?

Had there not been Vendetta?

Were there not Corsican brothers?

Should I not carry clothes for all sorts of weather?

Must THOU not have taken a dress coat?

Had HE not many letters of introduction?

Might WE not have taken extra pairs of spectacles?

Could YOU not have provided numerous walking
    boots?
Should THEY not have forgotten boxes of quinine
    pills?
  Shall WE possess flea-powder?
  Could YOU not procure copper money?
  May THEY not find cream cheeses?
    Should there not be innumerable moufflons?
    Ought not the cabin lamps and glasses to cease
      jingling?
    Might not those poodles stop worrying?—
thus and thus, till by reason of long hours of monotonous
rolling and shaking, a sort of comatose insensibility, mis-
called sleep, takes the place of all thought, and so the night
passes.

What might Edward Lear not have made of the Muzak-fed and
plastic-enclosed world of today?

In speaking of the making of poems, whether they well from
the deepest layers of sense or bubble out from the upper levels
of nonsense, I have described perhaps an impossible para-
bola. But then the writing of poety, as Walter de la Mare has
pointed out, is indeed the most curious of human activities.

    I used to go hunting mushrooms on a farm in Vermont,
and gradually I came to know one particular place where morels,
those rarest and most delicious of mushrooms, were to be found.
It was not far from the house at a bend of the road under large
maple trees. They would spring up overnight each year at the
same time, at the end of May after a night of rain. I had gathered them for several years when finally one day, having
brought them back to the house, I sat down, when they had been
cooked and eaten as they had been so many times before, and
wrote off a poem that I had not consciously planned to write. I

knew after it was written, however, that it was one I had lived
with for a long time, although it spoke only of the events of that
one afternoon and had seemed to spring up as quickly as the
morels themselves.

Poems do not always come so quickly to mind, nor do they
always spring up in the same place or in the same form. Five
years ago I took my younger son, then ten years old, deep-sea
fishing off Long Beach, California. I am a poor fisherman, although I love "messing about in boats." I certainly did not in
this particular instance relish the thought of this trip with some
sixty-odd tourists on board a ship "eighty-five feet long, twenty-
three foot beam, twin diesels, twin stacks painted red, white, and
blue." But I knew from the moment we went

> Through gray streets, at 10:00 P.M., down
> to Pierpont Landing, Long Beach,
> where, in the window of a shop offer-
> ing every type of fishing gear,

> Are displayed fish carved from driftwood by
> the natives of Bali, each representing in
> true colors and exact dimensions a fish
> found on their reefs,

> Colors derived from bark and root (each fish,
> when completed, is bartered for rice;
> no money is involved) . . .

that somewhere on this trip a poem lay waiting to be written.
Perhaps for this reason I began at once, while my son looked
around the shop on the pier, to write down in detail the descriptions of the fish in the window. It was not until we got back that
I realized that the poem I thought might grow out of this display
was really the journey itself and all that had happened on it, all
we had seen and done, from beginning to end. It was not a story
really; there was no story to tell: sixty-five people on a regular

fishing trip 135 miles off the coast of southern California had
caught 125 albacore. My son and I were among them; he had
caught one, and I, none. It had all been a bloody business, the
albacore coming up half-eaten by sharks, and then, on the way
back, we had come close to a pod of whales. But in sorting it all
out afterwards I knew that it was a narrative that I had to put
down just as I saw it, one whose whole meaning would gradually
become clear to me—and I hope to my reader—during the three
years that it took me to record "Fishing for Albacore."

The woods in Missouri on the banks of the Mississippi
through which I used to tramp endlessly as a boy had their terrifying aspects. All around in them were sinkholes left by an
earthquake; at the bottom of each was an overgrown black hole
that I was convinced was a bottomless pit that would surely swallow me up if I allowed myself to slip into it. As I went along
skirting the sinkholes, I would come at times on a snake and at
other times on a covey of quail. In the absolute stillness of the
autumn woods both were terrifying, but in the vision of the quail
there was not only terror but a haunting beauty as well. I have
tried to put it down in "Quail in Autumn":

Autumn has turned the dark trees toward the hill;
The wind has ceased; the air is white and chill.
Red leaves no longer dance against your foot,
The branch reverts to tree, the tree to root.

And now in this bare place your step will find
A twig that snaps flintlike against the mind;
Then thundering above your giddy head,
Small quail dart up, through shafting sunlight fled.

Like brightness buried by one's sullen mood
The quail rise startled from the threadbare wood;
A voice, a step, a swift sun-thrust of feather
And earth and air come properly together.

I wrote this thirty years ago as a college student and had never published it. Almost every word in it is just as I set it down with the exception of the first two lines of the final stanza. When I came on the poem a few years ago (I never throw any paper away even if it contains only a phrase or two), I found that I had written something like this:

> The quail rise startled from the autumn wood,
> Love makes its brief appearance as it should.

I realized, of course, that to a young man of twenty love is what always appears, or should appear, at any time of the day or night, but in middle age, I could see that what I had really experienced so long ago—and was still experiencing—was the chilling beauty, the terror, of poetry itself:

> Like brightness buried by one's sullen mood
> The quail rise startled from the threadbare wood:
> A voice, a step, a swift sun-thrust of feather
> And earth and air come properly together.

There is, I am told, a Poets' Competition in Barcelona. After the poems have been read aloud, the judges award the prizes in a most unusual fashion. The author of the third best poem receives a rose made of silver, the author of the second best, a rose made of gold, and the author of the best—the most enduring and most original—a real rose. One might think of these awards as a metaphor for the making of poems. What is given the poet—that phrase, that image, that scrap that circles around for months in his head, that God-given inspiration—is of silver. The second stage, that of composition and revision, when the poet must work constantly over every syllable, never at the same time losing sight of the whole, and when anything earned seems more precious than anything received—that stage is of gold. The third and final stage, when the poem is released and belongs to the reader and to the world, if the poet has succeeded and has been true to his vision, that final stage is the *natural* one, when the finished work may take its place, organically whole, beside the great work of life itself.

[1970]

A FRAME
FOR POETRY

William Plomer, a poet I much admire, has spoken of himself as a "solitary prospector" on the poetic scene, and the term is one that might apply to a number of writers in the vast, uneven literary expanse that is America. I, for my part, have staked out my claims, and legitimate claims in the area of lyric poetry I believe them to be; they may appear modest only because unannounced in gaudy and sprawling letters. I hate sloppiness of any sort and although I have belonged to no school, the fact that I can write a proper sentence places me, in the eyes of the recent resurgent literary bushmen, inevitably with the "academic" poets. In actuality, I have been associated with colleges only in recent years and then mostly on a part-time basis; and I deplore the way poetry is discussed in most classrooms. There is a vast amount of dull patter that passes for poetry today, both in and out of the academy; but the worst offenders are those "new" poets who go on interminably about their free-wheeling "poetics" derived from Williams and Pound. These self-expressionists had been quietly mimeographing their efforts for years (indeed, they themselves existed in a limbo of mimeography), but now that they have broken into print, their pretension is boundless. There is much dull talk about poetry of late; and although it can only briefly obscure the merits of good poems, it can unfortunately foster and promote many dull ones.

Variety in poetry, as in any art, is everything. It is the spice without which the cooking is glutinous and unpalatable. To repeat oneself *ad infinitum,* as even some extremely talented modern poets do, seems to me like locking oneself up with stale, unpleasant odors in the kitchen. I have always believed, as did Jean Cocteau, that the artist should find out what he can do and then do something else. The poet should always be venturing, trying out new things. One doesn't want experimentation for its own sake, the sense of the freakish doctor surrounded by retorts in the laboratory, but one does want the poet who is willing time after time to risk everything and play for the highest stakes. The poet must be constantly exploring, going out on a limb. This does not mean the continual development of wholly new styles, but rather the enlargement and expansion of one's basic style. It means putting out new shoots, growing as a tree grows up and out, feeding more and more on light and air. The following poem, "Tulip," seems to me to have something to say in this connection. The tulip, that favorite flower in the gardens of the mathematicians and philosophers of the eighteenth century, came originally from Persia (the word means "turban") and entered Europe by way of Constantinople. It became so famous that there developed the phenomenon of tulipomania when tulip bulbs were prized more highly than jewels. The tulip is, of course, the most metallic appearing of flowers, and one of its chief characteristics is that it has no scent.

TULIP

A slender goblet wreathed in flame,
From Istanbul the flower came
And brought its beauty, and its name.

Now as I lift it up, that fire
Sweeps on from dome to golden spire
Until the East is all aflame:

By curving petals held entire
In cup of ceremonial fire,
Magnificence within a frame.

Poetry for me should be continually expanding within its frame. Humor is itself a form of expansion; laughter, as Max Beerbohm said, is "but a joyous surrender." I have been drawn to light verse because of a firm belief that humor is one of America's greatest and most enduring characteristics. Children's poetry, with its wide use of stanza forms and the range of its nonsense, has been for me a liberating influence, giving me a chance to explore in a light vein themes that I have developed and expanded in adult work.

Some poems rise like mushrooms, full-grown, mysterious, complete in every detail, and one wonders from whence they have sprung. "The Peacock of Java" is for me such a poem, although it may seem otherwise in view of the facts of its composition.

THE PEACOCK OF JAVA

I thought of the mariners of Solomon,
Who, on one of their long voyages, came
    On that rare bird, the Peacock
    Of Java, which brings, even
To the tree of heaven, heaven.

412

How struggling upward through the dark
   Lianas, they beheld the tree,
   And in the tree, the fan
That would become a king's embroidery.

How they turned and on the quiet
   Water then set sail
   For home, the peacock's tail
Committed to the legends of the sea.

I remember not long after World War II copying out from a bird book at the Houghton Farm in Mountainville, New York, where I was then staying, the facts about the peacock and Soloman's mariners. I do not have the quotation now to refer to it; it reposes, along with the original typescript of the poem, in the Lamont Library at Harvard. I had the impression at the time that the reference might in some way be useful in connection with a group of poems on which I was then working that had to do with the Pacific. Some time later in New York, without referring to the piece I had copied out, I wrote the poem right off in a few minutes. The only word that gave me trouble was the first one in the last line. It took me a while to settle on "committed," which I now think is absolutely right and one of the best touches in the poem. When I had written down the piece as it stands, I still had the vague feeling that it was somehow incomplete and part of a longer work. But I realized later the reason for this. The poem clearly was concerned in some way with the years I had spent in the Pacific, but not with Java, where I had never been. In trying to locate to my own satisfaction what had given rise to the poem, I concluded that the experience itself had been omitted, or rather transformed, entirely and had to do with a peacock only metaphorically.

While I was liaison officer on board a French ship attached to the South Pacific fleet, we were requested by the French Admiralty to make a tour of the islands of the New Hebrides. We were received wherever we went with great excitement by

French planters who in some cases had not seen a French ship, nor often any of their metropolitan countrymen, for twenty-five years or more. On one island we trekked at length through what seemed impenetrable jungle, and finally, as we approached the plantation, the vegetation began to clear and the rotting bitter-sweet smell of copra and the other overrich odors of a tropical farm greeted our nostrils. As we emerged on the clearing, there rose, in a green circle before the low-lying plantation house, a superb traveler's tree, the great radiating fan of its branches flung up against a blazing sky. This marvelous sight made us all reflect on the appropriateness of the tree's name; it provided a rich and wonderful welcome. I thought of that vision afterwards and of the remainder of that day and that journey, and wanted to put it all down in some way. Years later I concluded that per-haps I had in "The Peacock of Java."

"Galileo Galilei" is one of my favorite poems by reason, I think, of the curious circumstances of its composition:

GALILEO GALILEI

Comes to knock and knock again
At a small secluded doorway
In the ordinary brain.

Into light the world is turning,
And the clocks are set for six;
And the chimney pots are smoking,
And the golden candlesticks.

Apple trees are bent and breaking,
And the heat is not the sun's;
And the Minotaur is waking,
And the streets are cattle runs.

Galileo Galilei,
In a flowing, scarlet robe,
While the stars go down the river
With the turning, turning globe,

Kneels before a black Madonna
And the angels cluster round
With grave, uplifted faces
Which reflect the shaken ground

And the orchard which is burning,
And the hills which take the light;
And the candles which have melted
On the altars of the night.

Galileo Gallilei
Comes to knock and knock again
At a small secluded doorway
In the ordinary brain.

In Oxford in 1947 an acquaintance of mine told me one morning that he had awoken the previous night and found that the peculiar happenings of his dream had suggested to him the lines of a poem. He began to write them down, but he could not get beyond the opening:

Galileo Galilei
Comes to knock and knock again
At a small secluded doorway
In the ordinary brain.

I noted the lines down, and forgot about them until that same night when I found myself unable to sleep. I got up and wrote the poem down more or less as it now appears.

This may all sound suspect—*à la* "Kubla Khan"—but it did really happen. The lines I now realize appealed to me particularly because I had just returned from my first trip to Florence, where I had been staying with friends in Pian dei Giullari, just around the corner from the house in which Galileo was living when Milton came to visit him. I was aware in writing the poem of many impressions of Italy, and of the movement of a kind of *mandala*, the dance of a priest around the altar.

In any case, I was rather pleased with what I had done and

showed the result the next morning to my friend. He said indignantly that what I had written had nothing whatever to do with what he had had in mind. *Tant pis*, I replied, then he could certainly not expect to get credit for the lines. He agreed that they were now mine; and we have not met since.

Oddly enough, those readers who have admired the poem have all commented on its strange dreamlike quality.

Poems grow out of dreams but dreams are often dreamt with one's eyes wide open. Once in St. Louis, when on leave during World War II, I was driving past a building that I knew well (I had passed it hundreds of times without ever giving it much thought). It was a school for the blind, run by the Sisters of Mercy. I had just heard that there was a power failure in this part of the city, and as I drove by, looking out at the sign, School for the Blind, I realized in a flash that this failure meant absolutely nothing to those whose eyes were already permanently sealed. The line came to me—one of those *données* on which we all subsist and for which we thank the gods:

The lights have gone out in the School for the Blind.

It traveled with me for a long time, that line, circling in the back of my head. I felt instinctively that I had the beginning of a poem. It was there: I had the rhythm, I had the title, "The Failure of Power." I felt the strength of some mysterious force pulling me forward, but I did not yet have the words. I remember, thinking back on it, of the story of the painter Degas excitedly taking some poems he had written to the poet Mallarmé. Degas had tried to put into them all his delight in dancers and race horses and when Mallarmé hesitated to give his approval, the painter protested that he had, after all, started the poems with very good ideas in mind. Mallarmé's rejoinder was, of course, that poems are written with words, not with ideas. In any case, the few words that I did have—not yet an idea even—traveled with me for some time, until I sat down one night in Noumea, New Caledonia, after an afternoon visit to a leper colony above the city

416

and wrote out the poem—with its title changed, rightly I think, to "Miserere."

MISERERE

The lights have gone out in the School for the Blind,
    And all the shades are drawn.
    Sisters of Mercy move over the lawn.

Sisters of Mercy move into the mind
    With steps that are swifter than any;
    Light on each pupil is perched like a penny.

The lights have gone out in the School for the Blind;
    The flare on the runway dies,
    And the murderer waits with dancing eyes.

The murderer waits in the quiet mind,
    While Night, a Negress nun,
    A Sister of Mercy, sweeps over the sun.

What I have been attempting to say about the peculiar genesis of poetry is something like what Charles Causley said recently—that all works of art must have their mystery, and although poems *can* be taken apart like clocks, when they are put back together they may still not be *explained*. They retain, they give off, as Garcia Lorca said every great work of art must, their *sonidos negros*, dark sounds. This, it seems to me, is the resonance that all great poetry possesses—that unfathomable mystery of the psyche that we can approach only with reverence and love.

Poetry for me always begins with the particular, and I can generalize only from my own experience. One of my poems that has become an anthology piece may serve as a peculiar and particular example of how poems—mine, at least—get written:

417

AMERICAN PRIMITIVE

Look at him there in his stovepipe hat,
His high-top shoes, and his handsome collar;
Only my Daddy could look like that,
And I love my Daddy like he loves his Dollar.

The screen door bangs, and it sounds so funny—
There he is in a shower of gold;
His pockets are stuffed with folding money,
His lips are blue, and his hands feel cold.

He hangs in the hall by his black cravat,
The ladies faint, and the children holler:
Only my Daddy could look like that,
And I love my Daddy like he loves his Dollar.

A poet friend remarked to me once that this was one of my poems that he most admired and that it must have been a delight to write it right off, as I so clearly had done. It was indeed a delight to write it right off—as it now stands—after working on it at odd moments for a period of five years. I cannot recall how many versions I put down during this period, most of them discarded. I knew exactly where I wanted to get to; the problem was getting there, and getting there with directness and *élan*— and without fuss. I had in mind a Mississippi River guitar tune —absolutely mechanical in its rhythm—an out-and-out child's innocent unadorned view of horror—horror with the resonant twang of strings to it. In its original version, the poem was very much longer. There were a good many little ballad bits, of which this is an example:

I fear the feel of frozen steel,
I fear the scarlet dagger;
But more than these I fear the eel,
I fear the carpetbagger.

I had indeed the vision of the carpetbagger who had made his money in some suspect manner; and with the sunlight and the screen door I wish to suggest the large, open, airy southern house that I remembered from childhood. The most difficult line for me to get in the poem was the one that now seems the simplest, and it is the turning point:

He hangs in the hall by his black cravat.

Poetry is all in verbs, in verbs and nouns, and it seems to me it is all here in the verb "hangs." I have frequently been asked to discuss this poem with grade-school children and, although it may appear a macabre choice on the part of the teacher, I have discovered that children respond to it without hesitation. They understand that a child is speaking and that the father has hanged himself for some reason involving money. College students, on the other hand, have often found this piece bewildering; they have lost the down-to-earth metaphorical approach of childhood and cannot follow the simple words to their unexpected conclusion. I think that I scarcely need add that although "American Primitive" is a bitter poem in the tradition of Edwin Arlington Robinson's "Richard Cory," it is certainly not intended as my sole view of the American scene.

My recent work has evolved in many ways and if I have in the past been attracted by the short poem—the lyric in which spirit is compressed—the fire in the brazier, to which Marianne Moore referred in speaking of the poems of Louise Bogan—I have been no less drawn to the opposite side of the coin, the long poem with the long line, slowly expanding, drawing the inner fire upward and outward. The danger of the long free-verse line is naturally a lapse into loose echoes of Whitman, but one must take the risk; one must break up the frame to make of the fractured frame a wholly new and different one. Poems must continually expand and contract, and I like to think of the lines in a long poem of

419

this sort as akin to the pleats in an accordion—each intact and trim but ready to open out resonantly to its full proportion. In conclusion then, I offer a poem that I hope illustrates in larger ways those qualities in verse that I have stressed and to which in any presentation of reality I feel one must return:

THE TIN CAN

One very good thing I have learned from writer friends in Japan is that when you have a lot of work to do, especially writing, the best thing is to take yourself off and hide away. The Japanese have a word for this, the *kanzume*, or the "tin can," which means about what we would mean by the "lockup." When someone gets off by himself to concentrate, they say, "he has gone into the tin can."

Herbert Passin, "The Mountain Hermitage:
Pages from a Japanese Notebook," *Encounter*, August 1957

I

I have gone into the tin can: not in late
    spring, fleeing a stewing, meat-and-fish
    smelling city of paper houses,

Not when wisteria hangs, a purple cloud,
    robbing the pines of their color, have I
    sought out the gray plain, the inde-
    terminate outer edge of a determined
    world,

Not to an inn nestling astride a waterfall
    where two mountains meet and the
    misty indecisiveness of Japanese ink-
    drawn pines frames the afternoon, pro-
    viding from a sheer bluff an adequate
    view of infinity,

But here to the tin can in midwinter: to a
sagging New England farmhouse in
the rock-rooted mountains, where wind
rifles the cracks,

Here surrounded by crosshatched, tumbling
stone walls, where the snow plow with
its broad orange side-thrust has outlined a rutted road,

Where the dimly cracked gray bowl of the
sky rests firmly on the valley and gum-
thick clouds pour out at the edges,

Where in the hooded afternoon a pock-
marked, porcupine-quilled landscape
fills with snow-swirls, and the tin can
settles in the snow.

I have gone into the tin can, head high, reso-
lute, ready to confront the horrible,
black underside of the world.

Snow-murmur! Wind-dip! Heart-rage! It is
now my duty to record, to enumerate,
to set down the sounds, smells, mean-
ings of this place. . . .

How begin? With the red eye of the choco-
late-brown rhinoceros? With the triple-
serrated teeth of the pencil-fed monster
with bright fluted ears and whirling
black tail? . . .

There is a skittering and scrambling in the
can: a trickle of sand and sawdust
from a sack, wet leaves blown back,
cracks spreading along the wall.

There is the chitter and clatter of keys, a
smudge of pencils, a smear of time. . . .

Stippled heaven! Snow-ruffle! Garnet-groove!
Black water winding through snow-
wounds! Ripple-roost!

Will the wilds wake? Will the words work?
Will the rattle and rustle subside? Will
the words rise?

A blue jay flashes by a window, the stripes of
his tail, chevrons torn from a noncom's
sleeve; and in the afternoon the snow
begins.

First: a hush—pit-stillness, black accent of
hemlocks up and down the mountain,
mist in the valley thickening and deep-
ening until it breaks

And the snow already fallen swirls up to
meet the snow descending—sky-dark-
ening, still-deepening, sky-hooded and
whirling, flakes flying,

Houses settling sidewise in the drifts—winds
wedging, snow-choked road lost, still-
winding, earth white-star-carpeted,
still-wheeling;

And in the tin can the same still, paper-
white, damp emptiness.

II

A door opens—is it a door?—and a woman
walks by in the tin can watering tropical plants that jut from the wall or
spring from the floor, their leaves great
green famished mouths—

Feeding the fish, distributing specks to the
  seahorses in their tank and meat to the
  turtle on his wet pillow;

Cats curling about her legs, she pats the dogs
  and caresses the heads of the children,
  and the children open their green
  mouths and grow upward toward the
  sunlight like plants.

A door opens: a woman walks by, and
  through her bobbing, mud-colored glass
  watches the movements of my pencil,

And a record turns, a black hemstitched
  whirlpool, and the woman wheels off in
  a trance of drumbeats, screaming of
  need and nothingness and money;

And money like wet leaves piles around
  my ankles, and I am sickened by its
  smell. . . .

Snow-madness! Leaf-mania! Green para-
  bolas! In the tin can there is no morning of revelation, no afternoon of
  appraisal, no evening of enchantment.

In the tin can a small boy in a nightmare
  kicks one leg from the bed overturning
  a glowing iron stove, and in seconds
  fire sweeps through a city of tin cans.

I wake thinking of the boy, and all about me
  are the smoking ruins of cigarettes;
  and the ashes descend through the half-
  extinguished afternoon with the smell
  of burning flesh. . . .

423

A weasel waddles along in a kind of trotting walk; a mole inches up through darkness, his blind trail, the workings of consciousness.

In the tin can I hear a murmur of voices speaking of life in other tin cans, of death sifting through them.

A vision of bodies blasted on the black earth; and I think of those photographs my father kept from the Nicaraguan Insurrection, was it?—that we played with as children on a sun-spotted floor—

Brown bodies spread out over the jungle floor, the figures beside them wide-eyed and bewildered, toy soldiers in ridiculous stances in a meaningless world;

I think of the photographs rubbed vinegar-brown in the sunlight; and of how we placed them around us, lined our toy fortress with them,

And talked to one another through tin-can telephones, while from out the photographs the jungle's green arm tapped our small brown shoulders.

III

The tin can is circling with beasts: dogs howl in the night, cats sidle through slats in the tin, wet field mice hanging from their mouths;

I step in the morning over the entrails of
rodents lying like spun jewels on the
carpet, offerings to the dark gods.

And the dogs rise from their corners, their
dirt-crusted rag beds, smelling of snow,
sniffing the roots, digging the floor, and
begin again to circle the can. . . .

Bright flashes of morning! Blue snow-peaks!
Fog smoking the valleys! Angels lighting the rubble: Children skating on a
blue pond! Deer stepping delicately
down through the pines! . . .

And always the face, the woman's face,
brooding over all, rising from the earth
beside me, disembodied; always the
woman clean and classic as sunlight,
moving about the room, sifting the dirt,
watering the shadowy flowers, polish-
ing the spotted tin.

I hear her speak softly; and there she is
again beside me; and again the face
turns, a small bat-face and the lips
draw back in a red wound and shriek;
and the room is filled with a smell of
mould and money. . . .

The woman turns, the bat-face again a
woman's face blue with shrieking, and
the woman walks to the end of the
corridor, climbs a broad white stair-
way. . . .

Leaf-fringe!   Sky-tingle!   Cloud-clatter!
Earth-blaze! All my underworld crum-
bles; and I am left with the one brood-

ing face, no face; with bat-wings
folding the black air into a shroud.

IV

When am I to emerge? Dirt falls; eyes blur;
memory confounds; multiple voices
move furred and batlike round my
ears; and then no sound—

Only the grating of a pencil over a page—
an army of ant words swarming up to
consciousness.

When will they break through to a bright
remembered world, up through the top
of the tin?

Snow-swirl—hemlocks hunching toward the
window—gray-black shadow cutting
over black, fan shaken over fan. . . .

From here the windows open their white
mouths to swallow the wind-driven
snow.

And I remember salmon sky, fine-boned
sunsets sweeping the spiny mountains;
and I have seen the snow

In banks driven back from the road, the
black edges scraggly and bearded, the
snowbanks under the birches like
milk from buckets overturned and
frozen. . . .

Will the words rise? Will the poem radiate
with morning? Here where I see nothing, I have seen the Cyclops-eye ballooning over a frozen world,

The wide fringe of eyelashes opening on all
existence, the single glazed dazzle of
the eye watching,

And I have lived with my eyes—watching
the watching eye, the eyeball swiveling
in nothingness, a huge black moon in
egg-white immensity,

And I have seen the edges of the tin can fold
in around it.

V

O bodies my body has known! Bodies my
body has touched and remembered—in
beds, in baths, in streams, on fields and
streets—will you remember?

Sweet vision of flesh known and loved, lusted
after, cherished, repulsed, forgotten
and remembered, will you remember my body buried now and forgotten? . . .

In childhood we played for hours in the sun
on a dump near a cannery; and the
long thin ribbons of tin rippled round
us, and we ran by the railroad track
and into the backyard behind the
asparagus and through the feathers of
green our bodies touched and the
strips of tin radiated their rainbows of
light—

And our bodies were spiraled with tin and
wondrous with light—

Now out of darkness here from the tin can,
through snow-swirl and wind-dazzle,

427

let the tin ribbons ride again and range
in newfound freedom;

Let the tin rip and rustle in the wind;
let the green leaves rise and rift the
wondrous windows, leaving behind the
raging women, and the sickening mould
of money, rust, and rubble. . . .

And the words clean-spun and spiraling orbit
that swift-seeing, unseen immensity
that will never be contained!

[1966]

The text of this book has been set in
twelve point Linotype Walbaum, leaded two,
with display in Weiss Series I initials
and Monotype Baskerville with its Italic.
It has been composed, printed and bound
by American Book–Stratford Press, Inc.

Design is by Ben Birnbaum.